Babies and Bosses: Reconciling Work and Family Life

Austria, Ireland and Japan

Volume 2

OECD

ORGANISATION FOR ECONOMIC CO-OPERATION AND DEVELOPMENT

ORGANISATION FOR ECONOMIC CO-OPERATION AND DEVELOPMENT

Pursuant to Article 1 of the Convention signed in Paris on 14th December 1960, and which came into force on 30th September 1961, the Organisation for Economic Co-operation and Development (OECD) shall promote policies designed:

- to achieve the highest sustainable economic growth and employment and a rising standard of living in member countries, while maintaining financial stability, and thus to contribute to the development of the world economy;
- to contribute to sound economic expansion in member as well as non-member countries in the process of economic development; and
- to contribute to the expansion of world trade on a multilateral, non-discriminatory basis in accordance with international obligations.

The original member countries of the OECD are Austria, Belgium, Canada, Denmark, France, Germany, Greece, Iceland, Ireland, Italy, Luxembourg, the Netherlands, Norway, Portugal, Spain, Sweden, Switzerland, Turkey, the United Kingdom and the United States. The following countries became members subsequently through accession at the dates indicated hereafter: Japan (28th April 1964), Finland (28th January 1969), Australia (7th June 1971), New Zealand (29th May 1973), Mexico (18th May 1994), the Czech Republic (21st December 1995), Hungary (7th May 1996), Poland (22nd November 1996), Korea (12th December 1996) and the Slovak Republic (14th December 2000). The Commission of the European Communities takes part in the work of the OECD (Article 13 of the OECD Convention).

Publié en français sous le titre :
Bébés et employeurs : comment réconcilier travail et vie de famille
Autriche, Irlande et Japon – Volume 2

Foreword

The reconciliation of work and family life directly involves two goals that are important both to individuals and societies: the ability to participate fully in the labour market, generating income but also seeking fulfilment in the most important social activity of modern life, and to provide the best for one's own children, giving them the care and nurturing they need. These aspirations need not be mutually exclusive.

However, all too often parents cannot achieve their preferred balance of work and care commitments. As a result, (potential) parents may adjust their family behaviour and decide to have children at a later age, not as many as desired, or not have children at all. Alternatively, parents (usually mothers) withdraw from the labour market, temporarily or permanently. Sometimes this is because of their wish to provide full-time care for their children, whatever their employment opportunities. In many other cases, however, it is despite the fact that they would like to work, or to work more hours, but cannot do so because of constraints in terms of time, access to services or limited opportunities to resume career tracks after childbirth. Other parents (often fathers) spend so much time working that they devote little personal attention to their children, which raises concerns about both partnership stability and child development. Hence, the demand for a better set of family-friendly social policies that helps the reconciliation of work and family life by fostering adequacy of family resources and child development, facilitates parental choice about work and care, and promotes gender equality in employment opportunities.

This second OECD review on the reconciliation of work and family life analyses how the existing mix of policies, including tax/benefit policies, childcare policy and employment and workplace practices, contributes to different parental labour market outcomes and other societal outcomes in Austria, Ireland, and Japan. The review is based on visits to the three countries that took place in September and October 2002, and the analysis concerns the situation at that time. The review was discussed by the OECD's Employment, Labour and Social Affairs Committee in May 2003. The report was prepared by Willem Adema (Project Manager), Katherine Fawkner-Corbett and Christopher Prinz, assisted by Yosuke Jin, Maxime Ladaique, and Valérie Nguyen, under the overall supervision of the Head of the Social Policy Division, Mark Pearson. This volume is published under the responsibility of the Secretary-General of the OECD.

Table of Contents

List of Charts

ISBN 92-64-10418-6
Babies and Bosses: Reconciling Work and Family Life
Austria, Ireland and Japan
© OECD 2003

Chapter 1

Main Findings and Policy Recommendations

This chapter presents the main findings and policy conclusions of the review of work and family reconciliation policies in Austria, Ireland and Japan. It starts with a summary of reform options that countries could pursue to help more parents find their preferred balance of work and care commitments. It then summarises key labour market outcomes, showing that the similarity across countries in overall female employment rates in 2002 masks marked differences in underlying trends and the extent to which these employment outcomes vary with the age of the youngest child. The chapter reveals how workplace practices, childcare policy and tax/benefit policy affect the behaviour of parents who are trying to find their preferred balance of work and care commitments. Notwithstanding the focus on employment outcomes, the review also addresses issues in current patterns of family formation and its impact on future labour supply. In all three countries policy objectives aim to "Provide Choice to Parents", but in practice policies and related outcomes differ markedly across countries.

1.1. Introduction to the review

Raising children and having a career both rate highly as important life goals for most people. Helping parents to achieve these goals is vital for society: parental care plays a crucial role in child development and parental employment promotes economic prosperity. For these reasons, helping parents to reconcile their work and family responsibilities is an important policy goal in its own right.

All three countries (Austria, Ireland, and Japan) covered in this review have experienced changes in female aspirations and labour force behaviour, while at the same time birth rates dropped significantly. For some (potential) parents having children (or having as many as desired) and fulfilling labour market aspirations have been mutually exclusive activities. As a result, current labour supply is less than what it could be, and human capital is underused. This result is not an efficient use of labour market resources, and were this situation to be perpetuated, it will limit economic growth relative to potential. At the same time, the declining number of children also has obvious implications for the shape of future societies.

Behind this general discussion of growth and societal development lie much more personal stories of unfulfilled lives. Parents may adjust their family behaviour and decide to have children at a later age, not as many as desired, or not have children at all. Alternatively, parents (usually mothers) withdraw from the labour market, temporarily or permanently. Sometimes this is because it is their wish to provide full-time care for their children, whatever their employment opportunities. In many other cases, however, it is despite the fact that they would like to work, or to work more hours, but cannot do so because of constraints in terms of time, access to services or limited opportunities to resume career tracks after childbirth. Other parents (often fathers) spend so much time working that they hardly see, let alone give personal attention to, their children, which raises concerns about both partnership stability and child development.

Work/family outcomes are influenced by a wide range of social policies, including tax/benefit policies (Chapter 6), childcare policies (Chapter 5), and employment and workplace policies (Chapter 3). Taken together, these factors help determine labour market outcomes (Chapter 2) but also impinge on family formation, parenthood, and family dissolution (Chapter 4).[1] Box 1.1 gives the country-specific policy recommendations arising from this report, with the rest of this chapter summarising main findings.

Box 1.1. **Policy recommendations**

Austria

- Generous income support to families with a very young child and parental leave entitlements mean that the Austrian version of "providing choice to parents" gives significantly more support to those families which choose to have a parent caring full time for a very young child than in Ireland and Japan (and indeed most other OECD countries). Policy should ensure that parents who wish to work more than a limited number of hours have access to similar support:

  i) Introduce an entitlement for part-time work throughout the existing employment-protected leave period or until the age when childcare becomes widely available.

  ii) Introduce higher Childcare Benefit payment rates for those who return to work at an earlier stage, for example, upon one year of parental leave. Similarly, the existing payment period reserved for the "second parent" could be shortened with higher payment rates to stimulate the use of parental leave among fathers.

  iii) Reform allowable earnings/income rules to reduce incentives to concentrate earnings at specific income levels thereby facilitating a greater range of work and care options to parents.

  iv) Link part of the Childcare Benefit payment with the use of formal childcare support.

- In any case, ensure that parents are fully aware of the different durations of Childcare Benefit (30/36 months) and the employment-protected parental leave period (up to the child's second birthday), to reduce the risk of parents not returning to work when the parental leave period is over.

- There is a risk that provinces (responsible for childcare policy) will see the introduction of Childcare Benefit as a signal to cut back, or not to increase, childcare provision. In order to address capacity concerns, extend childcare support for working parents of children at all ages through initiatives at different government levels. To improve efficiency among providers, consider focusing childcare subsidies on parents with such payments being conditional on the use of quality-licensed facilities only.

- Encourage more enterprises to participate in the work and family audit process.

Box 1.1. **Policy recommendations** (cont.)

Ireland

- Introduce an entitlement to part-time work for parents with very young children.

- Reduce the long-term benefit expectation among clients of One Parent Family Payment. This will require a comprehensive employment support approach, intervening more actively at an earlier stage of benefit receipt; providing training and childcare support, whilst ensuring that Family Income Supplement becomes a more effective tool in helping single parents back to work. If introduced, for such a comprehensive strategy to be effective it would need a system of mutual obligations requiring lone parents to seek work actively. This could include, for example, active full-time work-testing from when the youngest child reaches age 6 and in full-time schooling, and from age 4 (when infant classes are available), part-time activity testing (training or work).

- Encourage employers and unions to make workplaces more family-friendly, for example, through the introduction of initiatives that provide workplaces with tailored advice on family-friendly policy practices, while ensuring long-term commitment through regular assessment or audits.

- Explore options to use existing education facilities to address out-of-school hours care needs.

- Promoting child development and ensuring that childcare services are of good quality warrant additional public investment in childcare. Such public spending may best be focused on parents rather than providers, to increase their choice of work and care options, as well as providers and types of care; to improve equity in public childcare support across childcare providers; and to improve efficiency among providers. Income testing could be used to target expenditures on those most in need. To ensure quality of formal childcare, benefit payments can be linked to quality-licensed facilities only. There is a strong case for ensuring that "Childminding" that is currently in the informal sector should be subject to some basic quality controls in return for being eligible for public subsidies.

Box 1.1. **Policy recommendations** (*cont.*)

Japan

- Improve equity between regular and non-regular workers by extending coverage of employee health and pension insurance among non-regular workers.

- Enforce more actively gender equity and equal pay for equal work legislation.

- Reduce re-entry barriers to "mother returners" by enhancing the role of performance assessment in pay and promotion decisions for all workers (regular and non-regular employees).

- Another barrier to labour market re-entry by mothers is the use of age limits in recruitment: there is a need to change attitudes towards the use of such limits.

- Health and pension insurance provisions need to ensure that spouses do not face significant financial disincentives to work. Reform that reduces the financial bias against work for spouses needs to be considered.

- Encourage employers and unions to reform similar employer-provided spousal allowances.

- Encourage employers and unions to make workplaces more family-friendly, with a focus on measures that make working time practices more compatible with family commitments of workers. At the same time, the government should encourage more actively the notion of "work and family life reconciliation promoters" in the workplace to ensure that family-friendly measures fit the workplace in question.

- The family-friendly nature of workplace practices would be further enhanced by effective policing of overtime regulations and the application of working-time flexibility stipulations, as in the Childcare and Family Care Leave Act.

- Childcare policy aims to ensure a sufficient supply of high-quality childcare places to foster child well-being. This aim is to be achieved through an efficient use of public resources, while also generating equity among parents. Recent reforms towards a more market-oriented approach, such as allowing commercial licensed providers to enter the market thereby giving more choice to parents and providing guidance to non-licensed centres to improve their quality, should be extended. One possibility to improve efficiency is to consider focusing childcare subsidies on parents, with such payments being conditional on the use of quality-licensed facilities only.

1.2. Key work and family outcomes

In 2001, female employment rates were highest in Austria (at 62.3%) but are similar in the three countries and close to the OECD average of just below 60%. However, the underlying trends are very different (Chapter 2). In Austria, female employment rates increased rapidly from 50 to 60% during the 1985-1994 period but growth rates have abated since. In Japan, female employment rates gradually increased over the 1980-2002 period. Irish female labour market behaviour has changed dramatically, and is intrinsically linked with a rapidly expanding service sector and buoyant Irish economic growth in the latter part of the 1990s. The female employment rate increased by 15 percentage points since 1994, and employment rates of women aged 25-29 (almost 80%) are now higher than in the other two countries and are *double* that of Irish women of the same age 20 years ago. Employment rates for mothers with children not yet 3 years of age are about 70% in Austria, but only 32% are in work (the rest being on parental leave), compared with 25% in Japan and 45% in Ireland. However, despite the buoyant economy, employment rates among single parents in Ireland are only just over half of those in Austria and Japan where over 80% of single parents are in work.

Long-hours cultures characterize workplace practices in all three countries (Chapter 3). About one third of all Austrian and Irish men work over 43 hours per week, with 11% and 14%, respectively, working 60 hours or more. This is higher than in most European countries, but it pales in comparison with the Japanese record: three fifths of Japanese men work over 43 hours, two fifths work 49 hours or more, while one in five Japanese men put in over 60 hours per week. Combined with long commuting times and the fact that Japanese workers frequently dine together, the result is that on average, Japanese men with non-working wives contribute a mere 13 minutes to daily housework and care. As a comparison, in Austria this is about 2.5 hours per day. More than elsewhere, the long hours' culture in Japan ensures that mothers perform most unpaid housework.

Childbirth is a major determinant of female labour force behaviour, while becoming a parent hardly affects paternal employment behaviour. Usually this makes plain financial sense, as it is least damaging to family income when the spouse with the lowest earnings (usually the mother) reduces her hours of work. However, partly as a result, and despite broad gender equality in levels of educational attainment, women are at a much greater risk of being "trapped" in jobs that do not promote career opportunities. The gender gap in terms of job quality is larger than that in employment rates, and this is particularly the case in Japan because of the operation of its dual labour market. In terms of the proportion of workers involved non-regular employment is a much more important feature of the labour market in Japan (27% of workers) than in the other two countries (around 6% of workers).

Family developments cause concern in all three countries (Chapter 4). Fewer marriages take place than in the past, while divorce rates are increasing. Childbirth is being deferred, if not postponed indefinitely, until parents have completed more years of education and when one or both members of a couple are more securely established in their careers. Although falling rapidly over the past 20 years, the Irish fertility rate is still relatively close to replacement level. This is not so in Austria and Japan, where the total fertility rate (about 1.3 children per woman) has been low for some time. Concern about this issue is slowly creeping into the Austrian policy debate, usually in the context of pension reform, while in Japan concern over low birth rates is widespread.

1.3. The overall policy stance

In all three countries under review, the avowed objective underlying the pursuit of reconciliation policies[2] is to support parents so they have a real choice in making their work and care decisions. Work pays for most of those considering entering employment in these countries: compared with most OECD countries the tax burden on labour is low. However, public social spending on families with children varies considerably: in 2001 it was highest in Austria at 3.3% of GDP, compared with 2.1% in Ireland and 0.9% in Japan. Design of national policies also differs, and with it, the likelihood that parents choose one reconciliation solution over another.

By means of a long parental leave period and generous public income support for all families with a young child, the Austrian version of "providing choice to parents" gives significantly more support to those families which choose to have a parent caring full-time for a very young child than in Ireland and Japan. And there is a broad consensus in Austrian society about the importance of supporting mothers to care for very young children on a full-time basis. When children grow up, the tax/benefit system supports dual-earner couples, while "kindergartens" are widely available. This contributes to employment rates for mothers with children aged 6-16 being high at almost 75%, even though kindergarten opening hours and school hours generally do not facilitate full-time employment. The employment policy stance towards lone parents is one of immediate activation upon expiry of parental leave, which contributes to high employment rates among this population group. However, there are blemishes in labour market performance. In particular, only about one in four mothers return to their previous employer upon expiry of parental leave, while another 25% of mothers whose leave expires also returns to work, but does so by changing employer in order to facilitate working part-time or working limited hours in so-called "marginal employment" (see below).

Irish policy development is unfolding in a rapidly changing environment, with labour market behaviour being very different between older and younger female workers. Irish policy makers are keen to ensure equity between mothers regardless of their employment status, while otherwise using the huge economic gains of the past ten years to reduce tax rates and increase the returns to work for all. The social policy model for couple families with young children is characterised by the absence of direct policy intervention for a considerable period: paid maternity and unpaid parental leave give mothers the option of caring for their own child for about six months upon childbirth. Access to pre-school groups (in the education system) only becomes widely available from age 4 or 5 onwards. Subsidies for childcare of those aged between six months and four years is minimal. There has nevertheless been rapid growth in the number of mothers in work. One major challenge for Irish policymakers is to improve autonomy among single parents. The Irish social policy model provides long-term (until children are 18 or 22 years at maximum) benefits to single-parent families, with no requirement to be available for and seeking employment. This appears to be a significant contributory factor to the relatively low employment rate among single parents.

The social policy stance in Japan towards female employment is very comprehensive. With recent reform, started in 1991 and gradually extended since then, policy provides for one year of parental leave (paid out of Employment Insurance at 30% of previous earnings), and, innovatively, an additional payment worth 10% of previous earnings that is conditional on having worked continuously for six months upon the return from parental leave. Back in work, parents with young children often can reduce working hours until children are 3 years of age (see below), and there is public childcare and pre-school support available for older children. However, in practical terms the model is not fully used: many women still withdraw from work around childbirth. Furthermore, the benefit system discourages dependent spouses from earning more than JPY 1.3 million per annum (about 31% of the earnings of an average production employee), as above this level, spouses generally have to pay health and pension contributions. This effect is often reinforced by employer-provided spousal allowances as about half of the employers who pay such allowances, cease payment completely if the "dependent spouse" earns more than JPY 1.03 million yen per annum (approximately 24% of APE earnings) or JPY 1.3 million per annum. In addition, childcare constraints, especially in the Metropolitan Tokyo area, add to difficulties of finding ways of reconciling work and family life. However, the biggest stumbling block towards a more comprehensive integration of mothers in the labour market lies in prevailing workplace practices which all too often are inhospitable to women (see below), trapping them in low-paid employment. However supportive social policies are towards mothers who work, they are likely to have little effect unless the labour market changes dramatically.

1.4. Reducing workplace barriers to parental employment

1.4.1. *Gender equity in employment opportunities*

The gender employment gap in Austria (15%) is smaller than in Ireland (22%) and Japan (23%). However, the gender wage gap is smallest in Ireland (19%) and largest in Japan (35%), while in Austria estimates range from 20% to 30%. Women make up close to 30% of those in senior and managerial positions in Austria and Ireland, compared with 9% in Japan.

Female career prospects in Austria are hampered by the long time they are often not in work in the aftermath of childbirth. Many women use the full duration of the parental leave period up to the child's second birthday. Upon expiry of leave, almost half of the mothers do not return to work, often temporarily dropping out of the labour force until the child is older. Of those who do return to work about 40% engage in so-called marginal employment with limited earnings (see below). The "Returners Programme" run by the Public Employment Service is specifically designed to help those with long work interruptions back into the labour market (Chapter 6).

In Ireland, as leave entitlements and leave taken are both shorter than in Austria, more women with young children are in work. Compared with Austria and Japan, the increase in female employment rates in Ireland occurred only recently, and so relatively few Irish women have had time to climb up the managerial ladder. Nevertheless, there already is some evidence of a "glass ceiling" for women caused by a mixture of structural, institutional and attitudinal factors constraining female career progress.

Gender inequity in employment opportunities is, however, most prevalent to Japan, both within regular employment, and because of the substantial difference in terms and conditions between regular and non-regular (or "atypical" or "casual") workers. More than 85% of men in work have "regular" contracts, compared with about 55% of female workers. Career patterns are determined early on in working life. About half of the enterprises with more than 5 000 employees have adopted a "career-track system" that employs regular employees into one of two broad career streams: the fast-track "*sougou-shoku*" (where workers are groomed for management, with employment conditions generally involving longer working hours and transferability whenever the employer so desires) and the more routine track of "*ippan-shoku*" workers. Only 3.5% of "*sougou-shoku*" workers are female, while in just over half of all companies only men are in this stream.

Workers in regular employment receive in-house training and employer benefits such as spousal and dependents allowances while their compensation is essentially seniority-based and strongly linked to certified skills, age and tenure – loyalty to the firm. In return, such workers accept a "flexible" adjustment of working conditions, and signal their commitment to their employer and career by putting in long hours, including unpaid overtime and taking less leave than that to which they are entitled. Such arrangements all but preclude playing more than a minor role in childcare.

As over 70% of non-regular workers (who often work less than 35 hours per week) are female concerns about equity between the two types of workers are interwoven with gender equity issues. Non-regular workers are often paid by the hour, with wages that are frequently linked to the prefectural minimum wage. There are glaring wage discrepancies: on average a female non-regular worker earns 33% less than her regular counterpart. Yet in 60% of firms that employ non-regular workers at least some of them have similar workplace responsibilities as regular employees and in 23% of these enterprises there are many non-regular workers with similar duties as regular employees. In almost 50% of enterprises with non-regular workers at least some of them have worked for their company for over ten years, and in 15% of these companies this is true of a substantial number of non-regular workers. Also, in 20% of enterprises that employ both types of workers, at least some non-regular workers work the same hours as regular employees, work overtime and are being transferred within the company while in 10% of these companies there are a substantial number of such non-regular workers. Thus, a considerable number of non-regular workers have workplace responsibilities similar to regular workers. Mother returners who take time out to care for their children, often end up in non-regular employment. Once in non-regular work, throughflow to regular employment is very difficult to obtain. In some occupations age-related entry barriers to regular employment exist. For example, to become a public childcare worker in some municipalities an applicant has to be younger than 28 years of age (the specific age varies across municipalities), otherwise employment in the public childcare sector can only be under non-regular employment conditions.

In the other two countries reviewed, differences in employment contracts are less striking, but nevertheless there are of course employers who perceive women as less committed to their career than men, and are therefore less likely to invest in female career opportunities. To some extent this is a vicious circle: since female workers have limited incentives to pursue a career if they perceive the likelihood of advancement is more limited than for men, they are indeed more likely to withdraw from the labour force, only to return, if at all, in jobs that are often low in job-content compared with their potential.

As a result, employers do not use labour resources efficiently, and especially in Japan do themselves a great disservice by shutting out mothers and women more generally, many of whom have high levels of educational attainment. Changing workplace practices will require sustained effort over a long period, but one step forward in Japan would be to strengthen the link between employment patterns to performance, and reduce the role of seniority-based pay increments and the system of career progression that is based on rigid worker classification systems. There are indications that both employer and employee attitudes towards long-term employment with one and the same employer are changing, and evidence points to a weakening role of the seniority in remuneration. However, so far, employers and unions have not been able to agree on reform to improve the employment conditions of those non-regular workers who do similar work to regular employees (Chapter 3).

1.4.2. Working time flexibility

As it allows more time for caring, part-time employment is often regarded as an attractive way for parents to provide sufficient care for their children, whilst maintaining their labour force attachment, especially when children are very young. In Ireland and to a lesser extent Austria, the expanding service sector facilitated an increase in part-time employment, which since the 1990s has been remunerated on a *prorata* basis compared to full-time employment. By contrast, the recent recession in Japan contributed to part-time (non-regular) employment growth, because it is a relatively cheap form of labour (Chapter 3). Thus, not all types of part-time employment are equal, and its value as a reconciliation solution depends in part on it not becoming a trap for many (mainly female) workers in low-paid, dead-end jobs.

The Austrian system provides employment protection for workers with a young child up to their second birthday (as well as generous income support for such families, see below). However, on expiry of this period, almost half of the mothers do not return to work, and of those who do, 50% change employer, often because the desire to work part-time cannot be realised with the original employer. The leave system allows for taking part-time work (and since 2002, working full-time for a 13-week period), but this option is not frequently used as employers are often hesitant about introducing part-time employment on a regular basis. This contributes to many mothers temporarily withdrawing from the labour market or engaging in so-called "marginal employment" (in Austria defined as earning up to about USD 284 per month in 2002 which is equivalent to about 15% of average earnings).[3] The high rates of (temporary) withdrawal from work certainly reflect parental preferences to a degree. However, other parents are constrained in finding their optimal work and care balance because of the relatively limited regular part-time work options. The introduction of an entitlement to part-time work, as is being considered by the Austrian government (Österreichische Bundesregierung, 2003) would increase parental choice options, strengthen work-attachment during leave (see above) and increase future labour supply (see below).

The Japanese Childcare and Family Care Leave Act provides for one year of leave. Employers must provide work and family reconciliation support to workers with children not yet 3 years of age, and often do so through the reduction of working hours (the Act encourages employers to provide such measures until the child is 6 years of age). Although the Act is not specific on the number of working hours that can be reduced (there are guidelines), most employers who have introduced reduced working hours allow for a reduction of one to four hours per day. Since 2001, provisions also try to entice women to stay in regular employment by providing an additional payment to leave-takers who actually return to work (leave is paid at 30% of last earnings, but for leave-takers who return to work during or at the end of this period, the additional payment (also paid out of Employment Insurance) upgrades the overall payment to the equivalent of 40% of previous earnings). The impact of the Leave Act on current behaviour is limited at present (some of the provisions are restricted to regular employees): 70% of mothers still withdraw from the labour force around childbirth, most of them without using parental leave. Nevertheless, the policy model is valuable as it may help in discouraging many mothers from dropping out of the labour force upon expiry of leave, and also get employers more used to dealing with regular part-time workers.

In Ireland, the short parental leave period contributes to many mothers of young children being in work. During the economic boom of the latter part of the 1990s, mothers faced little difficulty choosing their working hours. However, with weakening labour demand, there is a risk that parents will have fewer opportunities to achieve their preferred working hours and adjust them with changing family circumstances.

1.4.3. Making the workplace more family-friendly

Family-friendly workplace measures are mostly time-related (part-time work, flexitime per day, week or month, tele-working, term-time leave, i.e. school-holiday adjusted working hours) but also include childcare support, access to family counselling services, and, in Austria, measures to assist re-integration after the prolonged parental leave period. Employers have good reason to provide such measures as they motivate and increase productivity of the existing workforce, increase workforce flexibility to meet peak-time demand, attract and retain qualified staff.

Especially in Austria and Japan, where so many female workers do not return to their original employer after childbirth, it is surprising that family-friendly workplace policies are not *more* common. In part, this may be because the "business case" for family-friendly policies is most strongly felt when it concerns (high-skilled) workers who are most expensive for employers to replace, thus limiting the potential target group of workers. Also, there appears to be limited awareness of the benefits of family-friendly policies to enterprises, and even if such notions are present, senior management (usually male) is often not sufficiently committed to their introduction and unions (predominantly male) give other issues greater priority. This lack of leadership limits the wider application of family-friendly practices in workplaces, and their use: workers only use such measures when they feel confident that take-up does not affect their position within the workplace.

Everywhere, take-up of existing family-friendly measures is predominantly a female affair, as illustrated by the proportion of eligible fathers taking up parental leave: 5% in Ireland, 2% in Austria and a mere 0.4% in Japan. The most common reason by fathers cited for not taking leave is the atmosphere in the workplace: traditional gender notions appear difficult to change.

Governments are reluctant to intervene directly in industrial bargaining processes, but even if they did, public directives alone do not easily change workplace cultures. However, there are some policies which reinforce gender stereotypes in the labour market and which should be changed, for example by tax/benefit reform (see below). In general, public policy towards changing workplace behaviour is one of encouragement, promotion of the virtues of family-friendly polices, or otherwise trying to raise awareness of the issue. For example, in the context of the Social Partnership Programme for Prosperity and Fairness, the Irish authorities established a National Framework committee to increase awareness and encourage a wider application of family-friendly policies. The Japanese authorities have set targets on leave take-up (80% for women and 10% for men), to help foster a change in societal attitudes (including among government, employers and unions) that will lead to a greater use of such measures in the workplace.

Policy initiatives could, however, go one step further, by extending the concept of encouragement to practical and tailored advice to improve the family-friendliness of workplaces. Both Austria and Japan provide a tailored approach to the needs of individual enterprises: the Austrian Work and Family Audit initiative, and the 2001 Japanese Childcare and Family Care Leave Act, which encourages enterprises to appoint a "work and family life reconciliation promoter" to oversee the implementation of flexible workplace practices. The strength of these initiatives is that they explore options best-suited to the individual workplace and involve feedback and assessment at a later stage, thereby generating long-term commitment to the process. So far, the number of enterprises involved in these initiatives is relatively small (Chapter 3), but both the "Audit" and "Promoter" initiatives deserve wider application in Austria and Japan. Given the call to develop more practical measures as formulated in the recently agreed Social Partnership Programme, Ireland should consider a similar initiative.

1.5. Tax/benefit systems and the choice of work and care

Low tax burdens across the three countries ensure that work pays for most individuals and the low effective tax rates on second earners in a household ensure strong financial incentives to work (Chapter 6). In each country, however, there are elements of existing policy that encourage mothers to provide full-time parental care rather than to engage in regular employment. The Irish system includes a Home Carer's Tax Credit, but its impact on work incentives is small. Austrian and Japanese benefit systems have a bigger effect on the work and care choice.

The incentives towards providing full-time care in the Austrian tax/benefit system vary with the age of children. Compared with Ireland and Japan, the Austrian tax/benefit system is most supportive to dual-earner couples when children are older than 3 years of age. However, for families with a very young child Austrian policy gives significantly more support to those families that choose to have a parent caring full time than in Ireland and Japan. One-earner couple families with a very young child receive cash transfers worth a considerable 38.1% of APE earnings in Austria, while similar support for one-earner couple families in Ireland (11.1% of APE earnings) and Japan (2.8% of APE earnings) is much lower (Chapter 6).

Recent reform in Austria dissociated the right to employment protection and the parental leave payment. Since 2002, the "Childcare Benefit" (that replaced a parental leave payment and which covers virtually all families) is paid at USD 410 per month (in addition to other child payments worth USD 147 per month) for up to 30 or 36 months. In line with the avowed policy objective, the increase in payment rates, duration, and coverage, certainly increased choice to parents: it improved the financial position of families, thereby making it more likely that families can afford to choose to have one parent caring full-time. Reform also changed the relative income position of parents choosing to work. The net increase in family incomes from a second parent working is far less than it would be if the Childcare Benefit did not exist, and this will also increase the likelihood of a household choosing to have one parent caring full-time.

However, interpreting the effects of this payment on employees is complex, because its provisions interact with those of parental leave legislation. In addition to some technical complications arising from different earnings/income thresholds in the two systems (Chapter 5), the key problem is that duration of payments to families with a very young child was extended to at least 30 months, and is longer than the duration of parental leave. There is a risk that parents will take advantage of increased financial support for the maximum period, not realising the consequences of losing their employment protection.

Recent reforms in Japan involved a move from regressive tax allowances for dependents towards cash benefits for children under age 6 (previously under age 3), and about 85% of families with children in that age group are eligible for the payment. Nevertheless, such payments are low (USD 40 per month for the first and second child) compared with Austria and Ireland. Within the Japanese income tax system, spousal allowances exist, but are designed so that additional spousal earnings always lead to an increase in net household income. Health and pension insurance regulations and employer-provided spousal benefits that have a bigger net worth are not always withdrawn at the same earnings thresholds and their design does not guarantee that additional spousal earnings always generate an increase in net household income (Chapter 6). These features provide clear financial incentives for dependent spouses to limit earnings. In view of concern about the coverage of the employee pension system amongst dependent spouses, reform of spousal pension contributions in 2004 is being considered, which along with income tax allowance reform, is likely to reduce the bias favouring the status of a dependent spouse.

In general, Japanese and Austrian tax/benefit systems and public employment services actively intervene to promote employment of lone parents. However, because around 50% of single parents are in non-regular low-paid employment in Japan, poverty rates are relatively high. The Irish tax/benefit system allows for long-term benefit receipt among single parents, while the role of public employment authorities is limited to "proactive information policy". This strategy is not achieving a satisfactory level of employment for single parents: compared with Austria and Japan, employment rates of lone parents in Ireland are low despite almost ten years of unprecedented employment growth. The "One Parent Family Payment" needs to be further developed to promote a speedy labour market return. The existing system of earnings disregards serves largely to encourage lone parents to top-up benefit income with small earnings, rather than help them back into regular employment. The Family Income Supplement (an in-work benefit for all families with children) could be better promoted as a tool for providing financial incentives for lone parents (not least because it is conditional on them working at least 19 hours per week) to enter employment. However, there are some issues surrounding awareness and take-up which need to be addressed to ensure that FIS reaches all eligible families.

Reducing the expectation of long-term benefit recipiency among new clients of One Parent Family Payment and a more forceful assistance in employment support policy are needed to help more lone parents in Ireland into work. The long periods of leave that lone parents can spend on benefit result in some children growing up in poor, workless and even socially excluded conditions. It is not in anybody's interest to accept passive benefit receipt over many years. There is a need for earlier and more active interventions to support work by clients with very young children, including childcare support, while for the existing long-term clientele comprehensive measures upgrading skills are likely to be necessary. For this to work effectively there would need to be a requirement for lone parents to take advantage of the opportunities open to them and made available through the increased resources provided by society to help them in this way. A system of mutual obligations should be embraced and enforced.

1.6. Improving access to affordable quality childcare

Formal childcare coverage for under 3 year olds is low: 18% in Japan and 12-13% in the two other countries. Of those children aged 3-6, however, 85-90% use some formal care or education facility. Public spending on care for children up to mandatory school-age is about 0.3-0.4% of GDP in all three countries. Support in Ireland is largely concentrated on 4 and 5 year olds, while in Austria and Japan – where local governments play a key role in childcare delivery – income-tested parental fee support is available to those using childcare from a very early age. In recent years, capacity concerns (driven largely by employment rather than child development considerations) have led to increases in public childcare investment in all three countries: the "Kindergarten Billion" in Austria; earmarked investment through the National Development Plan in Ireland; and additional funds through two "Angel Plans" (see below) in Japan. These initiatives have contributed to containing waiting lists, but capacity concerns continue to exist, especially in urban centres, and working mothers often use informal care. In Japan, increased public spending has rapidly improved access to out-of-school-hours care, often facilitated by using existing school-based facilities. Educational facilities are also increasingly used in Austria, and this has helped to meet out-of-school hours care needs, but they are not used in Ireland, where the lack of provision of this sort of care is prolonged.

To ensure a sufficient supply of high-quality childcare places to foster child development and child well-being is a major objective of childcare policy in all three countries. Despite significant increases in formal childcare capacity since the mid-1990s, especially in Austria and Japan, unmet demand persists everywhere, in particular for children under three. This suggests continued changes in parental preferences and work/care choices. Since 2000, Japanese policy reacted by developing a new market-oriented approach to childcare, thereby making it possible for commercial licensed providers to receive the same subsidies as public or non-profit providers. Nevertheless, the expansion of licensed provision has been insufficiently rapid to prevent the emergence of an unlicensed, poorly regulated market in childcare provision. While the proportion of children cared for in such centres is still low, the issue is pressing: parental fees for non-licensed day care are high, and quality is considered rather variable. In response, many municipal governments in Japan have started to provide subsidies to commercial providers of non-licensed day care who fulfill minimum standards – thereby gaining some form of influence over the quality of care provided.

In Austria, commercial providers had always been in the market, but most non-public provision is through well-established non-profit organisations, which also receive largely the same subsidies as public providers. While this has secured high-quality service provision throughout the country, such approach does, as in Japan, raise efficiency issues. In particular, providers in both countries face only limited incentives to keep costs low and, perhaps more importantly, to respond to parental preferences on matters such as the type of care provided, opening hours, etc. One possibility to improve efficiency of the childcare sector is to focus childcare subsidies on parents rather than providers, with such payments being conditional on the use of quality-licensed facilities only.

In many cases, parents prefer to use friends and family to care for their children. In Ireland, parents have an added incentive to look for such care as formal and informal care by paid childminders (mothers caring for their own in a couple family with children taking up to three other children in day care) is expensive: about USD 550 per child per month, twice as high as in the two other countries. As a consequence, a second earner with earnings at 2/3 of average earnings in a couple family with two young children in care has no net return from work after childcare costs. Informal care is provided by older women from those cohorts where female employment has been relatively low. This source of care will gradually dry up as younger cohorts are ever more likely to be in employment. Furthermore, the government has expressed concerns about the quality of care in the informal sector. Promoting child development and ensuring that childcare services are of good quality warrant additional public investment in childcare. When public resources devoted to childcare increase, there is a strong case for ensuring that paid childminding currently in the informal sector should be subject to some basic quality controls in return for being eligible for public subsidies.

In Austria and Ireland, policy has also responded by increasing generosity of child benefits (further increases in rates are projected for 2004 and 2005 in Ireland) that are in no way related to the use of formal care facilities. The underlying rationale is that extra money to parents increases their choice. However, as discussed above, while raising cash transfers to families gives parents more choice as it improves their financial situation, it also makes it financially more attractive for second earners in couple families to choose to stay at home. To counteract that effect, as well as enhancing objectives to increase female labour supply and gender equity (Österreichische Bundesregierung, 2003), one option would be to link Childcare Benefit payments and/or future increases in these payments to using childcare support, at least in part. This would facilitate the choice of parents in terms of work and care options, and in case of sufficient capacity foster choice among providers and types of care, while supporting equity among parents in public childcare support. Such a scheme also does not favour one particular provider over another, and would improve efficiency among providers.

Such a benefit programme can be income-tested, and so designed to have a basic payment for all users of childcare (say for 20 hours), but could also include higher payments (through allowing more hours) to parents in work. Rates of payment can be linked to the type of service used (full-time, part-time, out-of-school-hours care, centre-based or home-based care), while rates of financial support to children in childcare could be highest when a "quality-licensed" facility is used. This would give providers incentives to obtain licensee status and maintain quality, while national authorities can assure quality control. The Australian Childcare Benefit, for example, includes all these aspects (OECD, 2002f).

Demographic trends will also challenge childcare systems, as the working-age population will soon start to decline in both Austria and, most notably, Japan (see below). The need to mobilise additional female labour supply will therefore become more pressing in future. In part, such demands could be met by making part-time employment opportunities more generally available to mothers, but it is unlikely that further substantial increases in female employment rates can be achieved without extending childcare capacity.

1.7. Family formation: facing the future

This second review of family/work reconciliation policies brings together two countries with very low fertility rates – Austria and Japan – and Ireland where fertility rates were rapidly declining until recently. In the first two countries, there is increasing concern about the negative impact of low fertility, and interest in the role policy may conceivably play to counteract this trend. Unfortunately, reliable scientific analysis on the determinants of fertility behaviour is both limited and difficult to interpret: limited, because much of the available analysis only relates fertility trends to policy change without proving any causal link between the two; and, difficult, because fertility trends are affected by so many different factors that are difficult to control and/or identify separately.

It seems, however, that the relationship between employment and fertility is changing. While there was a strong negative causal relationship between employment and fertility in the 1960s and 1970s, in the 1980s and 1990s this relationship has become weaker to the point of insignificance in some countries. At the very least, in most OECD countries childrearing and employment seem to be less incompatible now than they were a few decades ago.

Japan's policy is most explicit in its aim to foster an environment conducive to parents having as many children as they want, and where it is acknowledged that rather than one or two "pro-birth rate" initiatives, a comprehensive policy package is needed to reverse existing trends. However, compared with the dominant role of concerns about fertility and child well-being in the Japanese social policy debate, budgetary allocations to support such initiatives have been modest. The new "Measure plan on support for the next generation" (Chapter 4), based on previous strategies, is a step forward in that it recognises that to have any hope of changing fertility trends, male attitudes and workplace cultures will have to change. Population projections clearly reveal that the Japanese and Austrian populations will undergo dramatic changes over the next 20 years or so in the absence of such changes. Otherwise, women will continue to feel that they face a choice – a career or a family. Childbirth is deferred or postponed by some, whilst labour market objectives are pursued. The result is that birth rates are so low that they are imposing high economic costs on (future) societies.

In both Austria and Japan, policy makers, as well as unions and employers, realise that something has to change in face of future labour supply concerns. However, this is not yet happening. In Austria, this is largely related to broad satisfaction with the current system in which mothers care for very young children, although there is growing awareness that the costs in terms of unused labour supply will increase in the future. In Japan, workplace practices seem very difficult to change. Japan will need "mother returners" to keep its economic engine going in future, and the labour market will have to change in order to provide them with the hours, jobs, wages and careers which will entice them (back) into employment. Reducing the "either/or" element when considering work and family choices seems to be the most promising strategy for improving birth rates.

Notes

1. More detailed information on social programmes can be found in the Background Annex to the Review.

2. Reconciliation policies are defined as all those measures that extend both family resources (income, services and time for parenting) and parental labour market attachment.

3. Throughout, "average earnings" refer to the annual earnings of an Average Production Employee (APE). This concept refers to the average gross wage earnings of adult, full-time workers in the manufacturing sector in each country. In 2002, these were USD 22 543 in Austria, USD 23 829 in Ireland and USD 33 926 in Japan, see also the Background Annex to the Review.

ISBN 92-64-10418-6
Babies and Bosses: Reconciling Work and Family Life
Austria, Ireland and Japan
© OECD 2003

Chapter 2

Families and Work: Labour Market Outcomes

This chapter discusses parental employment patterns in Austria, Ireland, and Japan. While the presence of children in the household hardly affects the labour market behaviour of fathers, it does have a significant impact on maternal employment patterns. It is worth noting, however, that trends across countries vary. Economic growth has procured a persistent increase of female employment in Austria, where three out of four mothers whose youngest child is in school are in work. The booming Irish economy of the latter part of the 1990s – sometimes referred to as the "Celtic Tigress" – facilitated a rapid change in female labour market behaviour: employment rates of women in their late twenties are now higher than in the other two countries and are double that of Irish women of the same age 20 years ago. The economic slowdown in Japan helps explain the growth of relatively cheap flexible labour (often female part-timers) at the expense of regular employment. As well as providing a comprehensive discussion of employment trends and how employment outcomes vary with the age and number of children, this chapter addresses gender equity issues, summarizes the different systems of public support for parents with children and, finally, briefly considers poverty rates.

This chapter discusses female and maternal employment patterns and how they have changed in recent years in the three countries. Labour market conditions are closely related to macroeconomic developments, and these have been instrumental in facilitating the rapid change in female labour market behaviour in Ireland, while the economic slowdown in Japan helps explain the growth of relatively cheap flexible labour (often female part-timers) at the expense of regular employment. Social policy is relevant, because it matters to parents how much support be it financial or in the form of services they get towards raising children. Such support is directly linked with how many hours parents may wish to be in paid employment.

The macroeconomic and social policy context in each of the three countries are summarised in the first section. Thereafter, the chapter describes labour market outcomes, differences between male and female employment behaviour and then moves on to maternal and family employment patterns, and finally briefly considers poverty rates.

2.1. The macroeconomic context

Austria and Ireland have populations of 8.1 and 3.8 million respectively, and the Austrian economy is about twice the size of the Irish economy (Table 2.1). With 126.9 million people, Japan is far larger and has an economy fourteen times the size of Austria's. In all three countries GDP per capita is above the OECD average, while the cost of living is well above average in Japan. The three economies have fared rather differently in recent years (OECD, 2002). Japanese annual average GDP growth of 0.6% in real terms (1995-2001) has been the lowest across all OECD countries, whilst Austrian growth has been modest at 2.5% (just below OECD average). By contrast, the Irish economy boomed in the latter half of the 1990s: economic growth in Ireland was unrivalled in the OECD area at 9.3% per annum. The slowdown in the world economy has affected all three, and projected GDP growth rates in 2003 are around 1% in Austria and Japan, and just over 3% in Ireland (OECD, 2003).

Government outlays are highest in Austria at a half of GDP, and balanced by equally high receipts, although slower growth contributed to a public deficit of around 1.5% of GDP in 2002. Outlays are lowest in Ireland at just below one third of GDP and receipts are slightly higher, and when the Irish economy was buoyant in the latter half of the 1990s, gross public debt dropped dramatically (OECD, 2001). However, after years of surplus, the slowdown of the economy contributed

Table 2.1. **A booming Irish economy, while growth halted in Japan**

Main economic indicators, 2001

	GDP	GDP per capita	Comparative price levels for GDP	GDP (real)	Compensation per employee in business sector	Consumer prices	General government outlays	General government receipts
	At current prices and current PPPs		OECD = 100	Annual average growth rate percentage			Percentage of GDP	
	Billions of USD	USD		1996-2001	2000-2001			
Austria	232.8	28 626	90	2.5	4.0	1.6	49.6	49.5
Ireland	115.8	30 052	98	9.3	7.9	3.2	30.6	32.0
Japan	3 359.6	26 410	136	0.6	−0.1	0.1	36.9	29.8
OECD	924.3[a]	24 152[a]	100	3.3	3.4	3.9	41.7[b]	41.6[b]

GDP: Gross domestic product.
PPPs: Purchasing power parities.
a) Unweighted average of 30 OECD countries.
b) Unweighted average of 27 OECD countries, i.e. not including Hungary, Mexico and Switzerland.
Source: OECD (2002) and OECD (2002a).

to a public deficit of around 1% of GDP in 2002. In Japan, outlays are just above one third of GDP, but 7 percentage points higher than receipts. Indeed, after more than a decade of low growth and high budget deficits, the Japanese gross public debt was around 130% of GDP in 2001 (more than twice as high as the other two countries) and is projected to continue rising (OECD, 2002b).

At 27% of GDP, public social spending in Austria is well above the OECD average, and more than 10 percentage points higher than in the other two countries.[1] During the 1990s, trends in Irish and Japanese social spending to GDP ratios have converged. Ageing populations in Austria and Japan had an upward effect on social spending in both these countries, in which 50% of public social spending is financial support for those in retirement (Chart 2.1).

Countries differ both in the scale and the structure of public spending on families (Background Annex to the Review). Austria is one of the OECD countries, which spends most on family policies at around 3.3% of GDP in 2001, and this is projected to rise to 3.5% upon the complete implementation of the new Childcare Benefit in 2004/05 (Chapter 5). At 2.1% of GDP in 2001 family spending in Ireland is around the OECD average, due to significant increases in child benefit payment rates (in 2001) and considerable spending on the lone parent benefit programme (about 0.6% of GDP). In Japan, the state plays a much smaller role in assisting families with children through cash transfers with spending on families at about 0.9% of GDP. Child benefits in Austria and Ireland are universal, while the Japanese child benefit is income-tested and stops when children turn 6. This explains a large part of

Chart 2.1. **Austrian and Japanese pensioner welfare states**

Public social expenditure by broad social policy area, 1980, 1990 and 2000,[a]
percentage of GDP

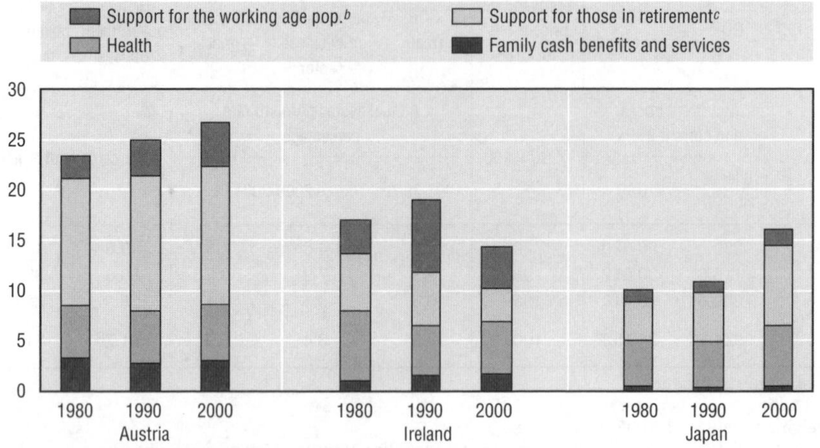

a) 2000 expenditures are estimates.
b) Disability, occupational injury, sickness, unemployment, labour market programmes, housing and other.
c) Old age and survivors cash benefits, and services to the elderly and disabled.
Source: OECD (2001a).

the cross-country differences in public family spending. In addition, over 75% of Japanese employers pay spousal and/or child allowances to their workers (Background Annex to the Review), and some Austrian firms also make child payments (BMUJF, 1999a), but the same is not true in Ireland.

2.2. Key labour market outcomes

Reflecting the diverse economic trends (Table 2.1), the labour market experiences of the three countries under review are very different (Table 2.2). During the 1990s, unemployment rates were relatively low and stable in Austria, and while male employment rates declined somewhat, female employment rates increased by almost 7 percentage points. Labour force participation and employment rates for the working age population for Austria and Japan are not dissimilar in 2001, except that male employment and labour force participation rates in Japan are about 5 percentage points above those in Austria and the OECD average. The underlying trend in Japan, however, is very different from the Austrian experience, with unemployment reaching record highs not seen since the immediate post-war period and projected to continue rising (OECD, 2002). The rapid increase in youth unemployment from 3.7% in 1990 to 9.3% in 2002 for those aged 20-24 is of particular concern (MCA, 1990; MPMHAPT, 2002). By contrast, the Irish economy boomed during the 1990s and unemployment rates dropped by 10 percentage points during this period. As female employment rates

Table 2.2. **The Celtic "tigress"**

Key labour market indicators

	Austria			Ireland			Japan			OECD	
	1984	1990	2001	1983	1990	2001	1980	1990	2001	1990	2001
Labour force participation (percentage of working age population 15-64)											
Men and women	..	67.7	70.7	60.7	60.1	67.5	68.2	70.1	72.6	69.4	69.8
Men	..	80.1	79.0	84.0	77.5	79.0	84.3	83.0	85.0	82.7	80.5
Women	..	55.4	62.3	36.9	42.6	56.0	52.5	57.1	60.1	56.4	59.3
Employment rate (percentage of working age population 15-64)											
Men and women	63.5	65.5	67.8	51.9	52.1	65.0	66.8	68.6	68.8	65.1	65.3
Men	78.2	77.7	75.9	70.8	67.5	76.0	82.6	81.3	80.5	78.0	75.6
Women	49.4	53.3	59.8	32.7	36.6	54.0	51.4	55.8	57.0	52.4	55.2
Women, aged 25-54	56.8	61.7	74.3	30.3	39.3	64.1	55.5	62.9	64.1	61.3	64.1
Women, aged 30-34	..	..	76.0	29.4	45.7	68.8	47.1	50.4	55.1	..	..
Unemployment rate (percentage of labour force 15-64)											
Men and women	..	3.2	3.7	14.4	13.3	3.7	2.0	2.2	5.2	6.0	6.4
Men	..	3.0	3.5	15.7	13.0	3.9	2.0	2.1	5.4	5.4	6.1
Women	..	3.5	3.8	11.3	14.0	3.5	2.1	2.3	5.1	6.9	6.8
Long-term unemployment (percentage of total unemployment)[a]											
Men and women	..	..	23.4	36.7	66.0	55.3	16.5	19.1	26.6	30.8	31.1
Men	..	..	23.8	42.3	71.1	59.5	16.7	26.2	32.1	31.0	31.5
Women	..	..	23.0	25.6	56.8	47.5	16.3	8.8	18.3	29.9	30.2

.. Data not available.

a) Long-term unemployment: 12 months and over. Ireland: 1999 instead of 2001.

Source: OECD (2002c) and OECD (2002d).

increased by almost 20 percentage points during the 1990s (male employment rates grew by about 10 percentage points), one can arguably speak of a Celtic Tigress. Nevertheless, as in Japan, in 2001 male employment rates were about 20 percentage points higher than female employment rates, while the gender employment gap was 15% in Austria. The recent slowdown of the world economy has decelerated employment growth rates in Austria and Ireland, and aggravated the relatively poor employment performance of the 1990s in Japan.

Female employment rates have been over 50% since the early 1980s in Austria and Japan (Table 2.2). In Austria female employment increased substantially from 1985 to 1994 (OECD, 2002d), and while growth rates abated thereafter, the female employment rate was 59.8% in 2001 – close to the EU Lisbon target (2000) of female employment rates of 60% by 2010. In Japan, after some increase during the 1980s, the female employment rate oscillated around its current level of 57% in the 1990s. Among the age group where young children are most likely to be present in a family (age 30-34) female employment rates increased to 76% in Austria and 55% in Japan (with this difference being partly related to the use of parental leave, see below).

Irish female employment rates increased modestly during the 1980s, but during the 1990s female employment rose dramatically, by almost 20 percentage points to 56% in 2001 (and although significant, the increase of employment rates among older Irish women was limited, OECD, 2002d). Much of this increase was facilitated by the booming economy, but attitudes to work have also been changing, most evidently among younger women. Age-related employment rates for women in their early thirties more than doubled from 29.1% in 1983 to 68.9% in 2001: employment rates among Irish women in their late 20s are now 77.7%, higher than in Austria (OECD, 2002d).

2.2.1. Part-time and non-regular employment

Employment growth has been concentrated in service sector employment (in which many women are employed) in all three countries, but particularly in Ireland where the proportion of women employed in services increased by nearly 4 percentage points between 1995 and 2001. The nature of such employment facilitates part-time work, and it is therefore no surprise that service sector growth contributed to increasing female part-time employment rates in all three countries during the latter part of the 1990s, especially in Ireland and Japan (Table 2.3).

Over 70% of all Japanese workers (and over 85% of male workers) are "regular" employees who have a long-term employment relationship with their employer. By contrast, sluggishness in economic growth has contributed to growth in "atypical", "casual" or "non-regular" employees who are treated very differently, and such workers are predominantly female (45% of working women compared with 13% of working men are in non-regular employment): three quarters of the growth in Japanese female employment between 1986 and 2001 was in non-regular employment (Fujiki et al., 2001). Non-regular workers in Japan frequently work part-time (often encouraged to do so by the tax system – Chapter 6), are paid considerably less and have few, if any, of the training and promotion opportunities available to regular workers (Chapter 3).

Atypical work is much less common in the other two countries. In Ireland, around 6% of employees are "casual" workers – i.e. they have less than 13 weeks of continuous service (provided this is not on a regular or seasonal basis) or have a casual employment agreement.[2] In Austria, "marginal" employment also involves around 6% of workers and concerns those with earnings up to just over USD 284 per month in 2002,[3] allowing students, benefit recipients, and maternal homemakers to supplement household income (Chapter 3).

Table 2.3. **The dual Japanese labour market**

Structure of employment

	Austria			Ireland			Japan		
	1990	1995	2001	1990	1995	2001	1990	1995	2001
Share of services[a] in percentage of civilian employment									
Men and women	55.2	60.3	63.2	56.1	59.9	63.8	58.7	60.7	64.6
Men	..	..	..	..	48.2	50.2	55.0	55.5	58.1
Women	..	53.2	54.3	..	50.1	53.7	44.3	45.6	47.0
Share of part-time (under 30 hours)[b] employment in percentage of total employment, aged 15 and over									
Men and women	6.0	11.1	12.4	9.8	14.4	18.4	..	..	17.1
Men	0.7	3.1	2.7	4.2	6.5	7.1	..	..	8.0
Women	15.6	21.6	24.8	20.5	26.6	33.0	..	..	30.2
Women's share in part-time employment	93.0	84.2	88.0	71.8	72.4	78.3	..	..	72.4
Share of part-time (under 35 hours)[c] employment in percentage of total employment, aged 15 and over									
Men and women	..	..	..	..	..	..	19.2	20.1	24.9
Men	..	..	..	..	..	..	9.5	10.0	13.7
Women	..	..	..	..	..	..	33.4	34.9	41.0
Women's share in part-time employment							70.5	70.2	67.5
Share atypical[d] employment in total employment									
Men and women	..	4.4	6.0	..	..	6.0	18.8	19.3	25.7
Men	..	..	..	..	..	4.5	8.0	8.1	12.7
Women	..	..	..	..	..	7.8	36.6	37.4	45.0

.. Data not available.

a) Based on United Nations ISIC (International Standard Industrial Classification) Rev. 3 for Austria and Ireland, ISIC Rev. 2 for Japan.

b) Part-time employment refers to persons who usually work less than 30 hours per week in their main job.

c) Part-time employment refers to persons who work less than 35 hours per week.

d) Marginal employment in Austria refers to workers earning less than the marginal employment threshold (USD 284 per month in 2002) – this figure includes many workers who have another job and persons in receipt of social (insurance) benefits – counting only those people who are only marginally employed reduces the proportion to 1.8% in 1995 and 2.7% in 2000; casual employment in Ireland in 2000, restricted to workers working 15 to 30 hours per week, based on Living in Ireland survey; non-regular workers in Japan.

Source: Services: OECD (2003a); Part-time: OECD (2002c) and OECD (2002d); Atypical employment: Hauptverband der Österreichischen Sozialversicherungsträger (various years); O'Connell (2002); MPMHAPT (2001).

2.2.2. Female labour force behaviour during the life-course

Male labour market behaviour is largely unaffected by changes in family status: Chart 2.2 shows that male employment rates are constant throughout

Chart 2.2. **Japanese women often withdraw from employment around childbirth**

Cross-cohort comparisons of employment rates[a] by age, percentages

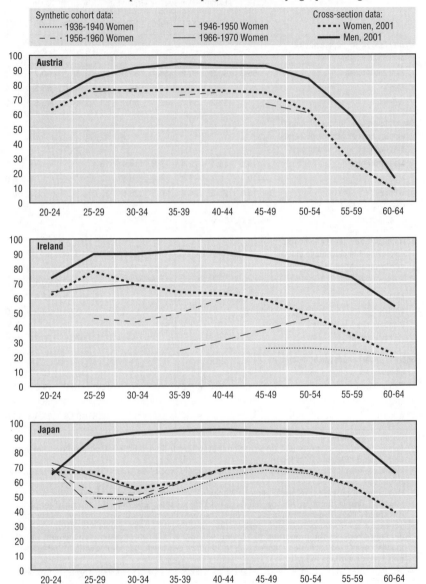

a) The chart combines cross-sectional data by age and gender for the year 2001 with "synthetic cohort" data for women belonging to selected age cohorts.

Source: OECD (2002c).

the childrearing years. Although different in level to male employment, female employment in Austria has a rather similar pattern over the life-course: apart from a slight decline in employment rates in the late 20s (the average age of first childbirth is 29, Chapter 4), female employment rates remain largely constant until age 50.[4] This is also due to the prolonged parental leave period in Austria, during which leave takers (usually women) are counted as "in employment" (Section 2.3). Irish cross-section data shows that female employment peaks around age 27 (the average age of first childbirth) and declines thereafter. However, as indicated above, successive cohorts of Irish women are much more likely to work than their predecessors at all ages, making it difficult to anticipate what the age-related profile over the life-course of younger cohorts will be.

Japanese female employment follows an M-shape pattern with employment rates peaking in the 20s and again in the late 40s, although with increasing work attachment for younger female workers (age 30-34), the "dip" in employment rates has become less pronounced with successive cohorts. Nevertheless, there remains a strong tendency for women to leave the labour market upon childbirth and return when the children are older: around 70% of married women stop work upon the birth of their first child (NIPSSR, 2000).

2.2.3. Gender wage gaps

As well as the considerable differences in employment rates, there are great differences in male and female earnings. Methodological and data differences make a direct comparison of results impossible, but available evidence suggests that the gender wage gap is smallest in Ireland, where median female full-time hourly wages are 19% below those of males (OECD, 2002c).[5] For Austria estimates of the wage gap vary from 20% (OECD, 2002c) to 30% (BMWA, 2002), with the latter study being based on a much larger sample with information drawn from social security files for all workers (excluding marginal employees). For both countries there is a clear decline in the gender wage gap compared to the 1970s, but, if anything, gender wage gaps increased slightly during the 1990s in Austria.[6]

Female labour market characteristics help explain gender pay differentials that increase at higher earnings levels. Despite similar education levels (Box 2.1), men and women tend to have different labour market experiences: women are more concentrated in a few occupations than men and occupational gender-segregation is higher among parents than childless workers (OECD, 2002c); female employment also tends to be more concentrated in low-paid sectors; and, women often have a relatively limited length of service, particularly in Japan (Barrett et al., 2000 on Ireland; MHLW, 2001 on Japan). The Irish situation is changing: younger women and men are more occupationally integrated than older cohorts whilst in Austria there is relatively little difference between cohorts (OECD, 2002c).

Box 2.1. **Educational attainment and employment**

Of the three countries under review, Japan has the most educated population – 83% of the working age population has at least secondary education compared with 76% and 58% in Austria and Ireland respectively (Table Box 2.1, Panel A). In Ireland and Japan educational attainment levels are not very dissimilar across the genders, while in Austria men have notably higher levels of education than women: almost one third of women have less than secondary education compared with one sixth of men. Table Box 2.1 masks the changing nature of the gender gap in educational attainment over time in Austria and Japan. In these two countries, men aged 55-64 had significantly higher levels of education attainment than women, and while males in the age group 25-34 in Austria still are marginally better educated than females, in Japan young women are now better educated than men. Remarkably among OECD countries, across all age groups, Japanese women are more likely to have at least secondary education than men (OECD, 2002e):

Table Box 2.1. **Irish and Japanese women are at least as well educated as men, but they are less likely to be in paid work**

Distribution of population and employment rates by level of educational attainment and gender, 25 to 64 years old, 2001

	Both sexes			Men			Women		
	Less than upper secondary education	Upper secondary education	Tertiary education	Less than upper secondary education	Upper secondary education	Tertiary education	Less than upper secondary education	Upper secondary education	Tertiary education
A. Distribution of population by level of educational attainment									
Austria[a]	24.3	61.8	13.9	18.1	65.3	16.6	30.5	58.3	11.2
Ireland	42.4	22.0	35.6	44.6	20.2	35.3	40.2	24.0	35.9
Japan	16.9	49.3	33.8	17.2	46.6	36.2	16.5	51.9	31.5
OECD	36.1	41.0	22.9	33.8	42.6	23.6	38.0	39.8	22.2
B. Employment rates									
Austria	53.6	74.6	86.5	65.3	81.9	89.3	46.7	66.4	82.2
Ireland	57.6	75.3	84.9	75.0	90.8	92.8	38.4	62.3	77.0
Japan	67.6	74.3	80.4	81.2	90.6	94.5	53.5	61.4	64.4
OECD	57.3	75.0	84.6	70.3	84.2	89.6	46.0	65.4	78.7

a) 2000 for Austria.

Source: OECD (2002c) and OECD (2002e).

> ## Box 2.1. **Educational attainment and employment** *(cont.)*
>
> In all three countries and for both sexes, employment rates improve with the level of educational attainment, but the actual rates and variance across education levels differs between countries (Table Box 2.1, Panel B). The employment rate of low-educated women is lowest in Ireland, but employment increases sharply with educational attainment. There is a similar increase in Austrian female employment as levels of educational attainment improve, and in both Austria and Ireland the gender employment gap is smallest for workers with tertiary education. The situation is very different in Japan where there is only a relatively small increase in female employment as education improves, and women with tertiary education are far less likely to work than their Austrian and Irish counterparts. Remarkably, 95% of Japanese men with tertiary education work compared with just 65% of similarly educated women. That so many well-educated women are not in employment reflects a considerable waste of investment in human capital.

For Ireland in 1997, Barrett *et al.* (2000) found that 53% of wage differentials is explained by observable attributes such as age and education, and that time out of the labour force (*e.g.* while caring for children) explains another 18% of the wage difference. There is no strong evidence that occupation segregation plays an important role, while working part-time seems to have had some impact. Thus 29% of the wage difference cannot be directly explained by observable characteristics. However, the authors estimate that the average woman's wage would only be around 5% higher if her characteristics were rewarded in the same way as are men's.

For Austria, BMWA (2000)[7] found that 20% of the earnings differentials is related to characteristics at the time of labour market entry (such as differences in educational attainment, Box 2.1, choice of occupation and sectors etc.), while another 30% is due to taking parental leave for a prolonged period (which can be taken until the child's second birthday) during which human capital may depreciate, while absence from work reduces future earnings and career prospects (*e.g.* Edin and Gustavsson, 2001; and Datta Gupta and Smith, 2002).[8] The remaining 50% of earnings differentials is related to limited career progression compared with men, but it is unclear what the reason for this may be and to what extent this can be directly related to observable factors. OECD (2002c) found that 23% of gender differences in adjusted hourly earnings in Austria could not be explained by observable variables.

Gender wage differentials are considerable in Japan where a full-time regular female employee on average earns 35% less than her male counterpart (MHLW, 2001). Moreover, non-regular workers (of whom 70% are female, MPMPHAT, 2001) earn substantially less than regular workers (Chapter 3), although the gender differences across this group of workers are smaller: average hourly earnings for female part-time workers, generally working shorter hours than their regular counterparts (Box 3.4), are 86% that of men (MHLW, 2001). The fact that women do not work as long as men, reflecting a different typology of work (see immediately below), and often drop out of the labour force upon childbirth is likely to be important in understanding wage differentials, as not being in work is penalised in a compensation system that heavily relies on age and tenure (Chapter 3). Kawaguchi (2001, 2002) concludes that much of the wage difference is because women are often in jobs below their potential (the next section discusses the challenges Japanese women face in career progression) and that women tend to leave the labour force or move into non-regular work upon marriage or childbirth and therefore have on average shorter tenure (and thus earnings, see Chapter 3) than men.

2.2.3.1. Female career progression

Despite similar education levels (Box 2.1), women are far less likely to be in managerial positions than their male counterparts in all three countries. Austrian and Irish female workers make up a far greater proportion of those in managerial positions – at around 30%, compared with 9% in Japan (ILO, 2003). However, even in Austria and Ireland, women tend to be concentrated in junior management positions, and are under-represented at senior management level. In Ireland, this may be partially explained by the fact that female labour market behaviour has only changed recently and so women have not had much time to climb up the managerial ladder. On the other hand, there is some evidence of a "glass ceiling" in Ireland caused by a range of structural, institutional and attitudinal factors (IBEC, 2002). The patterns of mothers taking leave, and whether or not they return to the labour market, along with specific recruitment and workplace practices, help explain differences in career progression in Japan.[9]

In Austria and Japan women with young children tend to stop working (though they may remain formally employed) for longer than the younger cohorts of female Irish workers (Section 2.3). This may contribute to more pronounced career progress amongst Irish female professionals in the future – as it does in the US when compared with Denmark (Datta Gupta et al., 2001). Indeed, international evidence suggests that, although the availability of parental leave increases the likelihood of continued employment with the same employer, longer leave periods tend to reduce the chance of return to the previous employer (e.g. Ronsen, 1999 on Finland, Norway and Sweden). The long period of Austrian parental leave may then dampen career progression opportunities: only around 50% of leave-takers go back to work immediately at the end of leave and about half of these stay with their "original" employer (ÖSTAT, 1992; Gisser et al., 1995; Lehner and Prammer-Waldhör, 2002).

The Japanese 1986 Equal Opportunity Law encouraged firms to provide equal opportunities to men and women in recruitment, hiring, assignment and promotion. However, firms could continue to advertise vacancies solely for women, and especially larger companies adopted a system that segregates male and female graduates and ensures they have different labour market opportunities within the company. Only 7.1% of all enterprises have adopted a "career-track system" (MOL, 2000), however, it is relevant to a substantial number of graduates because such systems are widely used in larger companies. Over half of large companies (more than 5 000 workers) and 40% of companies with 1 000 to 5 000 employees operate a "career-track system" that employs graduates into one of two broad career streams: the fast-track "*sougou-shoku*" (regular employees, who receive training, may be transferred and are groomed for management) whilst "*ippan-shoku*" workers do routine tasks and cannot be transferred or progress into management.[10] To some extent this sorting of workers into career paths reflects individual choice and preferences. Nevertheless, only 3.5% of "*sougou-shoku*" workers are female (JIWE, 2000) and in 53% of companies only men are in this stream, whilst in 61% of companies only women are in the "*ippan-shoku*" stream (MOL, 2000). The government has challenged this practice by companies through a revision of the Equal Opportunity Law in 1999: firms are now prohibited from only recruiting women into particular jobs.

Entry and the early years in employment are therefore important in determining future career patterns, and among regular employees in Japan, 57% of the difference in promotion between men and women arises in the first ten years of employment (MHLW, 2001a). This reflects both the career track system, and sectoral segregation – Chart 2.3 shows that over 50% of employers relate the lack of female promotion to the different types of work men and women do. Chart 2.3 also demonstrates the importance of tenure, and the willingness to travel, transfer jobs, or work overtime as determinants of promotion. Though more limited, there is also evidence that some employers feel that women and mothers are unable to be managers (Chart 2.3). Hence, despite high education levels (Box 2.1), female Japanese workers seldom have the same career opportunities as their male counterparts, and this contributes to their (temporary) labour force withdrawal. NIPSSR (2000) shows that better educated married women are more likely to quit work upon childbirth than those with a lower level of education attainment: only 27% of those with a university diploma continued work compared with 44% of those with a junior high school diploma.

Chart 2.3. **Why female regular workers struggle to be promoted in Japan**
Percentage of firms which answered "Yes"[a] to survey questions

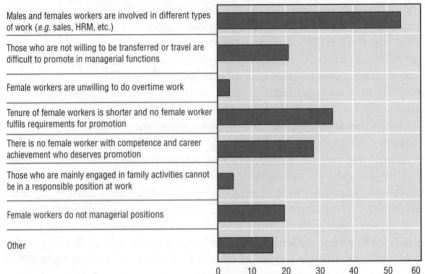

a) The chart shows the percentage of firms which answered "Yes" to each question: answers are not mutually exclusive, so responses do not add up to 100%.
Source: MHLW (2001a).

2.3. Mothers in employment

Age-related female employment profiles are closely related to the patterns of maternal employment, which vary with the age and number of children. Mothers generally drop out of the labour market in Japan, and until recently this was also true in Ireland. And while employment rates of mothers with children aged 6 to 16 are very high and close to 75% in Austria, maternal employment is by no means as high as for men. It is more often mothers than fathers who compromise their career to establish a balance between work and caring responsibilities. However, there is some evidence that a significant number of Irish fathers are adjusting working patterns: 27% of Irish men modified their working time behaviour upon becoming a parent, but a far higher 62% of women do so (TCD, 2002). Not only are participation rates low compared to fathers, mothers in employment often are engaged in different types of jobs in terms of hours and sectors. Prevailing attitudes to, and the policy framework for working mothers, the state of the labour market and workplace cultures, all play their role in explaining maternal labour market outcomes.

BABIES AND BOSSES: RECONCILING WORK AND FAMILY LIFE – ISBN 92-64-10418-6 – © OECD 2003

2.3.1. The policy framework towards working mothers

In all three countries, the policy stance is to "provide choice to parents" in making decisions regarding work and care responsibilities. In this respect, leave arrangements, financial support for families with children and the availability of affordable quality childcare bear on maternal (and far less often, paternal) employment decisions. Leave provisions differ substantially across countries (for detail on national leave arrangements, see the Background Annex to the Review) whilst the rates of *formal* childcare are more similar (Chapter 5). Overall public support during the early years is most comprehensive in Austria, followed by Japan, and more limited in Ireland (Chart 2.4).

In all three countries, participation in *formal* daycare is low for children aged 0-3, but far higher for those between the ages of 3 and 6 (the mandatory school age in all three countries) at over 80%. In all three countries, but particularly in Ireland, a large number of parents with very young children rely on informal care for finding ways to reconcile their work and care needs (Chapter 5).

The Austrian model gives the most comprehensive public support during the early years with 16 weeks of maternity leave (including maternity leave payment) followed by employment-protected leave up to the child's second birthday, Childcare Benefit, worth USD 410 monthly, is also available to families for the first 30-36 months after childbirth (subject to an individual income test). In addition, there are Child Allowances worth USD 147 per month (for the first child – there are supplements worth USD 12 for the second child and USD 24 for third and subsequent children). Low-income parents who use *formal* day care receive considerable support via income-tested fees (Chapter 5). Consistent with the long periods of leave and financial support, only 13% of children aged 0-3 are in *formal* daycare. This figure jumps to 86% for children aged 3-6, for whom kindergarten care is available at limited cost to the parents. Because of its generosity in terms of payment rates, coverage of the population and duration of leave entitlements and Childcare Benefit, the Austrian version of "providing choice to parents" involves giving significantly more support to those families which choose to have a parent caring full time for a very young child than in Ireland, Japan and the vast majority of other OECD countries (Chapter 6). There is a consensus in Austria about the importance of supporting mothers to care for very young children on a full-time basis. However, when children are older the tax/benefit system and formal care systems foster mothers to choose work, and as documented below, the extend to which mothers work in Austria varies a great deal with the age of children.

Until relatively recently, Irish policy reflected traditional gender roles: up to 1973 married women were banned from working in the civil service, and significant financial disincentives to second earners existed in the tax system

Chart 2.4. **Significant public support for Austrian parents of young children**

Policy models: key child benefits, leave and formal childcare support during the early years

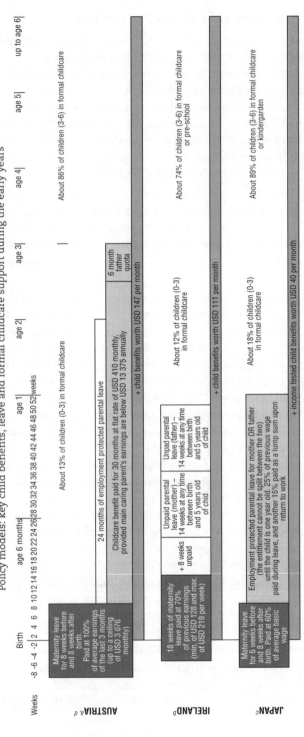

a) Austria: in 2002, public spending is 0.6% of GDP on leave, and 0.4% of GDP on childcare.
b) Ireland: in 2002, public spending is 0.1% of GDP on leave, and 0.3% of GDP on childcare (including pre-school).
c) Japan: in 2002, public spending is 0.1% of GDP on leave, and 0.3% of GDP on childcare (including kindergarten).
d) Income-tested fees for childcare in Austria and Japan.

Source: Information supplied by national authorities.

until the 1980s. A traditional position is still upheld by Article 41.2.2 of the Constitution, which stipulates that "The State shall (...) endeavour to ensure that mothers shall not be obliged by economic necessity to engage in labour to the neglect of their duties in the home". There is the possibility of 18 weeks of maternity leave (including maternity leave payment), another eight weeks of unpaid maternity leave, and a further 14 weeks of unpaid employment-protected leave each for the mother and the father. Perhaps surprisingly given the limited leave arrangements and number of working mothers, participation in *formal* day care is low at 12% for children aged 0-3: childcare solutions are often found in the informal sector. Child benefit payments are worth USD 111 per month (for the first and second child) and USD 139 (for the third and subsequent children), but there is no specific financial support for those using childcare. From the age of 4, Irish children can attend pre-school and around 50% of 4-year-olds and virtually all 5-year-olds do so.

In Japan, mothers can take 14 weeks of maternity leave (including maternity leave payment), and employment-protected parental leave is available up to the child's first birthday. The parental leave benefit (paid by employment insurance) is innovative in design as it provides financial incentives to parents to return to work: during leave parents receive 30% of their previous earnings in income support, and conditional on having worked continuously for 6 months on returning to work from leave are entitled to an additional payment worth 10% of their previous wage for each month on leave. However, it is only available to those covered by Employment Insurance, and not all non-regular workers are eligible (Chapter 5). Back in work, parents with young children often can reduce working hours until children are 3 years of age (Chapter 3). The income-tested benefit for children is worth USD 40 per month, and, as in Austria there is considerable financial support to families using childcare in the form of income-tested fees. However, with many mothers leaving the labour force upon childbirth the need for non-parental care may be relatively low. Participation in *formal* day care is higher than in the other two countries (also because use of informal care is less common): 18% of 0-3 year olds and 89% of those aged between 3 and 6 (with kindergarten generally available from the age of 3).

2.3.2. *Attitudes to mothers being in paid work*

Cultural attitudes play a role in influencing gender roles, though it is difficult to isolate or estimate their impact. The 1994/95 International Social Survey Programme included a survey of "Family and Gender Changing Roles" (ZA, 1997) and gives some indication of country attitudes and shows, albeit to a different extent in each country, the persistence of traditional values towards mothers providing parental care.

The feeling that both the man and woman should contribute to household income is far higher in Austria and Ireland (around three-quarters of those surveyed) than Japan (just over half). However, the extent to which people feel mothers should work varies with the age of children. In both Austria and Japan just over 60% of those asked felt women with pre-school children should not work outside the home, compared with almost half of those in Ireland. By the time the youngest child starts school around one quarter of those surveyed in all three countries felt the mother should stay at home. A smaller proportion feel mothers should work full-time when their children are under school age – 3% of Austrians, 11% of Japanese and 12% of Irish – than when the youngest starts school – 9%, 17% and 26% respectively.

The survey results suggest that in all three countries there is a strong feeling that women should stay at home to look after young children, and that those with school-age children should not work full-time. However, it is difficult to interpret this result when circumstances also play a part in shaping attitudes. Antecol (2000) tries to overcome this problem by looking at employment behaviour of first generation immigrants in the US. She finds that, after controlling for exogenous variables, gender employment gaps are higher than in the home countries for Austrian and Irish immigrants, though despite differences between the two countries, the gap for immigrants of both nationalities is 24.9. The gender employment gap amongst Japanese immigrants is considerably higher (at 39.7) than that in Japan which may reflect the strength of underlying cultural preferences.

There is evidence that traditional views on maternal employment are not as widespread as they once were in Japan. For example, the proportion of "professional housewives" saying they would like to start work at some stage in the future increased from 47% in 1989 to 66% in 1997. At the same time however, an increasing number of women feel it is not easy for them to work – increasing from 42% to 56% over the same period (Social Policy Bureau, 1999). Indeed, the inhospitable nature of the labour market toward mothers can help explain why the increasing preference to work translates into a very limited increase in actual employment rates.

2.3.3. Trends in maternal employment

About 70% of mothers with children age 0-16 are in employment in Austria, while maternal employment is just over 50% in Ireland and Japan. Irish mothers are more likely to work full-time than part-time, whilst the reverse is true in Japan and in Austria since 2001. However, being in employment is not the same thing as being in work. The long parental leave period in Austria (up to the child's second birthday) which mothers frequently use in full, and the one-year period in Japan (with average duration of about 8 months including maternity leave, Chapter 5), imply that female employment rates for mothers with very young children (aged 0-3) overestimate the proportion of mothers actually in work. This effect is limited for Japan, but huge in Austria, where 55% of mothers with children under age 3 are in employment but not in work. Hence, the proportion of mothers with a very young child who are in work is highest in Ireland at around 45%.

Considering maternal work patterns when children grow up, a very different picture emerges. Table 2.4 shows that maternal employment and in-work rates for those with children aged 3 to 6 are high in Austria at 66%,[11] and similar in Japan and Ireland at around 50%. By the time their children have reached school age, even more Austrian mothers are in work, 74%, while Japanese maternal employment rates for those with children aged 6 to 19 are at a comparable level (68%). It thus appears that mothers often return to work on a part-time basis when children enter kindergarten in Austria, while Japanese mothers do so when children enter elementary school. Austrian mothers with children at school age are most likely to work full-time. Employment rates among Irish mothers do not vary much with the age of children, which is related to changing cohort patterns of labour force participation (as discussed in Section 2.2.2), as also reflected in working hours. Mothers with young children in Ireland are more likely to work full-time than mothers with children of school age. Because of the change in labour market behaviour among young female Irish workers, the employment rates of mothers with older children can be expected to increase in the future.

These outcomes reflect very different national trends over the last two decades. Austrian maternal employment data for mothers with very young children are heavily influenced by parental leave reform, with the proportion of employed mothers on leave varying with changes in duration of leave and leave payment. As such the extension of leave (and associated payment) from one to two years in 1990 reduced the proportion of mothers with very young children in work. This proportion increased when leave payment for one parent (though not leave duration) was reduced to 18 months in 1996, but is likely to fall again after reform in 2002 extended leave payment for one parent to 30 months (with leave duration again remaining unchanged at two years, see Chapter 5). Although a comprehensive evaluation of the 2002 reform will not be possible until at least three years upon its introduction, initial evidence suggests that among "transition cases" (mothers who extended their parental leave entitlement under the old regulation in line with transition rules for the new Childcare Benefit legislation) the percentage of mothers returning to the labour market before their children reach the age of 27 months fell from 54% in summer 2000 to 35% in late autumn 2002 (Lutz, 2003). In any case, it should be stressed that labour force withdrawal is often temporarily, as Austrian mothers do return to work when children enter Kindergarten and about half of the working mothers with children aged 6-16 works full-time.

Table 2.4. **Irish mothers with very young children are most likely to be in work, but when children grow up Austrian mothers work most**

Female and maternal employment rates by age of youngest child, percentages

	Women				Mothers with youngest child aged:													
					0-16 years old[a]				Under 3 years old				3 to not yet 6 years old			6 to 16 years old[a]		
	All	Full-time	Part-time	On maternity/ parental leave[b]	All, of which:	Full-time	Part-time	On maternity/ parental leave[b]	All, of which:	Full-time	Part-time	On maternity/ parental leave[b]	All, of which:	Full-time	Part-time	All, of which:	Full-time	Part-time
Austria[c]																		
1980	50.0	40.7	8.2	1.1	44.1	29.7	11.7	2.6	39.1	17.4	7.6	14.2	40.7	30.0	10.7	46.4	33.2	13.2
1985	53.8	44.5	8.0	1.2	48.8	34.6	11.1	3.0	43.5	26.2	5.5	11.8	46.4	34.6	11.8	51.9	38.4	13.5
1990	57.8	45.2	10.9	1.7	54.2	34.4	15.3	4.4	51.2	25.5	8.9	16.8	50.2	33.9	16.3	57.0	39.0	18.0
1995	63.2	42.0	16.4	4.9	67.9	31.0	24.1	12.8	75.3	17.6	9.2	48.7	57.3	31.8	25.4	68.0	37.2	30.7
2000	63.8	41.3	19.0	3.5	70.4	30.5	30.2	9.8	69.6	13.4	15.4	40.9	66.0	29.6	36.6	72.3	38.0	34.2
2001	64.8	41.0	20.3	3.4	71.9	30.4	32.2	9.4	71.9	14.7	17.2	40.0	65.6	28.2	37.4	74.1	37.5	36.6
Ireland																		
1986	32.0	:	:	0.3	18.2	:	:	0.8	20.7	:	:	2.3	15.6	:	:	17.7	:	:
1991	36.4	:	:	0.4	28.5	:	:	1.1	33.5	:	:	3.7	27.3	:	:	25.9	:	:
1996	41.1	29.9	10.8	0.4	38.9	21.9	15.9	1.0	43.8	26.2	13.7	3.9	39.2	22.8	16.4	36.8	19.2	16.8
2000	53.3	36.5	16.3	0.5	49.8	27.3	21.4	1.1	52.5	28.9	19.5	4.1	51.8	30.5	21.3	41.8	17.8	24.1
2001	54.0	36.6	16.7	0.7	50.7	26.4	22.5	1.7	50.1	23.9	19.9	6.4	50.9	28.4	22.5	50.6	24.9	25.7
2002	55.2	37.7	16.7	0.8	51.7	27.7	22.2	1.9	51.1	25.6	18.8	6.6	52.3	30.9	21.3	51.1	22.0	29.1

Table 2.4. **Irish mothers with very young children are most likely to be in work, but when children grow up Austrian mothers work most** (cont.)

Female and maternal employment rates by age of youngest child, percentages

| | Women | | | | Mothers with youngest child aged: | | | | | | | | | | | | | | | |
| | | | | | 0-16 years old[a] | | | | Under 3 years old | | | | 3 to not yet 6 years old | | | 6 to 16 years old[a] | | |
	All	Full-time	Part-time	On maternity/parental leave[b]	All, of which:	Full-time	Part-time	On maternity/parental leave[b]	All, of which:	Full-time	Part-time	On maternity/parental leave[b]	All, of which:	Full-time	Part-time	All, of which:	Full-time	Part-time
Japan[d]																		
1980	50.7	36.1	14.5	0.1	..	..	..	..	..	..	..	..	..	..	..	..	..	..
1986	52.1	36.1	15.9	0.1	50.8	31.8	18.7	0.3	30.1	20.3	8.6	1.2	45.8	27.0	18.8	62.2	38.4	23.5
1991	54.0	35.4	18.5	0.1	54.3	29.6	24.4	0.4	29.6	16.8	11.3	1.4	50.3	23.7	26.5	66.9	36.8	29.6
1995	55.3	35.8	19.3	0.2	..	..	..	..	..	..	..	..	..	..	..	..	..	..
1999	56.2	33.7	22.3	0.2	52.1	21.7	29.5	1.0	29.4	10.1	16.2	3.1	47.8	19.4	28.4	67.4	29.0	37.4
2000	57.0	34.8	22.0	0.2	..	..	..	..	..	..	..	..	..	..	..	..	..	..
2001	55.7	32.6	22.8	0.2	52.4	22.2	29.2	1.0	28.5	9.9	15.4	3.2	47.5	21.3	26.2	68.1	29.7	38.1

.. Data not available.

Break in series in 1994 in Austria and in 1997 in Ireland.

a) Instead of 16 years old: to 14 years old in Ireland from 2000; in Japan, to 15 years old till 1990, to 19 years old from 1995 onwards.

b) We assume all mothers on maternity/parental leave are full-time workers.

c) It is not possible to comprehensively reflect on employment trends in Austria before and after 1995, as since 1993 all workers working more than 1 hour per week are counted, while beforehand the figures only included those working above about 13 hours per week. Persons working less than 12 hours per week are only counted as part-time workers since 1994.

d) Japan: the part-time/full-time share (under 35 hours/35 hours and more hours per week) for employees is applied to all working mothers.

Source: Information provided by national authorities; data for Japanese mothers are from MPMHAPT (2001).

The drop in labour force participation among Japanese women upon childbirth is illustrated again in Table 2.4. Japanese mothers do, however, often get back to work when children grow up particularly when children enter elementary school. Despite the fact that attitudes and policy have become more favourable to working mothers, the overall employment rate of Japanese mothers (disregarding the age of their youngest child) has been constant. The overall stability masks a slight fall in the proportion of mothers in full-time employment offset by an increasing proportion in part-time work, which, as indicated above, is related to a greater use of non-regular workers (often women) who are relatively cheap to employ (Chapter 3).

Employment rates among Irish mothers increased even faster than among other women, and although a series break makes it impossible to be precise on the exact magnitude, the proportion of mothers in employment at least doubled over the last 15 years. This spectacular increase in labour force participation was not prompted by changes in the social policy framework. As in Australia, Denmark and the Netherlands (OECD, 2002f), a substantial increase in formal childcare capacity did not precede expansion of female labour supply in Ireland (or in Austria and Japan). It thus appears that rapidly increasing maternal labour supply in Ireland has been facilitated by the informal sector which consists of two types, paid childminders (who are not cheap, see Chapter 5) and the traditionally strong Irish social network of relatives and friends. Hence, to some extent the Celtic Tigress was built on the back of older women (sisters are increasingly in work) who are full-time homemakers. However, the flipside of increasing numbers of women in work is a decreasing supply of informal care so in the future working Irish mothers will be far more dependent on formal care.

On the basis of costs structures and practical difficulties of arranging childcare (including after school care) for more than one child, one would expect to see both employment rates and working hours to decline with the presence of a growing number of children. Employment rates are clearly negatively related to the number of children in both Austria and Ireland (Table 2A.1 in the annex to this chapter). Furthermore, those with more children are more likely to work part-time in Ireland, but there is no such clear pattern for Austria. Data on working hours and the number of children are not available for Japan, but the employment rates for mothers remain remarkably stable whatever the number of children. Given the long working hours of men (Chapter 3) it is difficult to imagine that many woman with more than three children, are in paid employment for anything more than a limited number of hours.

2.3.4. *The need for more working mothers in the future*

In Austria and Japan, population size and in particular the size of the working-age population is projected to decline until 2050 because of low fertility rates (Chapter 4). The Japanese population will decline by around 20% and the

Austrian population by 6%, the respective working age populations will fall by over 35% and 20%.[12] These changes have considerable implications for the size of the labour force, economic output and the financial sustainability of social protection systems as the population ages and spending on pension and health care systems increases. Conversely, the Irish population is expected to continue to grow, reaching 4.8 million in 2050 – a 25% increase from 2000. The Irish population will however start to age, albeit more gradually, because of the very steep decline in fertility before 1990.

If rates of economic activity amongst the working age population stay the same, the size of the Austrian and, particularly the Japanese, labour forces will shrink dramatically (Chart 2.5). This effect could be, at least partly, offset by increasing employment amongst women and mothers. Indeed, Chart 2.5 shows that increasing female labour force participation rates to the same level as those for men could have a huge effect on the size of the labour force, especially in Japan. Both in Austria and Japan, the labour force would then be of a similar size as it is today. This projection is based on strong assumptions, but nevertheless clearly illustrates the size of the potential female labour force and its effect in alleviating concerns on future labour supply. This feature could also serve as an incentive for both governments and employers to make being in work more attractive to mothers.

2.4. Family employment patterns

2.4.1. Couple families

Joblessness rates (i.e. the proportion of households where no adult is in employment) in Austria and especially Japan are low, but in the latter country are nudging upwards with the recession (Table 2.5). Joblessness is much more concentrated in couple families in Ireland, at 14% in 1996, although this figure should have dropped with the strong employment growth since 1996 (more recent data is not available).

As discussed above, male employment rates are barely affected by the presence of children. Apart from other factors as for example, prevailing traditional gender notions, it generally makes financial sense for the mother rather than the father to provide parental care, because most female workers earn less than their male spouse. Family income is higher if it is the mother who takes leave, reduces hours of work or (temporarily) withdraws from the labour market because of the associated opportunity cost, and this pattern is clearly visible in all three countries (Table 2.5).

In Austria, dual-earner couples are now more common than single-earner families, because of the growth of partnered female part-timers in the late 1990s (see also Table 2A.2 in the annex to this chapter). In 1996, the traditional male-breadwinner model was still dominant in Ireland although

Chart 2.5. **Increase in female employment can prevent drastic shrinking of the labour force**

Total labour force from 1980[a] to 2000, and projections[b] from 2005 to 2030, in thousands

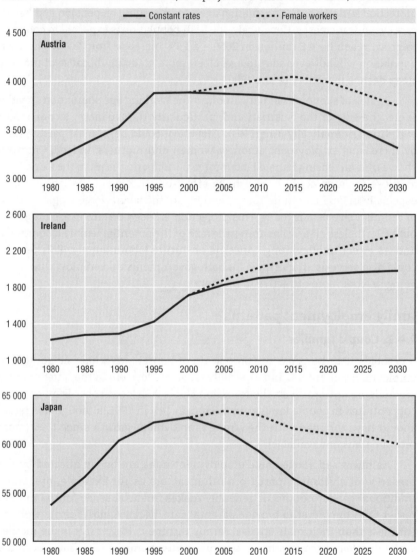

a) 1981 for Austria and Ireland.
b) "Constant rates": assumes constant labour force participation rates for men and women from 2000 to 2030; "Female workers": assumes that female participation rates reach current male participation rates in each country in 2030.

Source: OECD (2003b).

Table 2.5. **Traditional main-earner families still prevail**

Employment status of couple families with children,[a] percentages adding to 100%

	No one in employment	One in employment		Both in employment		
		FT	PT	2 FT	1 FT, 1 PT	2 PT
Austria[b]						
1980	3.0	56.2	0.9	28.4	11.1	0.5
1985	5.1	50.8	0.8	30.9	12.3	0.2
1990	2.8	46.2	1.4	34.0	15.2	0.4
1995	2.6	34.2	1.3	39.6	21.6	0.6
2000	2.7	30.1	1.7	35.3	29.4	0.7
2001	2.5	28.9	1.8	34.3	31.7	1.0
Ireland[c, d]						
1986	23.4			76.6		
1991	12.6	50.1		37.3		
1996	13.7	44.9	5.3	23.1	9.6	3.4
Japan						
1980	0.8	53.3		45.9		
1985	0.9	49.8		49.3		
1990	0.6			51.1		
1995	0.8	49.0		50.1		
2000	1.1	49.9		49.0		

a) Children aged not yet 17 years old, except in Japan until 18 years old in 1985, 1990 and 1995.
b) Austria: PT = part-time, working 35 hours or less per week; FT = full-time, working 36 or more hours per week.
c) Ireland: in the 1996 census the question of whether work was part-time (PT) or full-time (FT) was asked for the first time. The explanatory note that went with this question reads "What is required is the person's own assessment of whether their usual principal occupation is full-time or part-time". Therefore the figures provided may include some people who work over 30 hours and still said their work was part-time.
d) Head of household in employment.

Source: Information provided by Statistik Austria, Central Statistics Office Ireland, and the Japanese authorities.

the proportion of male-breadwinner families is likely to have fallen since (more recent data is not available). In Japan, the proportion of dual-earner couples has increased slightly since 1980. This should not be interpreted as some sort of parity, as many of these women are in low-paid atypical work. Indeed, in Japan, it appears that the decision to have two earners is partly related to economic necessity: low-earner families are more likely to have two earners than high earning families – around 65% of households where the husband earns under USD 32 900 were dual-income couples, compared to 46% where the husband earns over USD 79 750 (Social Policy Bureau, 1999).

These parental employment patterns, as well as gender earning differentials (see above) are reflected in Chart 2.6. Considering all families where men work full-time, it is clear that in all three countries there are very

Chart 2.6. **Women tend to have less income from work
than their male partners**

Distribution of two-earner couples where the husband worked full-time by the ratio
female to male of annual income from work, 1996 (1995 in Japan)

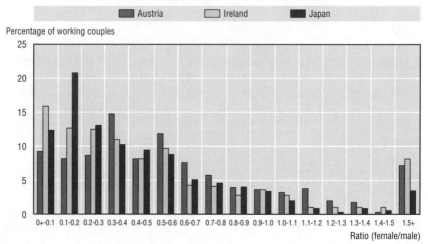

Note: Japanese data includes families where the husband is self-employed, family worker, director of
a corporation, general employee or employee with a contract for at least a month.

Source: Secretariat calculations from Eurostat (2001), ECHP UDB Version, September 2001 (wave 4), and
data supplied by the Japanese authorities.

few households where a female partner earns more than her working
husband. Indeed, the most likely scenario, particularly in Japan, is that the
female has no income from work, or otherwise earns less than half what the
male earns. In 45% of Austrian couple families the woman has no earnings
from work, compared to 54% in Ireland and 59% in Japan. Of couples where the
female partner is in paid work (not including those where either partner is
self-employed), the average female to male earnings ratio is 60% in Austria,
52% in Ireland and 44% in Japan (the Japanese figure rises to 52% if
self-employed workers are included). The proportion of Irish families where
the women is in paid work, and the average female to male earnings ratio is,
however, likely to have increased with female employment participation
after 1996.

2.4.2. Lone parent families

Reconciling work and care is even more of a challenge for lone parents
because of their more limited time. At 81% and 83%, lone parent employment
rates are considerably higher in Austria and Japan respectively than the 45% in
Ireland (Table 2.6). This difference is related to the very different policy
positions – lone parents are expected to work in Austria and Japan, whereas
the Irish policy stance is one of encouragement (Chapter 6). Albeit from

Table 2.6. **In contrast to Ireland, single parents in Austria and Japan are generally in employment**

Employment rates among lone parents, percentages

	1980	1985	1990	1995	2000	2001	2002
Austria	68.2	64.6	73.2	78.1	81.7	81.1	..
FT[a]	55.6	52.8	59.6	60.6	55.0	54.5	
PT[a]	12.6	11.8	13.6	17.4	26.7	26.6	..
Ireland[b]	..	31.2	33.4	40.7	43.2	45.1	44.9
Japan	..	82.6	86.7	84.6	83.6	..	..

.. Data not available.

a) Austria: PT = part-time, working 35 hours or less per week; FT = full-time, working 36 or more hours per week.

b) Census of population for years 1986, 1991, 1996; Quarterly National Household Survey from 2000 onwards.

Source: Statistik Austria, Central Statistics Office Ireland, and Ministry of Public Management, Population Census of Japan.

different levels, employment rates have been increasing in Austria and Ireland, and are generally lowest for families with young children (Table 2A.2 in the annex to this chapter). Meanwhile, employment among Japanese lone parents has been relatively constant in the last two decades, at a high level.

Single parents often work full-time in Austria. Indeed, Austrian lone parents are more likely to be in full-time work than mothers in couple families (AK, 2001). As with mothers in couple families, a large proportion of those with children under three counted as employed are on parental leave. However, in contrast to mothers in couple families, employment rates for single parents are higher for those with children aged 3 to 6, than for single parents with very young children. Although comparable data is not available, earnings evidence suggest that most Irish single parents in employment work part-time, and the majority of lone parents rely on social welfare as their main or only source of income (DSCFA, 2000). In Japan, about half of all single parents are in relatively low-paid non-regular employment (MHLW, 2001b), and average income of single mother households is around half of average earnings (MHLW, 2001b). Poverty amongst lone parents is therefore a much greater concern in Ireland and Japan, than in Austria.

2.5. Poverty

Across OECD countries, poverty rates tend to be higher amongst working age households with children than those without (Förster, 2000), and are therefore often a specific concern. Table 2.7 gives estimates of relative income poverty in the three countries in the mid-1990s. There are minor differences in definition of income and family across countries, so small differences in poverty rates cannot be interpreted as necessarily reflecting real differences.

Table 2.7. **Lone parent families are at risk of poverty**

Poverty rates[a] in the mid-1990s,[b] percentages

	Austria	Ireland	Japan
Entire population	7.6	8.6	16.8
Families with children	6.9	11.9[c]	11.6
Children	8.7	13.8	..
Lone parent families	17.1	24.0	44.4

.. Data not available.

a) Share of persons with income after tax and transfers under 50% of median income, except in Japan where poverty rates are based on income before tax and transfers.

b) 1997 in Austria and Ireland, 1994 in Japan.

c) Persons aged under 65 with children.

Source: Austria: ECHP 4th wave, 1998 (income data for 1997); Ireland: ESRI (1999); Japan: National authorities.

Nevertheless, the data are reliable for showing differences in poverty rates among household types within countries (Table 2.7), and it seems that children in the mid-1990s faced a somewhat elevated poverty-risk in Austria and, especially Ireland, but not in Japan. Compared with the overall population, poverty rates among single parent families are relatively high, especially in Ireland and Japan.

National studies suggest that child poverty has fallen and is low in Austria at 5.5% (Guger and Mum, 1999), at least in part owing to increases in family benefits in 1998. Further reform in 2002 is likely to contribute to additional poverty alleviation among families with very young children (Chapter 6). Strong employment growth in the second part of the 1990s further reduced the rate of joblessness among families in Ireland and helped along the implementation of the National Anti-Poverty Strategy introduced in 1997.[13] Reflecting the various improvements in Ireland, the Irish measure of "consistent poverty" which measures the percentage of children living in households where income is below 70% of median income and who experience "basic deprivation" shows a significant fall in child poverty from 15% in 1997 to 8% in 2000 (ESRI, 2002). This improvement is not reflected in relative income measures because although there was real income growth throughout the distribution, it was lower amongst low-income groups. In any case, the significant increase of Child Benefit in 2000 will improve the relative financial position of families. Meanwhile, Japanese national authority estimates suggest that poverty amongst families with children has been constant since the mid-1990s.

As employment is the best way out of poverty, *prima facie* lone parent families face an elevated poverty risk, as they have to be the main breadwinner and carer at the same time. Poverty concerns for this group are particularly relevant to Ireland, because of the low employment rates and to Japan because half of those lone parents in employment are in low-paid non-regular work (Section 2.4.2). In Austria, poverty of lone parents is less of a problem, because a high proportion is in full-time work. This is reflected in national data which despite not being fully comparable because of different underlying methodologies, show the expected pattern: poverty rates are lowest among lone parents in Austria (16%, see Guger and Mum, 1999) higher in Ireland (24% – ESRI, 1999) and considerably higher in Japan (47% in 2000, from national authority survey of 2001).

2.6. Conclusions

In 2002, female employment rates in the three countries were similar, after a period of dramatic increase in Ireland, and a smaller increase in the other two countries where rates were already relatively high. In all three countries, women are far more likely than men to work part-time, and are concentrated in certain types of jobs, often in the service sector in Austria and Ireland. In Japan the difference between male and female jobs is even more pronounced: men are more likely to be in a higher position in regular employment, whilst women tend to have more limited opportunities in regular employment, or have little choice but to take up low-paid, atypical work. In all three countries, there is a significant wage gap, though smallest in Ireland where women have progressed in the labour market in a short period of time, larger in Austria where long leave periods negatively affect female earnings progression, and biggest in Japan – related to the segregated nature of the labour market.

In all three countries, mothers rather than fathers adjust their working patterns to establish a balance between work and care responsibilities, whether by (temporarily) leaving the labour market or working part-time. Irish mothers are the most likely to be in work when children are not yet 3 years of age, and when in work it more often than not concerns full-time employment, while in Austria and Japan, working mothers with very young children are more likely to be in part-time jobs. Austrian and Japanese mothers often withdraw from the labour force on a temporary basis. Mothers in Austria often return to work on a part-time basis when children enter kindergarten, while Japanese mothers do so when children enter elementary school. Three out of four Austrian mothers with children in school are in work, which is a much higher proportion than in the other two countries, and more than half of them work full-time. Tax/benefit and childcare policy (Chapters 5 and 6) in Austria facilitates mothers with older children to work. On the other hand, Austrian policies supporting one parent in couple families to provide parental care to a very young child on a full–time basis are much more comprehensive than in Ireland and Japan. There is a consensus in Austria to support such mothers, but a long period out of work often has implications for career progression. In Ireland, the proportion of mothers in employment has doubled over the last

15 years, explained largely by a change in attitude towards work among Irish women, strong labour demand inherent to the booming economy, a strong informal care network (Chapter 5) and some policy developments favourable to working mothers. Compared to trends in the other two countries, Japanese maternal employment rates have not changed much in the last two decades: despite significant policy developments in support for working parents, workplace cultures are often inhospitable towards working mothers (Chapter 3).

Annex to Chapter 2

Table 2A.1. **More children involves less paid work, often on a part-time basis**

Employment rate and part-time share of women (of working age)
by number of children, 2002[a]

	Austria		Ireland		Japan	
	Employment rate, %	Share part-time, %	Employment rate, %	Share part-time, %	Employment rate, %	Share part-time, %
0	. .	. .	57.6	22.3	55.7	. .
1	77.3	42.5	55.4	38.4	53.4	. .
2	69.5	48.2	52.5	45.8	54.1	. .
3	58.9	44.7	45.7	50.6	56.6	. .
4+	52.9	37.0	31.9	49.5	52.8	. .
All	. .	. .	55.2	30.2	55.0	. .

. . Data not available.

a) 1995 in Japan.

Source: Information supplied by national authorities.

Table 2A.2. **Employment in households with children,
percentages adding to 100%**
AUSTRIA

	Two parents						One parent			All households with children
No one in employment	One in employment		Both in employment			Not in employment	In employment			
	FT	PT	2 FT	1 FT, 1 PT	2 PT		FT	PT		
A. Households with children (all ages 0-16)										
1980	2.6	49.4	0.8	24.9	9.7	0.4	3.9	6.8	1.5	100.0
1985	4.3	43.6	0.7	26.5	10.6	0.2	5.0	7.5	1.7	100.0
1990	2.4	39.5	1.2	29.1	13.0	0.3	3.9	8.6	2.0	100.0
1995	2.2	29.3	1.1	33.9	18.5	0.5	3.1	8.7	2.5	100.0
2000	2.3	25.6	1.5	29.9	24.9	0.6	2.8	8.4	4.1	100.0
2001	2.1	24.2	1.5	28.8	26.6	0.8	3.0	8.7	4.3	100.0
B. Households with youngest child under 3 years old										
1980	1.4	60.1	0.9	20.5	7.0	0.4	4.7	4.3	0.8	100.0
1985	4.3	47.9	0.6	26.5	5.7	0.1	6.5	7.0	1.3	100.0
1990	1.3	41.9	1.1	31.8	8.4	0.2	4.6	9.6	1.0	100.0
1995	1.1	24.0	0.8	52.0	8.3	0.3	2.4	9.8	1.2	100.0
2000	1.8	26.2	1.2	43.5	14.0	0.5	2.7	8.2	1.6	100.0
2001	1.6	24.9	1.2	42.4	15.9	0.6	3.1	8.2	2.0	100.0
C. Households with children with youngest child aged 3 to under 6										
1980	2.8	54.4	0.5	21.4	10.1	0.3	3.5	5.6	1.3	100.0
1985	4.0	47.8	0.5	24.3	10.9	0.1	4.6	6.2	1.6	100.0
1990	1.1	43.9	1.2	26.3	13.6	0.4	4.0	7.0	2.3	100.0
1995	2.0	37.3	1.3	24.4	21.6	0.6	4.1	5.8	2.9	100.0
2000	1.7	30.6	1.8	21.7	28.9	0.8	2.9	5.8	5.9	100.0
2001	1.7	30.2	1.9	20.8	30.3	1.1	3.1	5.9	5.0	100.0

Note: PT = Part-time, working 35 hours or less per week; FT = Full-time, working 36 or more hours per week.
Source: Statistik Austria.

Table 2A.2. **Employment in households with children,
percentages adding to 100%** (cont.)
IRELAND

	Two parents						One parent			All households with children
No one in employment	One in employment[a]		Both in employment			Not in employment	In employment		
	FT	PT	2 FT	1 FT, 1 PT	2 PT		FT	PT	
A. Households with children (all ages 0-16)										
1986	21.2		69.5			6.4	2.9		100.0
1991	11.2	44.5		33.1			7.4	3.7		100.0
1996	11.8	38.6	4.5	19.8	8.2	2.9	8.4	3.5	2.3	100.0
B. Households with youngest child under 3 years old										
1986	22.4		71.9			4.5	1.2		100.0
1991	12.9	47.2		31.8			6.3	1.8		100.0
1996	10.6	35.0	4.1	28.3	7.6	3.0	8.2	1.9	1.2	100.0
C. Households with children with youngest child aged 3 to under 6										
1986	20.9		71.1			5.8	2.2		100.0
1991	12.6	50.2		27.0			7.2	3.1		100.0
1996	11.2	38.5	4.5	20.0	8.2	3.2	8.7	3.4	2.3	100.0

Note: In the 1996 census the question of whether work was part-time (PT) or full-time (FT) was asked for the first time. The explanatory note that went with this question reads "What is required is the person's own assessment of whether their usual principal occupation is full-time or part-time". Therefore the figures provided may include some people who work over 30 hours and still said their work was part-time.
a) Head of household in employment.

Source: Central Statistics Office, Ireland.

Table 2A.2. **Employment in households with children,**
percentages adding to 100% *(cont.)*
JAPAN

	Two parents					One parent		All households with children
No one in employment	One in employment		Both in employment			Not in employment	In employment	
	FT	PT	2 FT	1 FT, 1 PT	2 PT		FT	PT	

A. Households with children (all ages, under 18)[a]

1985	0.9	47.8		47.3		4.0	0.7	100.0
1990	0.6	46.2		48.8		4.4	0.6	100.0
1995	0.8	46.7		47.8		4.7	0.7	100.0
2000	1.0	46.8		46.0		6.1	1.0	100.0

B. Households with youngest child under 3 years old

2000	1.5	71.9		26.1		..	..	100.0

C. Households with children with youngest child aged 3 to under 6

2000	1.0	55.2		43.3		..	..	100.0

.. Data not available.
Note: PT = Part-time, working 35 hours or less per week; FT = Full-time, working 36 or more hours per week.
a) Under 17 in 2000.
Source: Japanese authorities.

Notes

1. For these three countries, differentials in the tax burden on cash transfers explain some variation in *before tax* public social spending levels. About 9% of public social spending in Austria is clawed back by the Exchequer through taxation of cash benefits, while this is only 1% in Ireland and Japan. As aggregate indirect tax rates in Japan (about 6% on average) are so much lower than in Ireland and Austria (close to 20%), gross spending in Japan on cash benefits can be about 15% lower to obtain the same net transfer to households (Adema, 2001).

2. The 2001 Protection of Employees (Part-time Work) Act excludes casual workers from coverage, and all workers who put in less than 20% of the normal hours are not entitled to *prorata* pension entitlements. Coverage of some employment protection legislation in Ireland remains limited to those with longer tenure: to be covered by the Unfair Dismissals Act one has to have continuous service of one year, while for the Redundancy Payments Acts this is two years.

3. Throughout the report, the exchange rate used is the average of the daily rates in 2002, with USD 1 equivalent to EUR 1.063 and JPY 125.4 (OECD, 2002).

4. Compared to most other OECD countries female workers retire at a relatively early age from the labour force: In 2001, the labour force participation rate of older female workers (age 55-64) was 18.3%, compared with an OECD average of 39.4% (OECD, 2002c).

5. The standard way of measuring the gender wage gap is to use the percentage ratio of female to male earnings, and the closer this ratio is to 100%, the smaller the gender wage gap.

6. Equal pay for equal work legislation was introduced in 1979, and ever since the Austrian government has taken successive initiatives to encourage Unions and Employers to strengthen the position of women in the workforce. For example, legislation provides for company-based plans to facilitate female employment ("Frauenförderpläne"), e.g. through family-friendly policy measures. Recently, the Austrian Government (BMSG/BMBWK, 2002) published a study on gender-differences in many areas (containing indicators on, for example, schooling, employment, income, leisure, etc.) to increase awareness and assist the ongoing discussion on gender mainstreaming in Austria.

7. The BMWA (2000) study does not account for differences in working hours. It is unclear to what extent this reduces the robustness of the results, but the ensuing errors may not be that big: OECD (2002c) found that gender wage gaps are similar for full-time and all employees, including those working part-time.

8. In Austria in 1997, the earnings of women in work who took leave periods during the 1993-97 was some 9% lower in 1997 than in 1993, while earnings of those who had not taken leave had increased by about 20% in nominal terms over the same period (BMWA, 2002).

9. The incidence of sexual harassment of women does not appear to be very high in any of the three countries: of working women, 6% in Austria, 4% in Ireland (EFILWC, 2001), and 6% in Japan (MOL, 2000) report some form of sexual harassment.

10. Other smaller categories of career paths exist in Japan, for example, "senmon-shoku" workers do similar jobs as their "sougou-shoku" colleagues, but, apart from a few exceptions, they cannot be transferred or promoted.

11. Austrian maternal employment rates go down upon expiry of parental leave: employment rates of mothers with children aged 3-6 are 6 percentage points lower than those with children in the age groups 0-3. However, this conceals that in-work rates increase dramatically from 32% when children are 0-3 to 66% for mothers whose youngest child is 3 to 6 years of age (Table 2.4).

12. Population projections are based on Eurostat for Austria and Ireland (Eurostat, 1999), and the latest national projection for Japan (NIPSSR, 2002). The most recent national population projection for Austria (Hanika, 2001) expects a stable population size of around 8 million people until 2050, in contrast to the decline to 7.6 million projected by Eurostat. This difference is for the most part explained by somewhat higher assumed immigration, which would also dampen the decline in the size of the working-age population.

13. Originally, the Irish National Anti-Poverty Strategy focused on five themes: unemployment, educational disadvantage, income adequacy, disadvantage in urban areas, and rural poverty. The strategy was revised in 2001 adding two further areas of concern: health, and housing and accommodation.

ISBN 92-64-10418-6
Babies and Bosses: Reconciling Work and Family Life
Austria, Ireland and Japan
© OECD 2003

Chapter 3

Balancing Time at Work with Care Responsibilities

This chapter analyses how workplace practices affect the behaviour of parents who are trying to find their preferred balance of work and care commitments. The chapter contains a concise summary of industrial relations and prevailing employment conditions, which in all three countries, but particularly in Japan, are characterized by a long working hours culture. In practice, this means that fathers in Japan hardly spend any time with their children, while many mothers therefore find it difficult to imagine that rearing a child and having a career are not mutually exclusive activities. The chapter also analyses the duality in the Japanese labour market and explains why so many mothers with older children are in low-paid non-regular employment. The chapter ends with a discussion of persisting gender roles in workplace cultures and considers why family-friendly workplace measures are not more common. In that context, two recent innovative Austrian and Japanese initiatives are discussed which try to tie the concept of family-friendly workplace measures to individual enterprise needs, while also committing employers on a long-term basis. Such initiatives deserve a wider application in Austria and Japan, while Irish policy makers should consider adopting a similar approach.

It all used to be so simple. The male breadwinner model involved a clear allocation of responsibilities and time: men spent their time at work providing family income, while women spent their time caring for children at home. However, with changing female aspirations and female labour market behaviour this model has lost much of its relevance. Nevertheless, the previous chapter illustrated that in terms of employment outcomes, a gender equitable society is some way off. Societies do not change overnight, nor do labour markets. Moreover, changes in policy direction can be way ahead of behavioural changes in the workplace.

Potentially the gender equitable society holds the key to substantial labour market gains as it fosters a more efficient use of available labour market resources. However, these gains are not fully realised, as many mothers do not find the time to be in regular employment. They are often forced to either take up low-status part-time work – as this is the only way they can reconcile work and care responsibilities, or withdraw from the labour force for a considerable length of time, if not indefinitely. As a result human capital (and investment therein) goes to waste. Alternatively, when women's first commitment is their work, they may well decide not to have children, or fewer than originally desired, which has other negative consequences for societal development (Chapter 4).

The key towards more parents being in work thus lies in giving both fathers and mothers sufficient time to spend at work and with their children. Thus, working hour cultures, part-time work opportunities, and other, often time-related measures that facilitate the reconciliation of work and care responsibilities are crucial to reconciliation options. If working hours are long, childcare can become problematic in terms of time, costs and practicalities and often means that, particularly in Japan, fathers spend little time with their children and mothers bear the brunt of parental care.

This chapter takes a closer look at workplace practices that prevent parents from achieving their desired reconciliation solution. Compared to Austria and Ireland, such barriers are much more prevalent in the Japanese labour market. Inevitably, therefore, the discussion in some of the sub-sections below concentrates on the situation in Japan. Workplace practices depend on labour and social policy development as well as the industrial bargaining processes, and an overview of institutional aspects is given in the next section. Then prevailing long working hours' cultures are considered, upon which part-time work is discussed. Section 3.3 considers the dual labour market in Japan and its implications for maternal employment behaviour. Before concluding, this chapter also discusses the role of family-friendly policies in workplace practices and cultures.

3.1. Key institutional aspects

Workplace practices do not develop in a vacuum. Industrial bargaining outcomes and their linkage to labour and social policy development co-determine workplace practices. In all three countries, governments build labour legislation upon consensus among unions and employers, giving them considerable sway in the process while reform can be a lengthy process. In Japan, initial legislation on a particular topic often asks employers to "endeavour" to provide certain facilities, with entitlement being established at a later stage. In Austria and Ireland too, legislation sometimes provides for the possibility of certain reconciliation solutions, e.g. part-time work during the parental leave period or taking leave over different periods, while making their use contingent on employer consent.

Governments also avoid direct intervention in industrial bargaining processes, although it has happened in Ireland in recent years, when government intervention (often by fiscal means) was instrumental in achieving union and employer agreement on employment conditions within the context of the all-inclusive social and economic "Partnership" process. In all three countries, governments encourage unions and employers towards agreement on issues the government considers worthwhile (e.g. by promoting the virtues of introducing family-friendly policy measures in the workplace).

The industrial bargaining processes in Austria and Ireland takes place in an environment where the government attempts to preserve consensus through promoting negotiations between employers and unions (Box 3.1). By contrast, bargaining takes place at the enterprise level in Japan, which suits an employment system wherein the long-term nature of the employment relationship between individual employers and workers plays such an overriding role. Traditionally, such workers were male breadwinners (women were expected to leave upon marriage, and if not, then childbirth), where employers showed their concern for workers' families' well-being by paying child and dependant allowances. Unions otherwise staunchly defend the interests of these so-called "regular employees". Loyalty and commitment to the enterprise was, and is, key. Those who are not fully committed to their work and leave their employer (e.g. by having children), often end up in "non-regular employment" under very different employment conditions, and without having many prospects of returning to regular employment. Thus, a dual labour market has developed, which is sustained by employers (non-regular workers are relatively cheap) while unions have only recently decided to actively promote membership among non-regular workers.

Box 3.1. **Industrial bargaining and social and labour policy development**

Austria

Collective bargaining in Austria mainly takes place at sectoral level, with over 400 collective agreements being concluded each year. However, bargaining outcomes are not wildly different, as traditionally, the agreement in the "metal" sector is largely followed by other sectors. The traditionally two largest parties in government – Conservatives and Social Democrats, each have strong links with, respectively, employers and unions. Hence, there has been a high degree of consensus between unions, employers and the government.

For decades, this consensus model contributed to a peaceful industrial climate, overall wage restraint and generated considerable influence of unions and employers on social policy development. For example, as a result of the 1949 negotiations, employers started to finance public family payments, in return for wage restraint. With the support of both unions and employers, these payments have developed into the comprehensive Austrian family benefit system, which for over 70% is financed by employer contributions (Chapter 6). The consensus model, however, is under some strain, as the social democrats who have strong ties with unions, have not been part of government since 2000. Government proposals on social security reform thus did not reflect union interests to the extent that they have recently had a ballot and mandate to call a general strike (EIRO, 2002).

Ireland

Since 1987, social and economic policy in Ireland has been largely developed within the framework of national "Partnership Programmes" whose stipulations are often valid for a 3-year period. Typically, a report by the (tripartite) national economic and social council (NESC) taking stock of the economic situation while outlining possible policy avenues, provides the starting point for the consultation process (NESF, 1997). Subsequent negotiation leads up to a centrally agreed "Partnership Programme", the terms of which unions (ICTU) and the employer's organisation IBEC submit to their members for approval. Relevant stipulations are formalised in the few sectoral agreements that exist and numerous enterprise agreements.

The partnership programme consultations involve the government, unions, employers, the agricultural sector, and, since 1997, community and other voluntary sector groups. "Social partnership" in Ireland is thus understood in broad inclusive terms and built around a desire to generate and preserve social consensus. Given the inclusive nature of the partnership concept, it is no surprise that negotiations cover a broad set of economic and

Box 3.1. **Industrial bargaining and social and labour policy development** *(cont.)*

social policy goals and go well beyond the scope of more orthodox industrial bargaining agreements (O'Donnell and O'Reardon, 2000). For example, the most recent Partnership programme for the 2000 to 2003 period – the Programme for Prosperity and Fairness (PPF), covers four broad areas, apart from the strand evaluating the partnership process itself (DT, 2000): 1) "Living standards and workplace environment": wage stipulations, but also family-friendly policy initiatives; 2) "Prosperity and economic inclusion", *e.g.* macroeconomic policy goals, but also transport and infrastructural issues; 3) "Social inclusion and equality": poverty issues, rural development, social housing, gender and racial equality; and 4) "Successful adaptation to continuing change", including active labour market policies (Chapter 6) and childcare policies (Chapter 5).

Notwithstanding the inclusiveness of the process, the traditional strand of industrial bargaining on pay and work conditions plays the key role in the negotiations, and such wage agreements have been facilitated – explicitly so since 1997 – by government tax concessions (O'Donnell and Thomas, 2002). During the period 2000 to 2003 wages increased beyond what was agreed under the PPF (OECD, 2001): under the tight labour market conditions employers were not averse to additional pay rises. They therefore defaulted on the PPF terms agreed in return for government tax concessions. The PPF ran out at the end of 2002 (it applies to public sector workers until mid-2003), and a new partnership deal for the period 2003 to 2005 Sustaining Progress – was ratified in March 2003. It includes government subsidies to social housing and legislation towards union recognition, agreements on benchmarking public sector pay, but does not include substantial tax concessions (DT, 2003).

Japan

Industrial bargaining takes place at enterprise level and the main reason for its prevalence lies in its "functional excellence within Japan's system of long-term employment relations" (Araki, 2002). A large degree of standardisation of bargaining outcomes is obtained through the "*Shunto*" (Spring wage offensive) system. The national confederation of unions (Rengo) and the industrial federations of unions set bargaining targets and then co-ordinate the timing of bargaining rounds across enterprises first within, and then, across industries, with agreements in "leading" enterprises being followed elsewhere. The government does not directly intervene in the bargaining process. However, it may encourage Rengo and employers as organised in the Japanese Business Federation (JBF) to adopt policies by setting numerical targets on, for example, take-up of parental leave. If Rengo and JBF adopt these targets, enterprise unions and management may consider these in their bargaining round.

Box 3.1. **Industrial bargaining and social and labour policy development** *(cont.)*

In general, labour and social policy in Japan is developed in a step-by-step process that involves consensus-building and gives employers and unions considerable sway over policy development. The first step in the process of preparing legislation is for the Ministry of Health, Labor and Welfare (or any other ministry) to set up a committee of experts who prepare a report on the issue at hand upon consultation of stakeholders (employers, unions, other experts and, increasingly, members of the general public). The committee report typically identifies potential policy measures and is, in the case of labour policy, submitted to the Labor Policy Council or one of its sub-committees, *e.g.* on equal opportunities, labour conditions, etc (the government provides the secretariat to these councils). The Councils are made up of union and employer representatives as well as experts, and discussions in these councils can lead to proposals for legislative change. However, without council agreement there will be no such proposal. For example, unions are striving to improve the labour conditions of part-time workers, but thus far employers are unwilling to commit to this. Only upon reaching agreement within a council (*i.e.* on assent of both Unions and Employers) will the government propose legislation to the Diet.

Different Councils also make recommendations to each other. For example, The Council on Regulatory Reform (2001) suggests to the Labor Policy Council to reduce the restrictions on workers employed by a temping agency ("dispatch workers") who by law are not allowed to work on a "production site": under current draft legislation, such restrictions will be abolished for the manufacturing sector.

New legislation is often of an advisory nature, with mandatory stipulations possibly being introduced at a later stage. For example, the 1986 Equal opportunities legislation asked employers to make a "best effort" towards providing childcare leave; only with the enactment of Childcare leave legislation in 1995 did paid parental leave with employment protection become an entitlement.

3.2. Regular working hours

The standard number of hours employees are expected to be at work gives some indication of the challenge that parents face in reconciling work and family life.[1] In Austria, the standard working week varies across sectors, but ranges from 37.5 to 40 hours per week, in Ireland it is 39 hours, while in Japan, the standard working week is 40 hours.[2] However, compared to Austrian and Irish employees, the issue of time commitment to work is much more pressing than standard working hours seem to suggest: actual hours worked by employees in Japan are much higher.

Japanese men put in much longer hours than Austrian and Irish workers. Chart 3.1 shows that Japanese men often work long hours: almost two thirds of prime-age Japanese male workers put in more than 42 hours per week, and 20% work 60 hours of more. The comparative figures for Austria are 30% and 11%, and for Ireland 37% and 14%, relatively long by European standards, and in Ireland at least identified as a barrier to work and family reconciliation (TCD, 2002), but they pale in comparison to practice in Japan. In all three countries, long hours are most common among workers in their 30s and early 40s: i.e. when rearing young children (OECD, 2002d).

In all three countries, women tend to work fewer hours than men and are most likely to work between 15 and 42 hours per week. Everywhere, about 35% of women work 15-34 hours per week, while female working hours in Austria and Ireland are mostly concentrated in the 35-42 hours band. In Japan, 27% of women work more than 42 hours per week. Nevertheless, women in regular employment work considerably less hours (both scheduled and overtime hours are lower for women) than their male counterparts – averaging 135 hours and 165 hours per year, respectively (MHLW, 2001c). Long hours are much more a male than a female phenomenon.

3.2.1. Why do Japanese workers put in such long hours?

The reason for the long-hours culture in Japan lies in the nature of the prevailing employment relationship. About 70% of the Japanese workforce, and over 85% of male workers, are so-called *regular* employees. Such workers have a long-term (not to say, working life-time) employment relationship with their employer. In this system, employees are trained in-house and often receive spousal, child and/or housing allowances that reflect the traditional concern of employers for the well-being of the families of their male employees. In 2001, 96% of the recipients of employer-provided family benefits and 81% of the recipients of housing support were male (MHLW, 2002). Compensation is strongly linked to certified skills (*e.g.* university degree), age and tenure (which is seen as indicating loyalty, Box 3.2), while dismissals tend to be avoided, although the recent economic downturn has put that principle under pressure (see below).

Although the extent varies across different types of regular employees, in return for long-term employment, they accept a "flexible" adjustment of working conditions. Workers signal their commitment to their employer and career by putting in long hours, including unpaid overtime, and taking less leave than that to which they are entitled. Many regular workers perceive signalling less than complete devotion to work as inadvisable in terms of career progression and remuneration. To what extent this perception reflects reality is difficult to assess, but it certainly affects worker behaviour.

Chart 3.1. **Japanese men and women work longer hours than the Austrians and Irish**

Incidence of actual weekly hours of work among prime-age workers, 2001, percentages

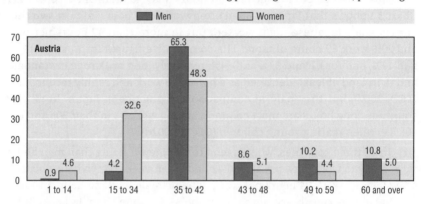

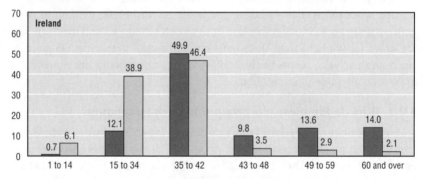

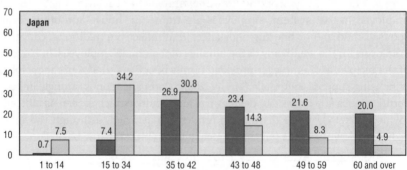

Note: In Austria and Ireland, the incidence of long hours is longest among managerial staff and agricultural workers (EFILWC, 2001). In fact, abstracting from self-employed workers (including those in agricultural sector), the incidence of very long hours (over 60 per week) among men and women in Austria is not 7.5%, but only 2.1% (AK, 2001a).

Japan: All industries, regular and non-regular employment.

Source: Eurostat (2001) and MPMHAPT (2001).

Box 3.2. **Seniority pay in Japan**

Remuneration and promotion in Japan are traditionally seniority-based, and are largely related to age, tenure and skills (qualifications). Of course, seniority plays a role in wage determination and career progression in other countries too, but its role is not as dominant: the age-related earnings profile in Japan is more pronounced than in most OECD countries (OECD, 2003b). Although a flattening of the tenure-related wage profile during the 1990s suggest some weakening in the role of seniority pay systems, the recession will also have played its part.

Considering the entire working life period it is possible that productivity and remuneration for individual workers match, but otherwise there is no link between employees' productivity and pay. Especially in the short-term, this may lead to a substantial gap between performance and pay for individual workers as well as inequity across workers. Seniority wage increments are not susceptible to international competition, and the impact of "market wages and external pay offers" on wage determination in Japan is relatively small. There are some signs of relatively rapid changes; MHLW (2001d) reports that market wages are the most important element in revising wages in 17.2% of enterprises in 2001, up from 10.6% in 1999. Nevertheless, in 1997, over 80% of enterprises identified the automatic seniority-based wage-increments as a problem in their compensation structure (NIKKEIREN, 2001). These weaknesses have become increasingly apparent with the economic slowdown in the 1990s, and have contributed to a growing interest in performance-related compensation in Japan – about a third of enterprises plan to introduce performance-related pay elements (MHLW, 2002a).

Compensation of regular employees in Japan consists of two main elements: 1) scheduled earnings that account for 58% of labour costs on average; and 2) bonus payments making up 18% of labour costs. In 2000, overtime payments (5%), social security and health contributions (10%), and direct employer payments as retirement allowances (5%), child, spousal and special allowances (3% – see below) and miscellaneous items (1%) make up the rest (NIKKEIREN, 2001).

Basic wage determination and progression remains largely based on skills (qualifications, certificates), age and tenure of workers (in some companies, payment systems try to ensure that across different sections (Sales, Finance, etc.) workers in similar work receive similar pay). In 2001, age and tenure automatically determined the basic wage increase for non-managerial workers in four out of five enterprises with more than 30 employees (this proportion is only slightly lower (74%) for managerial workers). However, in recent years the role of performance-related pay has increased: in 2001, almost two thirds of enterprises (up from 55% in 1998) reported that evaluation of performance plays some role in the basic wage determination. Enterprises also reported that the weight attached to performance-related elements in remuneration had increased (MHLW, 2002a).

Box 3.2. **Seniority pay in Japan** *(cont.)*

Bonus payments (usually twice per year) have declined in importance because of the state of the economy, in 2001, they constituted about three months of basic pay on average (MHLW, 2001). In the past the total bonus amount was allocated by industrial bargaining across the workforce, according to a fixed rate or amount. Recently, firms have started to allocate part of the overall bonus payments, according to the performance of a business unit as agreed by employers and unions, or link bonus payments with individual performance. Indeed, Morishima (2002) asserts that employers usually use the results of employee evaluation more to determine bonus payments than base pay, particularly for managerial staff.

Despite these changes the role of performance-related pay in Japan should not be exaggerated: the wage structure in Japan remains essentially seniority-based. Only 40% of the enterprises with more than 30 employees that report using performance-related pay experienced growing intra-firm wage disparity (Morishima, 2002), not least because employers experience practical problems with introducing performance pay (managers have difficulties in making the employee assessment). Employers seem also not (yet) convinced that staff will accept a full-scale replacement of the seniority system, while unions are wary of this as it would endanger solidarity within the workforce. Unions are often quite accepting of performance elements in bonuses, both because they mostly apply to managerial staff (who are less likely to be unionised), and as long as they are *additional* to the basic bonus. In sum, performance-related pay is not replacing seniority pay, but adding to it – "*Seikashugi*" or "*performance-ism*", making the wage system more complex.

Regular employees in Japan often hesitate asking for payment of overtime and taking up leave entitlements, as they perceive this could be interpreted as a signal of less than complete work attachment, and thus reflect badly on employment and career prospects. Overtime is an important feature of the long-term employment system: payments amount to 5% of labour costs (NIKKEIREN, 2001) and in 2002, a Rengo survey found that members put in an average 21 hours of overtime per month (Rengo, 2002).[3] 29% of respondents do unpaid overtime – often considered "part of the service", averaging 29.5 hours a month. However, the government is tightening up on this practice and will continue to do so: from April 2001 to November 2002, the Labour Standards Inspection Office directed 613 companies (found with overtime dues in excess of USD 8 000) to pay overtime compensation for 71 000 employees worth about USD 65 million (MHLW, 2001e). Similarly, leave entitlements are not fully used. In 2002, paid leave entitlements amounted to an average of 18 days paid leave per worker, of which only 48% was used (MHLW, 2002a). Workers either did not claim their full entitlement or the application for some days was met by refusal on the part of employers.

Although still predominant, traditional employment practices in Japan are being challenged. Over 60% of the employers are reconsidering their long-term employment strategy (MOL Study Group on Human Resource Management, 1999), and labour turnover is increasing despite the ongoing recession (MOL, 1991; and MHLW, 2001f). In contrast to older workers, over 60% of university students prefer regular job-change or self-employment over a long-term relationship with one and the same employer (Recruit Works Research Institute, 2001).

3.2.1.1. Implications for time to care

Of the three countries, Japan has the highest proportion of single-earner families (Chapter 2). The very long-hours culture means that if both parents were to work long hours they would not see much of their children. Instead, both potential parents may pursue a career and not have children (Chapter 4), defer having children until they are older, or one of the parents reduces working hours or (temporarily) withdraws from the labour force upon having children.

Men in their 30s (who are most likely to be the fathers of young children), work the longest hours in Japan, whilst the long hours culture is less widespread in Austria and Ireland and mostly concerns men in their 40s. In addition to the long hours, Japanese workers frequently dine together and face longer commuting times – averaging 48 minutes per day (MPMHAPT, 2001a) compared to 35 and 36 minutes in Austria and Ireland, respectively (EFILWC, 2001).

In all, it is clear that Japanese men in their 30s simply cannot be involved in many housework chores. On average, Japanese men with non-working wives contribute just 13 minutes to daily housework and care (MCA, 1996), compared to 150 minutes in Austria in 1992 (the latest year for which data is available, Gross, 1995). Irish evidence also suggests that fathers are more involved in these activities than their Japanese counterparts (Fine-Davis et al., 2002), as also illustrated by their wish to change workplace behaviour after childbirth (TCD, 2002). More so than in the other two countries, the prevailing employment conditions sustain the male breadwinner model in Japan, and Japanese family-life is heavily dependent on mothers providing parental care.

3.2.2. Part-time work

Part-time employment is frequently used as a reconciliation solution, although family-friendly considerations among unions and employers were not the major reason for its establishment or growth in any of the three countries. A mixture of labour demand and supply factors affects part-time employment trends. On the demand side the following, often interacting, factors can be identified:

- *Increase workforce flexibility.* Part-time workers can be useful to help employers have the appropriate mixture of employees in their workforce to meet demand at all times and deal with predictable peak hours and/or peak days. Because of the flexible labour input in many services activities, service sector expansion has contributed to the growth of part-time employment.

- *Reduce labour costs.* If labour costs are proportionally lower for part-time workers (as is most relevant in Japan) employers have a clear incentive to hire part-time workers.[4] Moreover, even if wages are pro-rated, part-time workers are likely to be cheaper per hour than paying overtime to full-time employees.

- *The stage of the business cycle.* In tight labour markets, employers can alter employment conditions to attract those workers who have a preference for working part-time (including many mothers). Conversely, in periods of economic stagnation and weak economic prospects employers may reduce working hours of existing employees, and/or take on part-time workers.

The desire among workers for part-time work solutions is often related to care commitments for relatives and spouses (not just for children), being in education, a desire for more leisure time (as, for example, among older workers), etc. Obviously, labour supply for part-time employment increases when relevant employment conditions and pay improve (relative to both full-time employment and being out of work). On the other hand, economic stagnation may lead to an increase of involuntary part-time employment: workers increasingly accept part-time work, as full-time employment opportunities are more restricted.

The design of tax/benefit systems impinges on both demand and supply side factors, as it affects: 1) (non-wage) labour costs; and 2) often provides incentives (to second earners in a household) to earn less than a certain amount and, thus supply a limited number of hours work. When relevant, such policies will be referred to below; Chapter 6 discusses the underlying intricacies in greater detail.

3.2.2.1. Economic expansion and mobilising labour supply

Although the trend in part-time employment has been upwards in all three countries, the underlying dynamics are rather different. The expansion of the service sector, the tight labour market, and policy measures improving employment conditions of part-time workers, contributed to an increase of part-time employment in both Austria and Ireland (Chart 3.2). Economic growth was particularly strong in Ireland, where strong foreign investment contributed to a service-sector driven expansion of employment, and while employment growth has been mainly in full-time jobs after 1993, the rate increase in part-time employment was even higher (O'Connell et al., 2003). In such buoyant economic conditions workers generally can choose their working hours and realise their preferences: in 2000, only 1% of Irish part-time workers reported having a preference for working more hours (CSO, 2000).

Chart 3.2. **Female employees increasingly work part-time**

Trends in the share of female employment in total employment, 15 years old and over, 1980-2001

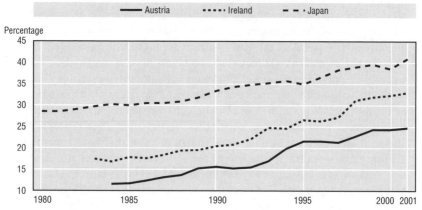

Part-time employment refers to persons who usually work less than 30 hours per week in their main job. Japan: data are based on actual hours worked, and part-time employment refers to persons working less than 35 hours per week.

Austria: part-time refers to 12-29 hours per week before 1994; from 1994 onwards, it refers to 1 to 29 hours per week.

Source: OECD (2002c).

During the 1990s, policy in Austria and Ireland has moved towards establishing a level-playing field among part-time (those who work less than 30 hours per week) and full-time employees in terms of labour costs. Despite there being women in part-time work, this equalisation means that gender wage gaps are similar for full-time and all employees (OECD, 2002c). Legislation in both countries was introduced that regulates the *pro rata* remuneration of (most) part-time and full-time workers. Regular part-time workers thus became relatively more expensive, but that did not abate the growth of part-time employment, which in Austria was helped along by an increase in cheap small-hours part-time work (Box 3.3). In the tight Irish labour market conditions of the second part of the 1990s, employers were anyway willing to pay more to workers and hire them on the conditions workers wished for, and many of those previously outside the labour force (including mothers) took the chance to work part-time when it was offered. In other words, part-time employment opportunities helped to mobilise otherwise unused labour supply (O'Connell *et al.*, 2003), particularly among mothers: 70% of "mother returners" over the 1994-1999 period did so through part-time employment (Russell *et al.*, 2002). Moreover, the design of earnings disregards in the Irish benefit system facilitates many lone parents on income support to engage in part-time employment (Chapter 6).

Box 3.3. **Marginal employment in Austria**

To facilitate small-hours employment among students and benefit recipients, marginal employment (*Geringfügige Beschäftigung*) is an important exception to Austrian reform towards proportional remuneration of all employees. The so-called marginal workers are those who earned less than USD 284 per month in 2002 (equal to about 15% of APE), and by law, these workers are only covered by accident insurance, although workers can opt-in to health and pension insurance at a low cost (and many do, while parents caring for children up to the age of 4 also gain pension credits), but they are never covered by UI legislation. With recent reform, exemptions to employers on social security contributions were limited to those that have fewer than 1.5 marginal workers in their workforce; nevertheless the number of marginal workers continues to grow. Further reform towards an equalisation of the status of these workers would run into resistance of small enterprises, as well as many students and pensioners involved in these activities.

Marginal employment constitutes about 10% of all part-time work, and at first sight, the use of marginal employment as a reconciliation option is limited: only 18% of the marginal employees report they combine such employment with care obligations at home. However, it is a popular option for mothers returning from parental leave: of those who returned to work upon leave expiry, 40% end up in marginal employment (Lehner and Prammer-Waldhör, 2002).

Austria's legislation provides for part-time leave – which keeps mothers in work and thus enhances their career opportunities – but this is subject to employer consent and only 3% of mothers taking leave actually use this option (BMUJK, 1999a). And while Austria and Ireland have introduced legislation to ensure *pro rata* remuneration of part-time employees, there is no legal basis to change working hours from full-time to part-time or *vice versa*, as in the Netherlands (OECD, 2002f). In Austria and Ireland, employers are *encouraged* to allow workers such flexibility, but part-time work is not necessarily part of regular employment career patterns.

3.2.2.2. Economic stagnation and "casualisation" of the workforce in Japan

Through *pro rata* remuneration of part-time workers in Austria and Ireland, the difference in overall labour costs (including employment adjustment costs) between full-time and part-time employees is relatively limited. Not so in Japan, where the concept of "part-time work" is tantamount to non-regular and relatively cheap employment (Box 3.4). In terms of the

Box 3.4. **The concept of part-time employment in Japan**

The Part-time Work Act does not explicitly specify an hours threshold (although less than 35 hours per week is considered as "part-time" in the statistics in Japan; the OECD threshold for comparative data on part-time work is 30 hours), but simply refers to "workers whose scheduled working hours per week are shorter than those of regular employees in the same workplace". This concept includes many so-called "quasi-part-time-workers" who work more than 35 hours per week, but less hours than is the norm in their enterprise, or work just as long as regular workers. For example, the 1995 General Survey of the Condition of Part-Time Workers considered all *non-regular* employees as "part-time" and of all workers surveyed 16% worked as many hours or more as regular employees (12% for women, and 27% for men – MOL, 1997). Part-time employment in the sense of less than 35 hours per week among regular employees is unusual.

While the majority of non-regular workers are part-time employees in the sense that they work less than 35 hours per week, it is more appropriate in the Japanese context, to discuss "part-time employment" in terms of "Casual", "Atypical" or "Non-regular" employment. Such workers generally do *not* have a *regular*, permanent, employment contract (although some "temps" or "dispatch workers" are regular employees of the temping agency for whom they work).

number of workers involved (about 25% in Japan vis-à-vis 3% in Austria and 6% in Ireland), non-regular employment is a much more important feature of the labour market in Japan than in the other two countries.

Non-regular workers are not entitled to the same degree of employment protection as their full-time counterparts (Kezuka, 2000). They would therefore be expected to be the first group of workers to be laid-off in times of economic adversity, while maintaining employment among regular employees. However, this does not hold for employment patterns in the late 1990s. Overall, in the current recession there has been some substitution of *regular* full-time employees by *non-regular* part-time employees, although employment dynamics vary across sectors.[5]

3.3. The dichotomy between regular employees and non-regular workers in Japan

Regular workers are hired into a company, often not in a specific job, but move around in the firm within their working-life. Their remuneration is essentially seniority-based (Box 3.2). In contrast, non-regular workers are taken on for a specific task: they are paid per hour and earnings are often linked to the minimum wage by prefecture (NIKKEIREN, 2001) plus a bit on top.

Table 3.1. **Substitution of regular employees by non-regular workers in Japan**

Shares in regular and non-regular employment[a] in Japan, in percentages

	Regular employees	Non-regular workers[b]			
		All	Part-timers	*Arubaitters*	Others
1990					
Men and women	79.8	20.2	11.6	4.7	3.9
Men	91.2	8.8	1.0	3.7	4.1
Women	61.9	38.1	28.3	6.1	3.7
1995					
Men and women	79.1	20.9	11.8	5.5	3.7
Men	91.1	8.9	1.0	4.2	3.7
Women	60.9	39.1	28.1	7.4	3.7
2000					
Men and women	74.2	25.8	14.5	7.3	4.0
Men	88.3	11.6	1.9	6.1	3.7
Women	53.8	46.2	32.7	9.1	4.4
2001					
Men and women	72.3	27.7	14.1	6.5	7.1
Men	86.1	13.9	1.9	5.6	6.5
Women	52.9	47.1	31.3	7.7	8.1

a) Except executives.
b) "Arubaito" workers generally concern students in very small hours jobs and short-term contracts. The category others include daily workers and "shokutaku": employees re-hired by firms upon reaching the mandatory retirement age and "dispatch workers" or "temps".

Source: MPMHAPT (2001).

Non-regular workers are often considerably less expensive to employers than regular employees unless they are young. Indeed, 65% of enterprises take on non-regular workers "to save on employment costs" (MHLW, 2002b). It is difficult to compare age-related wages of regular workers with hourly earnings of casual workers, but to give an indication, one estimate is that hourly earnings of a female employee of a temping agency are similar to that of a 27-28 year old female regular employee (Weathers, 2001). But even if wages are equivalent, non-wage labour costs are not. Non-regular workers are not covered by stringent employment protection legislation and are often not entitled to retirement and other (*e.g.* spousal and child) allowances. Whilst employers have to pay social security contributions for full-time employees, they do not for many whom work shorter hours[6] and as a result more than half of non-regular workers are not covered by employment insurance or employee health and pension insurance (MOL, 1997).

The distinction between regular and non-regular workers is more or less permanent: in 54% of enterprises, it is impossible to move from non-regular into regular employment (MHLW, 2002b). Similarly, age-related entry conditions in some occupations also deter older applicants from finding regular employment. For example, to become a publicly-employed childcare worker in Japan applicants has to pass the exam to enter the local civil service before their 28th birthday. There is no option of choosing to take up that career at an older age – for example, after returning to work after childbirth. Risk-averse behaviour among employers also plays a role. Stringent employment legislation makes it difficult and costly to lay off regular workers, even during the probationary period.[7] While employers may be willing to take hiring risks with young and inexperienced workers whom they can train, they are less certain about investing in older (30 years plus) female workers.[8]

In the absence of a viable alternative many female workers engage in non-regular employment. Almost 60% of women take up non-regular employment to supplement family income and choose non-regular employment because they cannot get regular employment (23%) and/or unlike regular work, atypical employment offers some working time flexibility (47%) (MHLW, 2002b). In addition, health and pension insurance regulations provide financial incentives to dependent spouses to limit their earnings to a maximum of JPY 1.3 million per annum (about 31% of average earnings). Up to that level, they do not pay employee health and pension contributions, while the husband benefits from tax allowances and employer-provided benefits for having a dependent spouse. This effect is often reinforced by employer-provided spousal allowances as about half of the employers who make such payments cease payment completely if the "dependent spouse" earns more than JPY 1.03 million or JPY 1.3 million per annum (see Chapter 6 for a detailed discussion). Evidence suggests that many married women deliberately limit their earnings, and thus restrict their hours of work, to avoid losing the spousal benefits (Chapter 6). For low-income families, favourable tax/benefit treatment of low-paid work thus helps in supplementing household income. However, the need to engage in low-paid work is limited for many high-skilled female workers as they are more likely to be married to men with high levels of educational attainment and earnings. Moreover, the job content of non-regular work is often not appealing to these workers, which contributes to their labour force withdrawal.

3.3.1. Discrimination of non-regular employees

Equal pay for equal work legislation aims to ensure "fair pay" across workers, but in Japan it is even more difficult than elsewhere to translate such a notion into practice. Regular employees are recruited into a company, unlike atypical workers who are recruited into a specific job. As earnings of regular workers are not set by type of job it is all the more difficult to compare remuneration across both groups of workers.

As men are much more likely to be in continuous employment than women, their earnings progression in the seniority-based remuneration system is on average stronger. Hence, the wage gap between regular and non-regular employees is more pronounced for men. On average, male non-regular workers earn 51% per hour of what their regular colleagues earn: for female workers this is 67% (MOL, 2000a). On occasion, wage gaps can be much higher. For example, the hourly earnings of a 50-year old public childcare worker can be about 2.5 to 3 times the hourly earnings of an otherwise not very dissimilar childcare worker on a non-regular contract. The glaring discrepancy in earnings between the two types of workers feeds the debate on whether such pay gaps are justified. As nearly three-quarters of atypical workers are female, such concerns are interwoven with gender equity issues.

The 1996 Maruko alarms case proved a landmark in practical terms (Kezuka, 2000; Osawa, 2001). The case was brought by 28 married women who had worked for the Maruko Company for between 6 and 27 years on renewable two-month contracts. They claimed that the wage gap with regular employees (between USD 8 760 and USD 11 960 a year) contravened equal pay for equal work legislation as well as gender equity legislation. The court ruling did not address the gender-related issue, but in the first instance the court did rule (the case was later settled out of court) that "(...) if plaintiffs' wages were less than 80% of female regular employees with the same tenure, the wage differential clearly exceeds the acceptable level, and to that extent the discretion of the defendant has violated public order and morals (...)" (Kezuka, 2000). On what grounds a wage gap of 20% for equal work was considered acceptable was not made clear, but it nevertheless illustrates that unexplainable pay discrepancies between regular and non-regular workers are the norm, not the exception.

It is frequently asserted in Japan that comparing earnings of the two groups of workers is inappropriate as regular and non-regular workers have different responsibilities in the workplace. However, a report released by the government established "Expert group on part-time work" in April 2000 (MOL and JIWE, 2000) found that in many enterprises that employ non-regular workers their work conditions were not all that dissimilar from regular employees. In almost 60% of enterprises that employ non-regular workers at least some of them have similar duties to regular workers and in 23% of these enterprises there are many non-regular workers with similar duties as regular employees. Almost 50% of enterprises with non-regular workers reported to have some non-regular workers who have worked for their company for over ten years, and in 15% of these companies have many such workers. Finally, in 20% of firms that employ both types of workers, some non-regular workers work the same hours as regular employees, work overtime and are being transferred within the company, while in 10% of these companies there are a substantial number of such non-regular workers. Thus, a considerable number of non-regular workers have workplace responsibilities similar to regular workers, and continuing the discrepancy in employment conditions seems unjustifiable.

3.3.2. *Improving the status of non-regular employees*

A government-established experts' group (a first step in preparing legislative reform – Box 3.1), has made some suggestions towards improving the status of non-regular workers. They have suggested dividing the group of "part-time workers" (read non-regular workers) in two groups: Type A – those workers who perform similar duties as regular employees, and Type B – those involved in different duties. The former type of workers should then be treated similarly as regular employees (in terms of wage structure, payment, access to training, etc.). Type B workers would still be subject to different treatment and payment from regular employees, but there would have to be a better balance between the wages of Type B workers and compensation of regular employees (Kezuka, 2000). However, difficult implementation issues in terms of how to identify Type A and Type B workers have not been addressed.

Since labour policy development in Japan is largely consensus based (Box 3.1), the minimum employers and unions can agree upon determines the scope for legislative reform. As employers and unions do not agree on the avenue towards improving the employment conditions of non-regular workers, reform has been slow in coming. Unions are in favour of upgrading the position of non-regular workers, as long as it does not impinge on the position of regular employees (of about 7.6 million Rengo members only 260 000 are "part-timers"). Employers are wary of the cost implications, and in any case are voting with their feet: in the present economic climate they are substituting expensive regular employees with relatively cheap non-regular workers.

3.4. Employer-provided family-friendly policies

Concepts such as promoting the *work-life* or the *work-family* balance have a common core: allowing workers more time to pursue their non-work related interests improves their well-being. For wide-ranging reasons governments, employers and unions, each have an interest in promoting measures that achieve a better balance between work and outside interests of workers.[9] The motivation of unions and employers to agree on the provision of family-friendly measures determines the extent to which such measures are available in the workplace, and the extent to which public encouragement to increase their coverage might be effective (Box 3.5). The Austrian Work and

Box 3.5. **Public initiatives to encourage employers to become more family-friendly**

There are two strands to Austrian policy encouraging employers to be more family-friendly. The most interesting is the Family and Work Audit which consults firms that want to become more family-friendly. The second strand is an annual national competition to find the "company providing the best conditions for female staff members and families". This is recognition of the importance of family-friendly policies, and can generate useful media coverage and publicity for the firms involved.

The Family and Work Audit is a small-scale initiative (directly involving 56 companies by the end of 2002), introduced in 1998 that attempts to raise awareness of family-friendly policy initiatives among companies and encourages and supports them to introduce such measures. The main advantages the Audit identifies for firms implementing family-friendly measures are improvements in employee motivation, commitment, reduced stress levels and associated costs as well as benefits from increasing retention rates. Enterprises taking part in the initiative are reimbursed for a large share of the costs, with 90% of fees being reimbursed for companies with up to 20 employees, down to 25% for companies with over 500 employees.

The Audit focuses on the needs of individual companies rather than setting benchmark standards for all companies. It looks at ten areas including working time, workplace practices, management competence, personnel development and support services. The strength of this initiative lies in its structured involvement of workers and management, and the possibility of regular follow-up. The first step is meeting with management, followed by a workshop with a group of employees, run by an external consultant, where workplace needs are identified. The consultant then makes a range of proposals and upon agreement with management practical goals to be achieved within a three-year time period are set. At the end of this period, an external auditor assesses achievements, and if the goals have been met, the company is awarded a certificate. Ideally the process is then repeated (with other goals) to ensure the ongoing nature of the process. As with any such scheme, its success is challenged by the difficulty of convincing employers of the benefits of introducing family-friendly policies (precisely because they are so hard to measure), and reliant on the support of managers who ultimately decide what measures will be introduced.

> Box 3.5. **Public initiatives to encourage employers to become more family-friendly** (cont.)
>
> The Irish National Framework Committee for Family-Friendly Policies was established under the Programme for Prosperity and Fairness (Box 3.1). Where Austrian policy works with individual firms, the Irish committee aims to identify what social partners can do at a national level to support the development of workplace family-friendly policies. Its main aims have been to establish a code of practice for parental leave, disseminate information on family-friendly policies (advocacy role), develop guidelines and best practices for flexible work practices (tele-working) and other measures difficult to legislate. One of the outcomes has been an annual Family-Friendly Workplace Day, held to raise awareness of and promote family-friendly policies. A scheme involving the provisions of practical advice to individual firms (as in Austria) is under consideration.
>
> In Japan, legislation itself is often of an encouraging nature, but the government also uses numerical targets to influence national unions and employer organisations, in the hope this will generate a behavioural change in priority setting at enterprise bargaining processes (see Box 3.1). For example, the government has set a target to increase the proportion of fathers and mothers taking parental leave to 10% and 80%, respectively. The government as an employer also tries to change the long-hours workplace culture. Government officials are encouraged to go home early one day per week, though individual ministries are responsible for establishing what time and day this is. Most recently, with the revision of the Childcare and Family Care Leave Act in 2001, the government encourages firms to appoint a "work and family reconciliation promoter" in charge of implementing the five measures towards reconciling working and family life as laid down in that Act (see Section 3.4.1). These "promoters" can also advice on family-friendly measures that are most suitable to the workplace in question. The Equal Employment Opportunity Bureau organizes seminars and generally disburses information on the promoters' role, and so far about 23 000 enterprises reported (which is not compulsory and thus likely to underestimate the "real" number) to have appointed a work and family reconciliation promoter. Compared to about 1.6 million enterprises this is small, but compared to the number of firms with more than 30 employees (157 000), the number of "promoters" appears more significant.

Family Audit and the Japanese "Promoter" are particularly interesting initiatives as they go beyond mere encouragement, and provide practical and tailored advice that fit best in the workplace at hand. Critically, the process involves feedback and assessment at a later stage, thereby generating long-term commitment to family-friendly workplace practices.

The majority of union members are male.[10] Part-time workers (or non-regular workers) are less likely to be unionised, or active within the union. For these reasons unions are often not particularly active in asking for family-friendly measures or such demands are not prioritised and are unlikely to remain on the negotiating table as long as pay claims (*e.g.* Ireland) or employment guarantees for regular workers in times of limited economic growth (Japan).[11] There is a "business case" for employers to introduce family-friendly policy measures, because such measures will contribute to:

● The quality of the enterprise-workforce by retaining some who would otherwise quit, and by attracting those who see family-friendly policies as an additional factor in a particular companies favour (being the "company of choice"). Both factors contribute to a reduction in recruitment and training costs.

● The motivation and productivity of the workforce.

● The flexibility in hours worked of the workforce.

● Companies being better prepared to deal with a shortage of workers – as recently in Ireland, while it is projected for Austria and Japan (Chapter 2).

As relevant potential (replacement) costs and gains are most substantial for high-skilled workers, employer-provided family-friendly workplace measures are likely to be distributed unequally, with low-skilled employees being least likely to benefit from such measures. Moreover, attempts in Japan to increase coverage of family-friendly measures mainly cover regular employees: atypical workers often do not have access to non-wage employer benefits.

3.4.1. The penetration of family-friendly measures in the workplace

Apart from the part-time employment solutions discussed above, there are broadly speaking two types of employer-provided measures: 1) those that are supplementary to public childbirth related leave and/or day-care provision; and 2) measures that facilitate a more flexible organisation of time spent at work. (Cross-nationally comparable information on the prevalence of such measures is not available, but the annex to this chapter provides national information.)

To start with the former, employers in Australia, but certainly in Denmark and the Netherlands were likely to provide some income support during the maternity and/or *parental leave* periods (OECD, 2002f). This practice is much less prevalent in the three countries in this review. The statutory leave provisions differ markedly across – in order of declining generosity, Austria, Japan, and Ireland (Chapters 2, Chapter 5 and the Background Annex to the Review). The long period of parental leave in Japan and particularly in Austria, mean that employers face costs in finding and paying replacement workers, which they, if the situation allows for it, will limit by replacing workers at the lowest level possible.[12] Therefore, few, if any, employers in these two countries feel obliged to also continue (partial) wage payments during the leave period. In Ireland where the childbirth-related leave period is much shorter and where there is no public income support directly linked to parental leave, around a quarter of employers make some payment during childbirth-related leave period (IBEC, 2001).[13] Collective agreements in Austria generally provide for paid leave for some days in certain family-related circumstances, while 58% of Irish enterprises offer *paternity leave* (TCD, 2002). It is unclear to what extent this practice exists in Japan.

In all three countries regulations on *leave to care for sick children* exist. Austrian workers can take up to two weeks per year to care for sick children under the age of 12, while Irish workers can take three days per year up to a maximum of five days in three consecutive years to care for sick family members. In 1999 only 11% of Japanese employers had introduced a system to provide sick leave for working parents with pre-school age children, while this care system was only been used by parents in 10% of the companies that introduced it (MOL, 1999): most workers took paid annual holiday to care for sick children. Because of the limited penetration of this measure in workplaces, the 2001 revision of the Childcare and Family Care Leave Act obliges Japanese employers to endeavour to introduce sick leave for parents with pre-school age children. Employers in these three countries hardly ever provide *earmarked childcare support* to their workers, instead most family-friendly measures relate to working time, and in Austria often used to relate to extending statutory parental leave provisions (Table 3A.1).

There are various ways of increasing *work-time flexibility* by reducing the number of hours over a specific period, making them more flexible on a daily basis or allowing for the possibility of working from home. In all three countries, the most commonly offered arrangement is some form of reduced hours (other than part-time), though flexitime is far more prevalent in Ireland than the other two countries. In Ireland, the most common possibilities are job sharing, flexitime and personalised hours (Table 3A.2). "Term-time" working (whereby parents can take unpaid leave for the school summer holiday period) is also offered by a small proportion of Irish companies, and throughout the Irish civil service. The impact of tele-working as a way of reconciling work and family life is small. For example, EcaTT (2000) finds that only 9% of tele-workers in Ireland were female. By contrast, and not surprising given the overall employment status mothers in Japan, tele-workers in that country typically concern mothers with young children and a high educational background (Ouchi, 2000).

Recognising that flexibility in workplaces is hard to legislate, the 2001 "Law on Childcare and Family Care Leave" stipulates that firms must take at least one measure out of five options (of which four relate to working time)[14] to assist employees who are bringing up a child not yet 3 years old, while employers are encouraged to do the same for those with children aged 3 to 6 – *i.e.* when the child enters primary school. In 1999, about two out of five enterprises adhered to the then recommendations of the Law (MOL, 2002), while 60% of companies with more than 30 employees did so, predominantly through measures adjusting working hours (Table 3A.3). Since reform in 2001, employers are legally obliged to introduce one of the five options for workers with a child not yet 3 years of age (previously, this concerned workers with children not yet 1 year old), which should have led to a significant increase in flexible workplace options, but data to illustrate that effect are not yet available.

In fact, the "Childcare and Family Care Leave Act", provides a comprehensive support model for parents, usually mothers with young children. It provides for one year of employment-protected leave (paid through the Employment Insurance system), while employers must provide (often working time related) support towards a better reconciliation of work and family commitments to workers until children are 3 years of age (Chapters 2 and 5). Although the Act is not specific on the number of working hours that can be reduced (there are guidelines), most employers who have introduced reduced working hours for workers with very young children, allow for a reduction of one to four hours per day. Nevertheless, 70% of mothers still withdraw from the labour force around childbirth (Chapter 2).

3.4.1.1. *The reasons for limited access to family-friendly policies*

The question is then why are family-friendly policies not more common, particularly in Japan and Austria where so many female workers do not return to their original employer after childbirth. An important reason is that the business case is strongest for high-skilled workers, thus limiting the potential target group of employers. The business case is felt less strongly in the current economic climate in Japan which reduces the risk of workers leaving voluntarily (and may contribute to hesitancy among Japanese employers to investing now in family-friendly measures). Also, regular employees in Japan have already strong incentives to remain with employers as their compensation strongly depends on age and tenure. Nevertheless, with so many women leaving employment upon childbirth, the low fertility rate (Chapter 4), and the obvious need to increase female labour supply in the medium term, it is surprising that employers (and unions) in Japan are not pushing harder for a wider application of family-friendly measures in workplaces.

Often the decision to introduce family-friendly measures is not the result of a cost-benefit calculation by management, but because of a personal decision by someone (or small group of people) in the leadership of an organisation about how the company should behave as an employer (*e.g.* Inzersdorfer in Austria, Aer Rianta in Ireland, NEC in Japan). Leadership is particularly necessary to overcome internal institutional barriers (in large firms) to introducing such measures. In general, limited awareness of the benefits of family-friendly policies and a lack of strong commitment to their introduction among senior management limit their wider application.

A general difficulty for employers in introducing flexible work arrangements or leave to care for sick children is that unlike the periods of leave around childbirth, they are not predictable. Hence, flexible practices are generally more common as an entitlement in large, rather than small firms – of which there are many in Austria, who are more likely to provide reconciliation measures on an informal basis (IBEC, 2002a; MOL, 2000).[15]

3.4.2. Gender roles in workplace cultures

Take-up of existing family-friendly measures is overwhelmingly by women. For example, the proportion of eligible parents taking parental leave in Austria was 95% of mothers and 2% of fathers, for Ireland 40% of mothers and 5% of fathers, and in Japan 58% of mothers and 0.5% of fathers. Similarly, 98% of Irish employees engaged in job-sharing were female (IBEC, 2000) and in Japan almost all workers making use of the reduced working hours option were women (MOL, 1999). The differential take-up rates clearly illustrate the persistence of traditional roles in terms of caring responsibilities, but will also reflect differences in the different types of employment of fathers and mothers.

In all three countries, the most common reason for fathers for not taking leave is the atmosphere in the workplace, which in Japan is exacerbated by the nature of employment relationships. Apart from anything else, and as shown above, regular workers are unwilling to use even their full quota of holiday entitlements, as this may signal less than complete work-commitment. Moreover, the lack of forceful leadership in introducing family-friendly policy measures plays a crucial role, as without such leadership, workers often do not have confidence that they can take advantage of the provisions without compromising the business objectives of the organisation and their own careers. For these reasons, it is unrealistic to expect a rapid change in behaviour of male (and female) workers with long-term employment relationships.

In the past, Japanese "women mainly performed routine tasks and sometimes served as flowers of the workplace, brightening the environment for male workers" (Weathers, 2001; The Japan Times, 2002). Workplace practices have been changing in response to equal employment legislation and the need to utilise more fully the skills of the whole labour force. Nevertheless, women still are often in low-status employment and it is difficult to find them in managerial positions. In Ireland, female employment rates have been lower for much longer than in Japan, but workplace cultures seem to have changed more rapidly and do not seem be burdened as much by traditional notions of gender roles.

3.5. Conclusions

Time is a crucial resource to parents juggling with work and care commitments. Workplace practices therefore affect how much time parents in employment can spend caring for their children. Simultaneously, workplace cultures also co-determine which (or whether both) of the parents reduces hours of work to provide care.

Long-hours workplace cultures contribute to female workers in particular being forced to make a choice between: 1) prioritising career and work commitments over spending a lot of time with their children (or not having any, or as many as desired – Chapter 4); 2) seeking a reconciliation solution which involves a significant number of hours spent with their children; and 3) becoming more or less full-time homemakers, at least for a few years. In all three countries long-hours cultures prevail, but particularly in Japan, the choice is a stark one, and it seems that many mothers have difficulties imagining that a long working week is compatible with caring.

Employers are aware that parents, usually mothers, have to make work and family choices. In all three countries reviewed, there will be employers who perceive women as less committed to their career than men. Particularly in Japan, many employers expect women, regardless of their educational attainment level to withdraw (at least temporarily) from the labour force upon childbirth. When women are rightly or wrongly perceived as less committed to their career than men (and willingness to put in long hours is seen as a relevant signal), employers are less likely to invest in female career opportunities. To some extent this is a vicious circle, since female workers have limited incentives to pursue a career if they perceive the likelihood of advancement is more limited than for men, they are more likely to leave the labour force.

As it allows more time for caring, part-time employment is often regarded as an attractive reconciliation solution, especially when children are very young. In Ireland, and to a lesser extent Austria, the nature of the expanding service sector facilitated an increase in part-time employment that since the 1990s is remunerated on a *pro rata* basis compared to full-time employment. In Ireland, buoyant economic conditions helped parents to realise their preferred employment conditions in recent years, but with weakening labour demand, there is a risk that parents will have fewer opportunities to achieve their preferred working hours. In Austria, many mothers do not return to their original employer, as they find they cannot combine full-time work with caring responsibilities, and although many find regular part-time employment, others end up in low-paid marginal employment. In Japan, part-time employment is hardly ever of a regular nature, except for mothers who return from parental leave. Indeed, recent policy reform tries to keep women in regular employment by providing one year of paid parental leave and two subsequent years wherein employers – often through reduced working hours, have to provide measures supporting the reconciliation of their work and care commitments. However, reform does not cover mothers who withdrew from the labour force in the past and a considerable number of female workers currently in non-regular employment.

In Japan, part-time work is essentially synonymous with non-regular employment and concerns 40% of female workers. The ensuing (gender) equity issues are considerable: an "acceptable" wage gap between regular and atypical employees of 20% for equal work illustrates that unexplainable pay discrepancies are the norm, not the exception. To facilitate work and care reconciliation, workers can use these flexible so-called "non-regular", "casual", "atypical" or "marginal employment" relationships, certainly for a short period. However, as a long-term reconciliation solution this type of low-paid employment is of limited value. Moreover, once in non-regular employment it is very difficult to obtain regular employment in Japan. This may be because of age-related entry conditions for some occupations or simple cost considerations: atypical workers are relatively cheap and are not covered by stringent employment protection legislation. While employers do not hesitate to invest in young graduates, they are far more reluctant to make a similar investment in mother returners who are therefore severely constrained in their re-employment options.

As a result, employers in all countries do not use potential labour resources efficiently, but particularly in Japan, they do themselves a great disservice by shutting out a large part of labour force potential. Changing workplace practices is difficult but one step forward in Japan would be to strengthen the link between employment patterns and performance, and to further reduce the role of seniority-based pay increments and the system of career progression that is based on rigid worker classification systems. Increasing equity among non-regular and regular workers, while improving the throughflow between the two types of employment, would increase the likelihood that "mother returners" find a job, which suits their ability and training.

The penetration of family-friendly workplace practices seems low in view of the many women that drop out, or drop down to low-paid employment. The business case for providing such measures is strongest for high-skilled employees, but management also does not appear to be fully aware of the virtues of family-friendly measures. Leadership among senior staff could be far more forceful in implementing workplace measures, also to give workers the confidence that they can use these policies without jeopardizing their career.

Governments are reluctant to directly intervene in industrial bargaining processes in order to promote the adoption of family-friendly policies, but even if they did, public directives alone do not easily change workplace cultures. In recognition of diversity in workplace needs, the Japanese Childcare and Family Care Leave Act offers employers a choice out of five measures of which they have to offer at least one to workers with children not yet 3 years of age. Nevertheless, public policy towards changing workplace behaviour in all three countries is largely one of encouragement, promotion of the virtues of family-friendly policies, information campaigns and otherwise trying to raise awareness of the issue.

Policy initiatives could, however, go one step further, by extending the concept of encouragement to practical and tailored advice to improve the family-friendliness of workplaces. Both Austria and Japan provide a tailored approach to the needs of individual enterprises: the Austrian Work and Family Audit initiative, and the Japanese Childcare and Family Care Leave Act which encourages enterprises to appoint a "promoter" to oversee the implementation of flexible workplace practices. The strength of these initiatives is that they explore options best suited to the individual workplace and involve feedback and assessment at a later stage, thereby generating long-term commitment to the process. Both initiatives deserve a wider application. Irish policy development explicitly recognises the "consultancy" option, and there is a good case for this option to be pursued more intensively.

Annex to Chapter 3

Table 3A.1. **Family-friendly policy measures in Austrian enterprises**
Percentage of companies which took family-friendly policy measures in Austria, 1998

	Percentage of companies
Working hours reduction because of care commitments	23
Teleworking	8
Extended leave with insurance coverage and employer payment	2
Extended leave with insurance coverage	2
Extended leave	12
Career planning support for female employees	32
Reintegration support for those on leave	26
Training for those on leave	13
Employer paid supplement to child benefit	4
Employer payment towards childcare costs	1

Source: BMUJF (1999a).

Table 3A.2. **Flexible working arrangements in Ireland, 2002**

	Percentage of companies
Permanent part-time	62
Job sharing	29
Flexi-time	36
Personalised hours	26
Teleworking 5 days per week	7
Teleworking 1 or 2 days per week	12
Compressed working week	10
Career breaks	23
Term-time working	5

Source: IBEC (2002a).

Table 3A.3. **Japanese measures for employees with young children, 1999**

	Percentage of companies with more than 30 employees
Total proportion of firms providing measures	59.6
Proportion of firms providing:	
Short-time working hours	70.6
Flexitime	17.5
Adjustment of time to start/end work	46.9
Exemption of non-scheduled work	51.5
Providing childcare centre	2.7
Financial aid for childcare	3.3

Source: MOL (2000).

Notes

1. Across OECD countries, the actual number of hours put in by workers varies across occupations and positions within the workforce. For example, farmers and (senior) managers (and those who have aspirations in that direction) generally work relatively long hours.

2. Older workers in Japan sometimes express the sentiment that "the younger generation of workers does not know what hard work is". They can be forgiven for this reflection: on average total actual hours worked (both scheduled and overtime hours) in 1960 amounted to 2 432 hours per annum (in 1970, it was still as high as 2 239), while in 2001 it was a "mere" 1 848 hours per annum (JIL, 2002).

3. For workers to work long hours, employers have to have an agreement with the union. This agreement has to be submitted to prefectural authorities for approval in Japan, which is not automatic.

4. In general, even though wages, bonuses and non-wage labour costs as social security contributions and employer costs related to private (pension) insurance, dismissal and training costs could theoretically be pro-rated across workers on basis of the hours they work, recruitment costs are more likely to be fixed per worker.

5. The increase in non-regular employment in Japan has been strongest in the "wholesale, retail, eat and drink sector" where the share of atypical workers is 34.9% in 2001 up from 23.7% in 1992, while in the service sector (including hotels, entertainment, broadcasting, information services, advertising, medical/health services, social insurance, education), the share is 17.0% in 2001 up from 12.9% in 1992 (MHLW, 2001f). In these sectors laying off (older) workers is least prevalent, while large companies are currently downsizing their workforce laying off staff while adjusting the mix of new hires in terms of adjusting recruitment of graduates, specialists and atypical workers (including temporary workers recruited via a temping agency).

6. Employers in Japan do not have to pay pension and health insurance premiums for non-regular workers who work less than three-quarters of the hours put in by full-time employees in that firm. Employers do also not have to pay employment insurance for non-regular workers who work less than 20 hours per week and/or have an employment contract that is for less than a year.

7. Stringent employment legislation also affects hiring of older workers into regular employment in Japan. There is a national pilot project that supports hiring middle-aged and older workers on a trial period of three to six months, during which dismissal is possible. Initial results are favourable and indicate that many workers are kept on.

8. Even when Japanese mothers are able to return to regular employment at a later stage, a seniority-based remuneration system punishes those who withdrew from regular employment on a temporary basis for whatever reason, including caring for young children. As long as those "exiters" are women, seniority pay *de facto* hampers female career and earnings progression, perpetuates gender inequity, and limits the attraction for mothers to return to the labour force.

9. The notion of promoting *workforce diversity* in Japan (making a better use of the different assets of different workers, *e.g.* women, older workers – MHLW, 2003), also embodies the provision of measures that facilitate mapping working life and outside interests.

10. In Austria, 52% of male employees and 33% of female employees are unionised. 44% of Irish union members and 28% of Japanese union members are female.

11. Together RENGO (Unions) and the JBF (employers) issued a statement in April 2000 strongly supporting a more family-friendly workplace in Japan. However, although the general gist of the document is broadly supported, practical progress has been limited as priorities have changed in view of the economic climate (Government, Employers and Employees' Agreement on Diversified Working Style and Work Sharing (December 2002).

12. In Japan, many employers replace workers on leave on a "domino basis". Several worker(s) replace the worker at the level immediately above them, so that in the end, a cheap non-regular worker replaces the lowest grade worker. Assuming that colleagues have sufficient knowledge of the job of their immediate senior colleagues, this practice limits replacement costs associated with workers taking parental leave.

13. In general, the practice of individual employers to (partially) continue payments to their employee during leave may negatively affect gender equity, as employers thus face strong financial incentives to hire men rather than women in their childbearing years. To avoid this risk, and spread the costs among all employers, a publicly financed system (distributing the costs among all taxpayers or all employer and employees) would be more desirable.

14. The five legislated options to help employees with a child not yet 3 years combining their work and care commitments are: short-time working hours (there are only guidelines and no legal stipulation on the amount of reduction), flexitime, adjustment of time to start/end work, exemption of non-scheduled work, setting up and operation of a childcare centre.

15. In general, public sector employers are among the employers who are most likely to offer family-friendly measures for a broad group of workers.

ISBN 92-64-10418-6
Babies and Bosses: Reconciling Work and Family Life
Austria, Ireland and Japan
© OECD 2003

Chapter 4

Family Formation: Does More Work Lead to Fewer Births?

Birth rates have declined continually over the last decades, while at the same time female employment has steadily increased. Are these two features related? To what extent are pursuing a career and establishing a family mutually exclusive activities, or does dual earnership in couple families lead to postponement of having children or to having fewer children than otherwise desired? What, if anything, can policy do? This chapter addresses these issues . It starts by describing socio-demographic changes in recent years, and the factors behind these changes. It then addresses the changing relationship between fertility and female employment. This leads into a discussion of different policies and socio-economic trends (and theories thereon) that affect fertility behaviour. The chapter concludes by considering what role family-friendly policies may possibly play in, if not reversing, then at least abating the downward trend in birth rates. It concludes that policies that focus on reducing the indirect costs for mothers to work by offering affordable quality childcare, regular part-time employment opportunities and, generally making the labour market more inclusive, seem to be the most promising avenue towards improving birth rates.

Governments in many OECD countries are increasingly concerned about the possible consequences of low and/or declining fertility. This second review of family/work reconciliation policies draws together two countries with very low fertility, Austria and Japan, and one country, Ireland, with one of the most rapid declines in fertility ever observed in Europe. Low fertility will alter the structure of populations, raising concerns about the financial sustainability of social protection systems, future labour supply, and the vitality and strength of family units and networks (Box 4.1), which in many ways are the most important building block of society.

Box 4.1. **Family concepts**

Despite its pivotal role in society, across countries there is no broadly accepted definition of exactly what "families" are because of cultural and historical differences. These differences relate to different views of partnerships between adults but also to differences regarding the wider concept of family relations. In all three countries under review, the nuclear family is predominant. The practice of extended families – in general three generations living in one household – still prevails to some extent in Japan (see below). Both in Japan and in Austria, however, legal obligations on family members go beyond the nuclear family; immediate relatives – parents, adult children and siblings – are supposed to financially support a potential social assistance claimant, for example.

In order to maintain comparability across countries throughout this review, a *family* is defined as "a household of one or more adults living together with, and taking responsibility for the care and rearing of, one or more children". This definition comprises nuclear as well as extended families. *Family formation*, then, is "the establishment of families (or living units) as defined above".

Improving the well-being of families in general and of disadvantaged families in particular is an important goal of social policy. Child and family policy also promotes child development (Kamerman et al., 2003), and the promotion of child well-being is an important concern in all three countries (Chapter 5). At the same time, Japan's family policy is most explicit in its aim to foster an environment conducive to parents having as many children as they want.

Fertility rates have been declining in Austria and Japan for a long time, and – after a baby-boom in the mid-1960s in Austria and in the late 1940s in Japan – fell below replacement level in the early 1970s. Female employment has steadily increased over this period (Chapter 2). In Ireland, female labour force behaviour changed rapidly in the 1990s, while fertility fell sharply between 1970 and 1990 but not during the 1990s. Are these two features related? To what extent are pursuing a career and establishing a family mutually exclusive activities when both parents in couple families wish to stay in work? Does dual earnership lead to postponement and/or deferral of having children or having fewer children than otherwise desired? What, if anything, can policy do?

This chapter addresses this debate. It starts by describing how marriage, cohabitation, divorce and fertility has changed in recent years, and the factors behind this change. Then it addresses the changing relationship between fertility and female employment. This leads into a discussion of different policies and socio-economic trends (and theories thereon) that affect fertility behaviour. The chapter concludes by considering what role family-friendly policies may possibly play in, if not reversing, then at least abating the downward trend in birth rates.

4.1. Fertility and family dynamics

Population growth rate differences between the three countries are largely explained by different fertility developments and migration patterns. Austria experienced modest population growth in the past three decades, with almost zero natural growth and steady immigration during the 1970s and 1980s, mostly guest-workers from Turkey and Yugoslavia. Considerable immigration of over 350 000 people from the Balkan states in the 1988-1993 period has led to population growth of 0.5% per annum over the last decade (Table 4.1). Today, almost 10% of the Austrian population is foreign born, contributing 17% of all annual births.[1]

Japan also experienced little natural population growth, especially since the late 1980s, and with immigration being virtually non-existent, the Japanese population has been roughly at the same level since the beginning of the 1990s. Ireland, on the other hand, had significant natural growth over the last 30 years, which was partly compensated by large emigration streams. Immigration is a rather recent phenomenon in Ireland that has only emerged in the mid-1990s (OECD, 2003d).[2]

As a consequence of these trends, Austria and Japan already have relatively old populations today, with about 16-17% of the population over age 65, compared with only 11% in Ireland (Table 4.1). Uniquely for Western Europe, Ireland still has a very young population: 22% of the population is not yet 15 years of age. Despite these different trends, the share of the working-age population is almost identical in all three countries.

Table 4.1. **Migration affects population patterns in Austria and Ireland**
Demographic indicators

	Population						Share of the population		
	Total	Density	Net average annual increase over previous ten years	Degree of urbanisation	Foreign population	Average net migration	Children 0-14	Working-age 15-64	Elderly 65+
	Thousands	Inhabitants per km^2	Percentage		Percentage		Total population = 100%		
	2001^a			2000		1991-2000	2000		
Austria	8 110	97	0.5	67.0	9.3	3.3	16.6	67.8	15.6
Ireland	3 839	55	0.9	59.0	3.3	2.9	21.6	67.1	11.3
Japan	127 210	337	0.3	79.0	1.3	0.0	14.7	68.1	17.2
OECD^b	37 347	32	0.6	. .	5.8	. .	19.2	67.0	13.8

. . Data not available.
a) 2000 for Austria.
b) Weighted average.
Source: OECD (2002d, 2003a, 2003d); UN, World Urban Prospects.

4.1.1. Family change

In all three countries, average household size has continuously been falling (Table 4.2). This is explained by declines in the share of families with three or more children and an increase in one-person households, which in turn is a consequence of changing partnership behaviour (see below). The decline in average household size throughout the 1980s and 1990s was fastest in Ireland, which, however, by today still has the largest households. Almost 40% of all Irish households include at least one child under age 17, compared to less than 30% in both Austria and Japan.

Despite similar fertility levels, as will be discussed later, Japanese households are larger than Austrian ones. This is explained by the prevalence of extended families (usually spanning three generations) still living in one household in Japan. In 2000, 14% of all households in Japan fell in the category of extended family households, and some 28% of all children were living in an extended family household – compared with only 11% in Ireland and less than that in Austria (Table 4.2).

Family life of children under age 17 also differs in other dimensions. In Austria, in the 1980s children used to live predominantly in male breadwinner families, while, reflecting the increase in mothers' employment rates, in the 1990s dual earner couples became the most frequent family "type" among couple families (Table 4.2). In Japan, on the contrary, changes were relatively

Table 4.2. **In what sort of families do children live?**

Trends in households and children, 1980 to 2000

	1980	1985	1990	1995	2000
Austria					
Average household size	2.8	2.7	2.6	2.6	2.5
Share of households with children in all households	37.2	33.6	31.3	30.3	28.3
Share of one-parent households in households with children	12.2	14.2	14.4	14.4	15.2
Number of children (aged under 17)	1 768 662	1 585 215	1 515 224	1 580 698	1 535 421
Share of children living in (percentages adding to 100%)					
One-parent households	8.9	9.7	10.3	10.5	11.6
Two-parent households	79.1	79.0	79.1	80.3	80.6
Extended families[a]	12	11.3	10.6	9.2	7.8
Share of children in household (percentages adding to 100%)					
With no parent in work	5.2	8.8	2.7	4.9	5.6
With one parent in work	60.5	55.7	52.7	42.2	39.9
With both parents in work	34.3	35.5	44.6	52.9	54.5
Ireland[b]					
Average household size	3.7	3.6	3.4	3.2	*3.0*
Share of households with children under 17 in all households		46.6	43.3	39.8	38.3
Share of one-parent households in households with children					13.4
Number of children (aged under 17)	1 144 758	1 133 652	1 038 936	954 174	..
Share of children living in (percentages adding to 100%)					
One-parent households	4.5	5.7	7.6	10.2	..
Two-parent households	78.3	80.1	79.8	78.6	..
Extended families	17.2	14.2	12.5	11.2	..
Share of children in household (percentages adding to 100%)					
With no parent in work	..	..	18.9	17.3	..
With one parent in work	..	..	51.5	53.9	..
With both parents in work	..	..	29.6	28.8	..
Japan					
Average household size	3.3	3.2	3.0	2.9	2.7
Share of households with children in all households		43.1	36.3	29.9	27.9
Share of one-parent households in households with children		4.0	4.4	4.7	5.0

Table 4.2. **In what sort of families do children live?** (cont.)

Trends in households and children, 1980 to 2000

	1980	1985	1990	1995	2000
Number of children (aged under 17)		29 714 214	26 318 529	23 150 565	21 315 461
Share of children living in (percentages adding to 100%)					
One-parent households			3.1	3.4	4.5
Two-parent households			64.2	64.9	66.9
Extended families			32.3	31.5	28.3
Share of children in household (percentages adding to 100%)^c					
With no parent in work			. .	. .	. .
With one parent in work			57.5	57.8	57.3
With both parents in work			42.5	42.2	42.7

. . Not available.

a) Extended families: shares estimated from BMUJF (1999), assuming equal number of children in nuclear and extended families.

b) For Ireland, 1981, 1986, 1991, 1996.

c) As data for "no parent in work" is not available for Japan, these percentages cannot be compared with those for Austria and Ireland.

Source: Austria: data supplied by CSO based on the Microcensus; Ireland: data supplied by CSO; Japan: data supplied by Japanese authorities based on the Population Census of Japan.

small and in 2000 more than half of all children were living in a family with only one parent in work, a consequence of the still rather high proportion of mothers leaving the labour force around childbirth (Chapter 2). Data on Ireland is not available but is likely to reflect the Austrian pattern with some time lag.

Japan also differs from the other two countries in that only a very low proportion of children live in one-parent families: less than 5% compared to around 10% in Ireland and Austria (Table 4.2). The proportion of lone parent households is increasing everywhere, reflecting in turn rapid changes in marriage and divorce rates. Total first marriage rates have fallen most dramatically in Ireland (Chart 4.1). Current behaviour suggests that in Austria only about 54% of the population will eventually get married, compared with 60% in Ireland and still 72% in Japan. At the same time, divorce rates – crudely measured as the number of divorces per 100 marriages in the same year – are rising rapidly in all three countries.

Duration-specific divorce rates, which are only available for Austria, suggest that with current behaviour in this country 43% of all marriages will end in divorce, compared to 26% in 1980. Many divorces take place in childless couples, or after children have reached adulthood. Again for Austria, data show that one in five children experience a divorce of their parents before they reach the age of 19 (BMUJF, 1999) – which also implies that even with such high divorce rates the large majority of all children is living with both of their

102

Chart 4.1. **Fewer marriages that are more likely to end up in divorce**

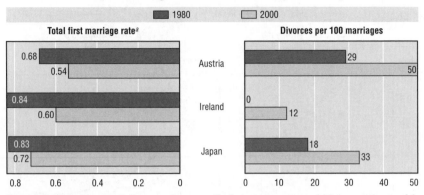

a) Total first marriage rate is the sum of age-specific first mariage rates, which is an estimate of the likelihood of getting married.

Source: Eurostat, Demographic data, NewCronos database 2002; Japan: MHLW (2001g).

parents during their entire childhood. This is confirmed by findings according to which most lone parents have children over age 15 rather than very young children.

4.1.2. Fertility trends

Since the early 1970s, fertility trends have been very similar in Austria and Japan. In both countries, the total fertility rate (TFR) fell below replacement level in 1973, and continued to decline gradually since then to a very low level of only 1.3 in 2002 (Chart 4.2). Completed family size measured from a cohort perspective (see Box 4.2), however, is still a bit higher in Japan (1.8-1.9 compared to 1.6-1.7 in Austria), which is due to a short-term fertility recovery in the mid-1980s. The total fertility rate in Ireland remained high until 1970. Since then, it dropped very sharply until the early 1990s and remained virtually constant at around replacement level throughout the last decade. Completed fertility fell from 3.5 children for women born in the 1940s to a little bit above 2 children for those born in the 1960s (2.2 for the cohort born in 1965).

Up until age 30, fertility rates are very similar in all three countries. The higher fertility level in Ireland is due to significantly higher birth rates of women in their thirties, with Irish women in their late thirties having more births than, for example, Austrian women in their early thirties (Chart 4.3). Teenage motherhood is extremely low in Japan, with only 0.5% of women in the 15-19 year age range having a baby each year, the lowest figure across the OECD. This proportion is three times higher in Ireland, which, however, is still less than half of the UK and only a third of the US level – the two OECD countries which are known for their high number of teenage births.

Chart 4.2.   **Declining fertility rates in all three countries**

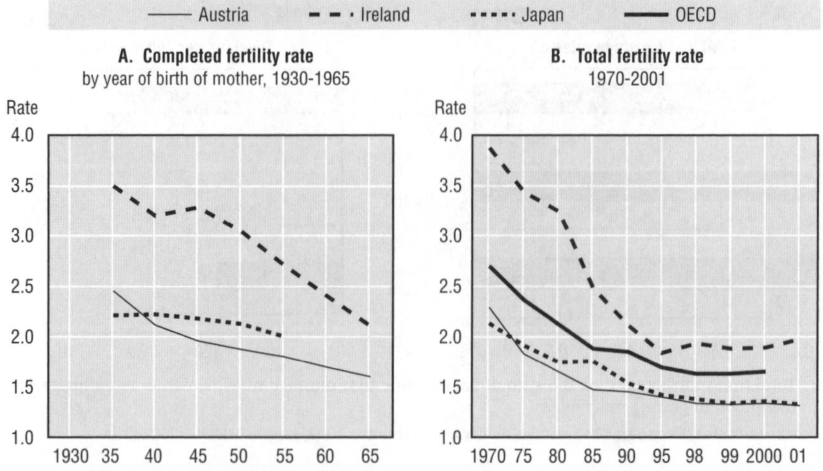

——— Austria   ▬ ▬ · Ireland   ····· Japan   ▬▬▬ OECD

A. Completed fertility rate by year of birth of mother, 1930-1965	**B. Total fertility rate** 1970-2001

The completed fertility rate (CFR) measures the number of children that a cohort of women who have reached the end of their childbearing years had in the course of their respective life. The CFR is measured by cumulating age-specific fertility rates in a given cohort as they aged from 15 to 49 years.

The total fertility rate (TFR) in a specific year is the average number of children who would be born to a synthetic cohort of women whose age-specific birth rates where the same as those actually observed in the year in question.

Source: Eurostat, New Cronos database, Theme 3; MHLW (2001g).

4.1.2.1. *Underlying demographic transformation*

The following changes in family formation behaviour underlie the decline in the fertility rates:

1. *The postponement of marriage.* The first marriage increasingly takes place later in life, and as a consequence – though also depending on the other factors discussed below – the age at first birth gradually increases. This upward trend started around 1970 in Japan, 1975 in Austria, and 1980 in Ireland (Chart 4.4). There are a number of related trends that have contributed to this rise. Participation among women in higher and tertiary education has risen over the last few decades (see Chapter 2), increasing the average age of entry into employment. In some countries, during this period also the average age at which young people leave the parental home has increased, a trend that in Japan was shown to be related to rapid urbanisation and the increasing number of young people growing up in metropolitan areas (Suzuki, 2001).[3] Postponing marriage and first births for at least partly socio-economic reasons leads to a concentration of childbearing in an ever narrower age-interval: in demographic theory this phenomenon is known as the "rectangularisation of fertility" (Kohler and Ortega, 2001).

Box 4.2. **Measuring fertility rates**

There are two different perspectives on fertility. The period perspective considers the reproductive behaviour of the total population, and the ultimate indicator to measure period fertility is the annual number of births (possibly measured relative to the total population, the so-called Crude Birth Rate). The cohort perspective looks at the reproductive behaviour of female individuals over their lifetime. The ultimate indicator to assess cohort fertility behaviour is the completed family size of a cohort, i.e. the average number of children a woman of a particular cohort has over her lifetime. This indicator can only be correctly measured once a particular cohort has reached the end of its reproductive life, or at least an age after which the additional number of births will be small. Estimates for women age 35 are commonly used (Chart 4.2).

Obviously, there is a relationship between the period and the cohort perspectives (e.g. van Imhoff, 2001), but how to correctly derive cohort fertility from data that are essentially collected on an annual (periodic) basis is a contested issue. The most frequently used synthetic summary indicator of period fertility is the Total Fertility Rate (TFR), which essentially measures what completed family size would be in the long-term should current age-specific fertility rates remain constant in future (Chart 4.2). Thus, it attempts to measure cohort fertility on the basis of assumptions which are unlikely to hold. Especially during periods of rapidly changing fertility behaviour, such as when first births are postponed, the accuracy of the TFR in predicting cohort fertility diminishes. Various measures have been developed to account for changes in the timing of births (Bongaarts and Feeney, 1998) or for timing and the birth-order distribution of children (Kohler and Ortega, 2002). Estimates suggest that completed fertility would be higher by about 0.2 children for Austria and Japan, and by 0.3 for Ireland, than current age-specific fertility rates suggest (Bongaarts, 2002). Note that, relative to the observed fertility level, these timing distortions tend to become more important in a low-fertility context.

2. *The decline in marital fertility.* Later marriage could merely lead to a postponement of fertility, leading to a temporary dip in birth rates. However, marital fertility has also declined, suggesting an increasing preference for smaller families. In Austria and Ireland, recently this has meant a decline in the proportion of married women having a third or fourth child (Buber, 2001; and Fahey and Russell, 2001), while in Japan the decline seems more general although at a lesser speed (Retherford et al., 1999). Furthermore, evidence for Austria suggests that people aged 20-34 now prefer to have only 1.7 children per woman on average, down from over

Chart 4.3.   **Irish women over 30 make all the difference**

Age specific fertility rates, per 1 000 women, 2000[a]

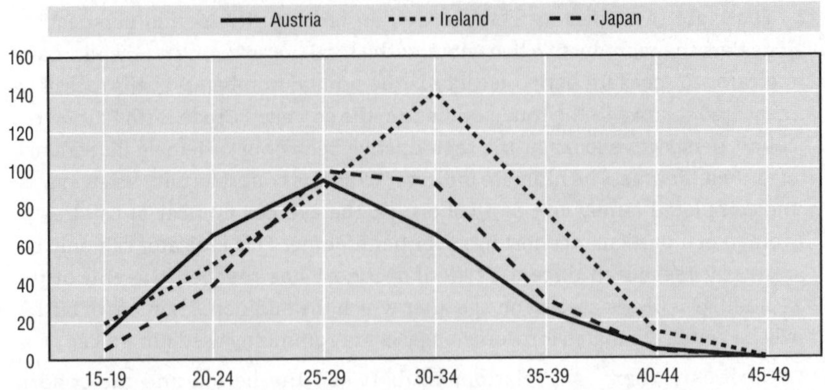

a)   2001 for Ireland.

Source: Statistik Austria (2002); and data supplied by the Irish and Japanese authorities.

two children in the mid-1990s (Goldstein et al., 2002).[4] As birth rates in Austria have been low for some time, this might suggest that through "social learning" younger generations adapt their ideals to the reality for the previous generation. In line with this hypothesis, the ideal number of children reported for Ireland is still higher than in Austria at 2.5 children on average, although down from 3.6 in 1979 (European Commission, 2001). Changes in ideal family size are as strong in Japan, down from 4.3 children in 1977 to 2.7 in 1997 (NIPSSR, 1997), but the ideal is still lacking "behind" actual behaviour.[5] The concentration of childbearing in a narrower interval caused by later marriage also simply means that, for pure physiological and biomedical reasons, parents cannot have as many children as they initially wanted, thereby contributing to the decline in marital fertility rates.

3. *The increase in the proportion never marrying.* Not only does marriage take place later and have women fewer children once married, but fewer people get married at all (Chart 4.1). This trend has been identified as the main cause of fertility decline in Japan (*e.g.* Ueno, 1998). While marriage used to be a matter of course, living as a single person has increasingly become a life choice. The degree to which this is accepted as a permanent condition varies both between countries and between different social strata within each country, but everywhere tolerance is growing. In Austria, young adults often live together in consensual unions, the preferred way of life for people in their late twenties (Prinz, 1995). Once expecting a child, or soon after childbirth they still tend to get married. In Japan, unmarried cohabitation is virtually non-existent. Instead, young people often have so-called LAT (living apart together) relationships.

Chart 4.4. **Young people delay marriage and parenthood**

Mean age at first marriage, first birth and at (all) births

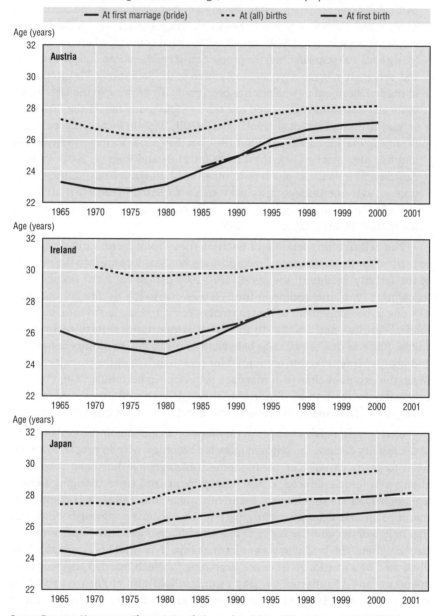

Source: Eurostat, Newcronos, Theme 3, Population and Social Conditions; Japan: MHLW (2001g).

4. *Lower fertility outside marriage* (compared to marital fertility). At every age, unmarried people have much lower fertility than married people. This is particularly true for Japan, where having a child outside marriage occurs only rarely – and therefore any changes in marriage behaviour translate into a similar change in fertility. Austria is an unusual country, where historically (going back 100 years in time) the proportion of children born outside marriage was very high in some regions, like Kärnten or the Steiermark. The proportion of children born out of wedlock has been gradually growing in the last twenty years and now stands at around one third – 45% among first births, 20% of all second births and 15% of all third births (BMUJF, 1999). In Ireland, the incidence of non-marital births was low until 1980, but their share increased very rapidly and has also reached one third in 2000 (Fahey and Russell, 2001). In both Austria and Ireland, as much as in other Western European countries, most unmarried women expecting a child were shown to live in a stable relationship of some kind (cohabiting, engaged), while births to "solo" mothers are rare (Kiernan, 1999; and Mahon et al., 1998).

The relative importance of each of these four factors differs across countries. For Japan, a recent decomposition analysis looking into the reasons of the fertility decline in the period 1970-2000 (Hirosima, 2001) revealed the following: 57% of the decline in the TFR was due to the decline in marriage, 13% due to postponement of first marriage (Box 4.3), 25% due to the decline in marital fertility, and 5% due to the delay of non-marital fertility. In other words, 70% was due to marriage behaviour and 30% due to fertility behaviour, and postponement factors accounted for less than 20% of the overall change. Given the extent of change in marriage behaviour in both Austria and Ireland this factor is likely to be important, although high and increasing fertility among unmarried mothers counters this trend to a large extent.

If, at least in Japan, changes in marriage behaviour dominate explanations of the fertility decline, the relevant question becomes: why do people no longer want to get married? The postponement of marriage has been related to changes in female education and employment, and so to changing female aspirations. Japanese feminists frequently argue that women's perception of marriage life has changed rapidly, with men's awareness lagging behind, and that only women who are ready to follow traditional gender role patterns still have children. The lack of any significant change in marital life is arguably best illustrated by statistics on time use, according to which married Japanese men spend around 13 minutes per day on household and childcare activities, irrespective of their wives' employment status (Chapter 3). Even working women spends more than four hours a day on these activities, while every second Japanese husband was found not to spend any of his time on such activities (Tsuya et al., 2000). Under these conditions, it is not all that surprising

Box 4.3. **Do education and housing costs affect birth rates?**

Education and housing costs (and the perception thereof) are often referred to as important financial factors that affect fertility behaviour, if not in levels of birth rates, then in timing. Housing costs can be a factor in explaining the timing of demographic events, such as leaving the parental home and, in turn, marriage and first birth. In Ireland, house prices have soared over the last decade (OECD, 2001), which at least in part reflects the rapid increase in household income that in turn is related to female employment growth. The high cost of housing poses the greatest difficulty to first time buyers, and although this only affects about 5% of all households, many of those are young families with children. A similar situation has occurred in Japan where housing costs are often cited as a main reason for having fewer children, especially among younger adults (NIPSSR, 1997). If, and to what extent, housing costs affect fertility trends is uncertain. For Ireland, the evidence is weak because the TFR remained stable during the 1990s when house prices exploded, whereas it fell very rapidly during the 1970s and 1980s (Chart 4.2). For Japan, Takayama *et al.* (2000) found a statistically significant negative effect of housing costs on the fertility rate, while Kato (2000), found that housing costs affect the first marriage rate, thereby indirectly affecting the birth rate (see also below).

Especially in Japan, education costs (and high costs of childrearing in general) are perceived as a major problem, as surveys consistently show that education spending, like housing costs, is among the top reasons given by parents for having less children than they consider as ideal (NIPSSR, 1997). Primary and secondary schools are almost exclusively public in all three countries. But while in Austria tertiary education is also entirely public, 20% of university education spending in Ireland and 60% in Japan (compared with 50% in the USA) is private (OECD, 2002e). Education costs account for 7% of total household budgets in Japan, compared to only 0.2% in Austria and 1.1% in Ireland (MPMHAPT, 2002a; Eurostat, 1999a). The reason for this difference is the use of private education in Japan, frequently throughout the period of mandatory school attendance, and the costs of university education – with tertiary education attendance rates being higher than in Austria and Ireland (Chapter 2).

To have access to top (private) universities in Japan, it is virtually necessary (although not a formal precondition) to attend one of the few top private (junior) high schools. Access to these schools is highly competitive. To make sure their offspring succeed, many parents send their children to *juku* classes: private extra-school education of a couple of hours per day that is offered after the standard school hours. The number of children enrolled in *juku* is high: one third of all children in elementary school and almost one in two in junior high school (Hirao, 2002). Due to the smaller number of hours per day,

> ### Box 4.3. **Do education and housing costs affect birth rates?** *(cont.)*
>
> costs for *juku* attendance are about the same as the average fee paid in licensed day care for pre-school children (and lower than the full fee in daycare), but the duration of this payment stretches over a very long period. Overall, costs for *juku* account for about 20% of total private education spending. The direct impact on fertility is difficult to assess, but both the awareness of the issue and the actual costs are high. Estimating simultaneous equations, Kato (2000) found that along with household income, real wages, and the first marriage rate, education costs have a significant impact on birth rates.

that marriage is no longer a particularly attractive option for Japanese women who value their job and career (*e.g.* Mason *et al.*, 1998).

4.1.2.2. Will birth rates continue to fall?

To postpone the marriage decision could lead to deferment of marriage, and eventually contribute to an increase in the number of women who do not have any children. This notion is supported by evidence on the increasing incidence of childlessness among women, especially among women with relatively high levels of education attainment. Data for Ireland and Austria suggest that among women born in the late 1960s, childlessness will probably reach 25%, up from around 15% twenty years before (Freijka *et al.*, 2001). Japan used to have lower levels of childlessness than other OECD countries, involving only 8% of all women born in the 1920s (Rowland, 1998). Since 1985, childlessness is slowly increasing (Ogawa and Retherford, 1993), though probably still lower than in most countries of Europe.

In all three countries in this review, as much as in most other developed countries, demographic projections in the past have always overestimated future fertility levels. Until recently, it was assumed that in the long run fertility levels would balance out at population replacement level of a TFR of 2-2.1 children per woman. However, with the dramatic political and economic transition in the 1990s, a new phenomenon of "lowest-low fertility" has appeared. Today there are about twenty countries with a fertility level below 1.3 children per woman, and in several sub-regions, *e.g.* in Northern Italy, it is even below 1.0. Recent fertility projections in Japan assume a long-term TFR of less than 1.4 children (NIPSSR, 2002), and of 1.5 for both Austria and Ireland (Eurostat, 1999), but there is a risk that fertility rates may well end up being lower than that (Kohler *et al.*, 2001).

From a socio-economic point of view, there are several reasons why fertility rates are rather unlikely to recover very much or may even continue to decline. First, the efficiency of measures of birth control can be expected to improve.[6] Second, without improved reconciliation options, the growing number of female high-skilled workers for whom childbirth has considerable opportunity costs can lead to an increased risk of childlessness and smaller families. Third, increasing partnership instability may lead to prospective parents deciding against having children. And fourth, the postponement of fertility will significantly increase the number of couples who fail to realise their intentions for pure physiological and biomedical reasons (Kohler *et al.*, 2001). It may not have been until the beginning of the 1990s that the possibility of enduring below-replacement fertility was seriously discussed, but today it seems pretty unlikely that fertility levels in developed countries will ever return to replacement level (Demeny, 1997).

However, other dynamics are at work, too. Very low fertility rates will result in substantially smaller cohort sizes. This is likely to improve the opportunities of people in these small cohorts – in the education system and on the labour (and housing) market. This potential positive effect of cohort size was first proposed by Easterlin (1980) who argues that smaller cohorts because of higher earnings resulting from better opportunities are likely to have more children, thus resulting in waves of lower and higher fertility (the so-called Easterlin-cycle). Very low fertility in Austria and Japan will result in particularly strong cohort size effects, although in Austria this is partly compensated by immigration trends.

4.2. Employment and fertility

The male-breadwinner model involves a clear allocation of responsibilities, with men providing family income, and women providing care at home. Female employment was incompatible with caring for children, but as long as most women accepted this gender division of responsibilities (as many did until the 1960s in many countries), fertility rates remained stable and high. With changing female aspirations, as for example reflected in changing labour market behaviour, the relevance of this traditional model diminished, and fertility rates started to decline.

Various authors have recently reported a change in the relationship between fertility and female employment that has occurred during the last 30 years or so (Ahn and Mira, 2000; Brewster and Rindfuss, 2000; and Esping-Andersen, 1999). Cross-country correlations suggest that, in the 1970s and early 1980s, countries with high fertility rates had low female employment – a finding that seemed consistent with the conventional wisdom of a trade-off between work and family life. Today, however, OECD countries with higher rates of female employment also tend to have relatively high fertility rates (Chart 4.5).

Chart 4.5. **Is work compatible with having a child?**

Total fertility rate (TFR) and female employment rates (age 15-64), 1970, 1985 and 2000

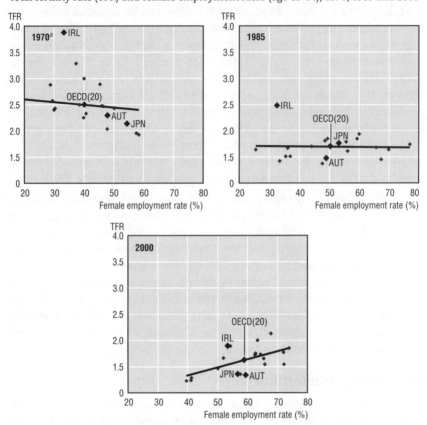

Note: As data is not available for the complete 1970-2000 period, OECD(20) does not include the Czech Repulbic, Hungary, Iceland, Luxembourg, Mexico, Poland, Portugal, Slovak Republic, Switzerland and Turkey.

a) 1976 for Belgium, 1971 for Greece, 1975 for the Netherlands.

Source: OECD (2002h).

More recent analysis based on time-series correlations rather than cross-country correlations moderates these findings and suggests a slightly revised conclusion. Engelhardt *et al.* (2001) found that the relationship between fertility rates and female employment is still negative in any single country, but that the degree of incompatibility between the two activities had diminished. They found a strong negative correlation for all countries in the 1960s and 1970s, with causality in both directions (i.e. childbearing reducing employment, but also employment reducing fertility). In the 1980s and 1990s, in some countries the negative relation became weaker to the point of insignificance, while in others – such as Italy – the relation remained significantly negative.

Kögel (2002) corroborates this finding, and further suggests that combining childrearing and being in employment is most incompatible in Mediterranean and least incompatible in Scandinavian countries. While it may not be possible to devise a policy that leads to a simultaneous increase of birth rates and female employment, at the very least, in most countries childrearing and employment seem to be less incompatible with each other than in the past.

4.3. The policy response to family and fertility changes

Establishing a family has implications for society as a whole. Children ensure the continuation and development of societies and their institutions, and contribute to future economic prosperity. Thus, societies have an intrinsic interest in providing an environment wherein having children is a desirable life option and in which children receive adequate care.

Governments do not wish to interfere in what is a personal decision to have children, but since societies have a clear interest in children being born, a low fertility rate can justify a public policy response, as it has in Japan. For such a policy initiative to be successful it is necessary to understand what determines the decision to have children. A large number of different individual as well as cultural, societal and economic factors affect the decision to have one or more children (Box 4.4).

4.3.1. Partnership instability

Rapid changes in marriage and divorce rates have made partnership instability a policy concern in all three countries, although not always for the same reasons. It clearly is a major issue in Ireland, a country with a predominantly Roman Catholic population, where the constitution explicitly recognises families as the cornerstone of society. Only recently has legislation been changed allowing for families to dissolve: legal separation was introduced in 1989 while the ban on divorce was lifted in 1995.[7] Keeping families together is an explicit policy objective. This does not mean that married couples should be kept together at all cost – although there is public consensus that marriage is desirable and should be supported – but that each child should have the chance to develop a decent relationship with both of its parents.[8] In Austria, partnership stability is not an explicit public policy concern, but it arouses activity among some of the influential NGOs. In this country, the family lobby, although diverse, is strong and often closely linked to political parties.[9]

In both Austria and Ireland, family services, often provided by NGOs, have a strong element of relationship counselling. Counselling centres in Austria were introduced following legalisation of abortion in 1974. There are 336 such

Box 4.4. **Theories on fertility behaviour: an overview**

There are different, but often related, theories which try to explain fertility behaviour, as summarised below:

● In broad terms, the theory of *Demographic Transition* asserts that it is socio-economic development, which, through medical advances, first reduces mortality, which is then sooner or later followed by a decline in fertility towards a new equilibrium with the new low mortality rate. Other authors refer to this as the *Socio-Economic Threshold* hypothesis of fertility decline. On the whole, this theory is more of a description of the trend in developed countries from a traditional society with high mortality and fertility to a modern society with low mortality and fertility. Population ageing is an inherent and unavoidable longer-term outcome of that transition.

● The *Rational Choice* theory is based on the framework of the maximisation of utility given a budget constraint. In deciding to have a child, people make the considered calculation that the psychological and social benefits of an additional child outweigh the economic costs of having and rearing a child (Becker, 1981). A decline in fertility thus implies that the relative price of a child has increased, that (couple) incomes have fallen, or that there has been a change in the shape of the couple's utility function for children *versus* other consumption goods.

● The *Risk Aversion* theory adds a dynamic dimension to the rational choice theory. Costs and benefits of having children lie largely in the future and are relatively uncertain at the time the decision has to be made. Having a child changes the future life course of people and hence depends upon the future orientation of potential parents (McDonald, 1996). If potential parents perceive their future as uncertain – *e.g.* in terms of their employment or partnership – they may avoid the risk of having a child. The recent experience with limited economic growth in Japan, may thus have reinforced the downward trend in fertility rates. Instead, potential parents invest in security through increasing their employment attachment or opportunities by upgrading education (as in Sweden in the early 1990s, see Hoem, 2000) or work longer hours. This reallocation of individual resources to other areas can substantially reduce or at least delay childbearing.

● The *Post-materialist Values* theory identifies "value change" (individual self-realisation, satisfaction of personal preferences, liberalism and freedom from traditional forces of authority) as the driving force for the decline in marriage and birth rates and the increase in divorce rates (*e.g.* Lesthaege and Moors, 1996). According to this theory, otherwise known as the *Second Demographic Transition* theory, the value of children has changed, both in the sense that quality overrides quantity and that other consumer goods have taken precedence over children: both aspects resulting in fewer children being born.

Box 4.4. **Theories on fertility behaviour: an overview** (cont.)

● The *Gender Equity* theory (Chesnais, 1998; and McDonald, 2000 and 2000a) asserts that the degree of (in)coherence between the levels of gender equity in different social institutions determines fertility rates, and differences between those rates in advanced countries. This theory argues that there is a gradual shift from the traditional male breadwinner model, which is characterised by a clear distinction of gender roles in terms of paid market work and unpaid care and domestic work, to a gender equity model, which is characterised by a symmetric division of labour. This shift has started in areas such as education and market employment, but may not have spread in equal force to other societal institutions such as family units, family services, or tax/benefit systems. For example, a *high* degree of gender equity in institutions that deal with people as individuals, as for example education, combined with a *low* degree of gender equity in institutions that deal with people as members of a family, the family itself or the tax/benefit system, results in particularly *low* fertility. The greater the level of *incoherence* in gender equity between institutions and the stronger the influence of the traditional male-breadwinner notion on some workplace practices, tax/ benefit systems and family units, the lower are birth rates.

centres at present, plus a couple of dozen centres run directly by the provinces. In addition to regular counselling, these centres often offer other services *e.g.* regarding pregnancy, violence, divorce, disabled children or, since recently, reconciliation of family and work life. The latter would focus on family skills, raise self-awareness, and help ease to return to work (this Family Competence Programme is discussed in Chapter 6). Counselling is non-directive, it just makes individuals aware of their options.

The different services that exist alongside each other in Ireland include marriage and relationship counselling, family resource centres (with a strong focus on tailored service provision to local needs, including childcare), and family mediation services. These offer help in the conflict resolution process ("comprehensive multi-party mediation"), involving fact-finding, considering options, negotiation, agreement, and evaluation of that agreement a year later. The Department of Family and Social Affairs is in the process of bringing all such services under the umbrella of the Family Support Agency.

In Japan, there is no particular policy concern regarding partnership stability per se, but the issue entered the policy debate in the context of fertility concerns (see below). Counselling for parents who provide full-time care to their children is still rare, but is increasingly discussed.

4.3.2. Fertility in Japanese family policy

The persistent decline in fertility rates has fuelled the policy debate on the long-term sustainability of public pension systems in both Austria and Japan. However, where the Austrian debate has not moved much beyond that, in Japan this has led to public policy change. Today, low birth rates are the overriding family policy concern (*e.g.* Atoh, 2000). This has been so since the early 1990s, when it was realised that the gradual fertility decline since the early 1970s was likely to be of a permanent nature.

Since then, the government has established various committees[10] and prepared several reports[11] to identify the causes of this trend, while a special unit within the MHLW was created to formulate and co-ordinate the public policy response. Having identified the incompatibility of work and care activities and the fixed division of gender roles as the main causes of the declining birth rates, there have been sequential initiatives: the Angel Plan (1995-99) with a focus on extending nursery care services (Chapter 5) and the New Angel Plan (2000-04), which focuses on promoting an environment conducive to the reconciliation of work and family life. In addition, other measures that were taken include: the introduction of parental leave, the introduction and subsequent increase of payment rates during leave, and the extension of child benefit from those aged 3 to age 6. The trend to defer marriage (and childbirth) to a later age also led to concerns about young Japanese finding a suitable partner.[12]

In March 2003, the "Measure plan on support for the next generation" was introduced to the Diet with the aim to further improve child well-being and the living and working conditions of potential parents. This plan, which builds on and further enhances previous initiatives approaches the challenge of the declining birth-rate along four strands (in addition, in 2001 an initiative to reduce waiting lists in childcare had been launched, see Chapter 5):

1. Change prevailing working patterns, including those of men: reduce overtime work during the child care period (until child reaches age 6), promote fathers taking five days paternity leave, and set targets for parents taking childcare leave (see Chapter 2).

2. Recognize the value of childrearing for society: examine possibilities to account for periods of childcare leave in the contributory record of the public pension system.

3. Strengthen the position of children in society: fostering social skills, independence and self-reliance of children, through interaction between older and younger children.

4. Strengthen community-based support for parents: Local governments are responsible for family service delivery (Chapter 5) and involved in

counselling parents on family issues, including fostering an exchange between older parents, grandparents and new parents to alleviate parenting anxiety among the latter group. This initiative should be seen in light of concerns of weakening extended family networks, however, it remains to be seen whether such initiatives have a strong upward impact on birth rates.

The major difference between the Measure Plan and previous strategies, such as in particular the Plus One initiative, is that it provides a more concrete procedure: it determines which further pieces of legislation the government plans to introduce in the coming years, and what measures will have to be implemented by whom and when.[13] For instance, the Measure Plan includes an obligation for employers with at least 300 employees (including public employers) to draw up an action plan which first has to be accepted by the government and then be implemented over the period 2005-2010 with support from the government. While there are over 13 000 such large employers throughout the country, there is a best-practice obligation for other employers.

However, compared to the dominant role of concerns about fertility and child well-being in the Japanese social policy debate, hitherto budgetary allocations to the various initiatives to foster a child-friendly environment have been relatively modest. For example, the MHLW estimates that overall spending on the New Angel Plan amounted to USD 2.6 billion in 2002 or about 0.07% of GDP. The overall pressure on public budgets goes some way in explaining this.

Similarly, attempts to change workplace practices are mainly limited to promotion and encouragement. This is very much in line with the Japanese practice of consensus-based labour policy development (Box 3.1), but it effectively means that practical changes in workplace practices are slow to materialise. Given the considerable number of female workers that withdraw, at least temporarily from the labour force around childbirth, and the increasing need to mobilise female labour supply, it is surprising that employers do not invest more often in keeping female workers in their workforce, although around a quarter of Japanese employers report to have taken some action to improve the position of their female workers (in terms of hiring, promotion, etc. – MHLW, 2002). The current poor economic climate may explain some of the hesitancy among employers and unions to prioritise a wider application of family-friendly workplace measures. This is understandable, but increases the pressure on the government to be more forceful in its attempt to change workplace practices. In this respect, the Measure plan on support for the next generation is a step forward, as it recognises that to have any hope of changing the current fertility trend in Japan, male attitudes and workplace cultures will have to change.

4.3.3. The role of reconciliation policies

Public financial support towards the costs of children increase family resources and alleviate concerns among parents on the cost of raising children to some extent. However, cross-country studies (*e.g.* Blanchet and Ekert-Jaffe, 1994; Gauthier and Hatzius, 1997) and the experience in different countries[14] suggests that there may be a link between child-related financial support to parents, but that its effect on birth-rates is weak and temporary. The Austrian experience is an example: with one of the highest levels of family spending in the OECD it also has one of the lowest fertility rates, and increasing generosity of family benefits in the past has not apparently affected the downward trend in fertility.

It is hard to avoid the conclusion that the provision of child-related cash transfers is very costly, and the effect of such policies on birth rates at best temporary. If at all, parents appear to react to certain stimuli by either postponing births or bringing them forward, without this leading to anything more than only a limited effect on the long-term fertility trend (Lesthaege, 2000). However, analogies with other policies suggest that some caution in drawing such a conclusion is advisable, as aggregate studies often ignore a great deal of difference in the effects which policies can have on individual behaviour.

Reconciliation policies beyond merely increasing cash benefits may have a stronger positive effect on birth rates as they can potentially reduce the opportunity costs of women of having a child, and help them realise their increased individual aspirations. Public financing of childcare makes it less expensive to individual parents to combine work and family obligations, while parental leave gives parents some valuable time to care for their children.

There is some evidence that reconciliation policies can help. OECD (2002f) illustrates how an increase in the Danish fertility rate coincided with increased generosity of leave arrangements. Kravdal (1996) found a weak positive effect of the provision of more day care on the fertility rate for Norway, while Castles (2002) reports a strong association between childcare availability for children under age 3 and the TFR across OECD countries. In Singapore, the fertility rate increased by 15% in response to a comprehensive package of cash benefits and reconciliation policies (Lutz, 2000), although it is too early to assess the long-term impact of this reform. Although significant, these effects are generally small – smaller than the impact the increasing female wages and returns to human capital have had over the years on female opportunity costs related to childbirth (Walker, 1995, on Sweden).

Most analyses compare current fertility rates with the very high base in the past. However, the male-breadwinner society is not coming back, and expecting reconciliation policies to bring fertility rates back to levels experienced in the 1960s is unrealistic, and given the paradigm shift that has taken place, inappropriate. Nevertheless, some women feel that they face a choice – a career

118

or a family. Childbirth is deferred or postponed, whilst labour market objectives are pursued. What reconciliation policies realistically may be expected to accomplish is to contain the decline in birth rates, and possibly raise them at some point in future.

This is important as maternal labour force withdrawal, even if not permanent, involves considerable (opportunity) costs for the society as a whole. From a labour market perspective this represents a waste of investment in human capital and an inefficient use of labour force potential. Strong investment in female higher education has led to much higher female economic activity and this substantially contributes to economic growth. Long career breaks, let alone career terminations, and the persistence of unequal opportunities for male and female workers involve a considerable waste of personal potential, as well as being a waste of resources to employers and society as a whole. These issues are particularly important for Japan (but also apply to Austria to a lesser degree), where large numbers of women with high levels of educational attainment still leave the labour market at least temporarily around the birth of a child, and/or work in jobs that are low in job content compared to their potential.

4.4. Conclusions

During the last three to four decades, profound social changes took place that have considerably altered demographic regimes and family life. Young adults marry in fewer numbers and later in life, marriages are more often dissolved, and couples have fewer children. These changes have far-reaching consequences for societies: populations are ageing rapidly, and eventually may get smaller, challenging the financial sustainability of social systems, and to a lesser degree also the economic operation of a country.

Having fewer children is by and large a conscious choice. At least partly, however, people seem to have fewer children than they would want to have. Some women feel that they have to choose between a career and having a (smaller) family, and childbirth is deferred or postponed, whilst labour market objectives are pursued. To a large extent this social transformation that is turning the work and care balance reflects changing female labour market aspirations. However, labour markets have not yet fully responded to help women realise their aspirations, while changes in the division of unpaid work have been limited.

It seems, however, that the relationship between employment and fertility is changing. While there was a strong negative causal relationship between employment and fertility in the 1960s and 1970s, in the 1980s and 1990s this relationship has become weaker to the point of insignificance in some countries. At the very least, in most countries childrearing and employment seem to be less incompatible.

It is unclear what role policy may conceivably play to counteract the decline in birth rates, as there is limited evidence on what type of policies work, and how. Simple pronatalist policies that focus on cash benefits (to compensate the direct costs of having children) have shown to be ineffective in influencing individual behaviour. At best, such policies may be able to influence the timing of births. Policies that focus on reducing the indirect costs for mothers to work by offering affordable quality childcare, regular part-time employment opportunities and, generally, making the labour market more inclusive, seem to be a more promising avenue towards improving birth rates.

Notes

1. Both Ireland's and Japan's populations are fairly homogenous with only some relatively small minorities.

2. Recent immigration to Ireland differs from that to Austria, because half of the immigrants are Irish nationals who return to their economically booming country (Kiely, 2000).

3. In the Japanese discussion of the increasing age at which young people leave the parental home, this phenomenon is frequently (and misleadingly) referred to as the "Parasite Singles" problem, which has been explained by both the delay in marriage and a decline in the number of young people leaving home before marriage. While the same phenomenon is characteristic of the development of many low-fertility European countries, in particular in the South, this is not the case in Austria, where young people tend to leave their parental home earlier despite getting married later. Young men leave their parental home earlier than young women in Japan, while the opposite is observed in Europe.

4. Survey-based data on fertility preferences can be used with some degree of reliability to illustrate trend changes in such preferences. However, fertility preference data derived from surveys are unreliable predictors for future behaviour. For example, Noack and Ostby (2000) found only a weak relationship between fertility intentions and subsequent births among Norwegian women 5, 11 and 22 years after the interview. Short-term as well as long-term expectations overestimate future childbearing, with only one exception: women who do not expect to have any or more children are highly trustworthy.

5. According to the International Social Survey Programme, which collected data on desired family size for all three countries in 1994, differences in preferences on family size were as follows. In Austria the two-child norm dominated (with 70%), with a significant proportion of respondents wishing to have only one child (5%, compared to only 1% in the ISSP 1988). In Japan, the three-child norm dominated (over 50%), but almost no respondent wanted to have more than three children. Ireland stood out as the only country in which still about one third wanted to have four or even more children – a figure that has declined down from 50% in the ISSP 1988 (ZA, 1990, 1997).

6. Birth control is still far from perfect and a lot of children are unplanned. In Austria, 40% of all first births and more than 50% of all third births are not planned (BMSG, 1999). Some of this reflects a timing failure that may not reduce the ultimate number of children born, but it nevertheless does illustrate that human fertility behaviour is beyond theoretic modelling to some extent.

7. In order to obtain a divorce in Ireland, one has to be separated for four years beforehand. Following the introduction of divorce legislation in 1995, its incidence increased in 2000 and 2001 (Fahey and Russell, 2001).

8. In line with Ireland's strong focus on the right of the child, upon divorce the Courts often grant joint parental custody. This legal option has recently been introduced in Austria.

9. The main family-oriented NGOs in Austria are: the Austrian Family Association that is formally independent, but *de facto* closely related to the ÖVP – the Conservative People's Party; the Austrian Friends of Children which is affiliated to the SPÖ – the Social Democrats; the Freedom Party's family Association that is affiliated to the FPÖ – the Liberal Conservatives; and the Roman-Catholic Family Association. All these organisations provide services (sometimes including formal childcare) and have a strong advocacy role, not least through influencing political parties. These organisations also participate in the Austrian family committee: they are consulted on public family policy proposals.

10. Notable committees dealing with the declining birth-rate in Japan were the Inter-ministerial liaison committee for "Creating an environment where people can bear and rear healthy children" (1991); *ad hoc* committee of experts to "Consider policy Responses to declining fertility" in the Prime Minister's Office (1998).

11. Important reports on the declining birth-rate in Japan include the White Paper on Health and Welfare 1998: reflecting a society with fewer children to build a society where people can have dreams to bear and rear children (MHW, 1998), and a report by the Advisory Council on Population Problems (MHW, 1998a).

12. The past tradition of pre-arranged marriages in Japan has rapidly lost ground: in 1960, 60% of new marriages were pre-arranged, while this is less than 10% today (Retherford *et al.*, 2002). Thus, marriage partners are no longer found through the family but increasingly at work (40%) and through the network of friends (30%). As a consequence, the courting period has increased from one year to three years, implicitly affecting the age at marriage and thus birth-rates (Iwasawa, 2001). This has prompted some local governments to support initiatives to promote mating. In an evaluation of such an initiative for one prefectural government, it was estimated that an investment of USD 150 000 over a three-year period has eventually resulted in seven marriages and four babies: a lot of money with little effect (Asahi Shimbun, 2002a).

13. The new "Measure plan on support for the next generation", which will turn into law in June 2003, was a cabinet decision without the involvement of the social partners. The law has been designed as a framework law with specific targets and social partners are still to negotiate on specific items such as labour conditions, before these may become legal obligations.

14. There are other examples of cross-regional or cross-country findings on the impact of family policy on birth-rates. For example, in the aftermath of adopting of a series of pronatalist measures in 1989, including a large third birth bonus, Quebec's fertility rate has not developed strikingly differently from that of the rest of Canada without such a policy (Gauthier, 2001). Similarly, although comprehensive family support is generally held responsible for the relatively high fertility rates in France (Ekert, 1986), the trend of Britain's fertility rate has been remarkably similar, with a much less generous public system of family support (Gauthier, 1996).

ISBN 92-64-10418-6
Babies and Bosses: Reconciling Work and Family Life
Austria, Ireland and Japan
© OECD 2003

Chapter 5

Families and Care: Who Minds the Children?

Childcare systems differ greatly between Austria, Ireland and Japan, but in all three countries the proportion of 3-6 year old children using some type of non-parental childcare is high, while it is relatively low for children under age three. For very young children, many working parents rely on informal (or formal but poorly regulated) childcare. This chapter provides detailed information on the three countries' childcare systems, on the use of formal and informal non-parental care, and on recent childcare policy initiatives. It also reviews each country's system of parental leave, with a particular focus on the recently introduced Austrian Childcare Benefit. The core of the chapter discusses policy concerns and policy responses along four critical dimensions which can be seen as the major targets of childcare policy: to increase childcare capacity, to increase equity among parents, to increase user choice, and to increase service quality. Realising these partly interrelated targets would help to achieve the broader objectives of childcare policy: to improve child welfare, to promote child development, and to raise gender equity and female employment.

Children need to be minded. The younger they are, the more intensive care they require. Couple families are still the predominant household structure in which children are being raised (Chapter 4), but changing female labour market aspirations and family instability have increased the demand for childcare solutions beyond parental care.

Countries are faced with different problems, resulting from different historical developments of the childcare sector, which has a long history in Austria and Japan (going back to the middle of the 19th and the early 20th century, respectively) but not in Ireland. Major concerns today include, to a varying degree, supply-demand mismatches for different age groups, equity issues (access, parental costs), choice issues (provider choice, service flexibility), and quality issues.

In the first section of this chapter, the broader childcare policy objectives are summarised: child welfare, child development, female employment, and (in the case of Japan) increasing birth rates. Next, each country's system of parental leave is reviewed. This is followed by a summary of the key childcare indicators. The core of this chapter is the section on policy concerns and responses in relation to supply, equity, choice and quality of childcare services. The chapter concludes with a few recommendations that address these policy concerns while aiming to improve efficiency of current childcare systems. Childcare in this chapter comprises all services provided by education authorities, local governments and private providers for children age 0-6 (see Section 5.3).

5.1. Childcare policy objectives

If private childcare markets deliver desirable results, there is no need for public interference. In cases of market failure or externalities which accrue to society as a whole rather than just to the family purchasing childcare, however, there is a strong argument for government intervention. Research for the US concluded that demand for high-quality high-priced childcare may run short of what would be desirable from a society's point of view (Blau, 2002).

Another reason for government intervention in the provision of childcare is distributional: to strengthen families in need of help by providing childcare services at little or no cost to people living in economically disadvantaged areas or circumstances. The aim is to promote the inclusion of such families in society and to combat educational disadvantage. This motive is reflected in the provision of community childcare such as the community nurseries in

Ireland. Providing childcare places for child welfare purposes was the major objective upon introduction of day care in Japan about 100 years ago, and is still important in Japan and Austria, where childcare is provided (almost) free of charge to low-income families.

For children aged 3-6 a main objective in all three countries is to foster child development. Kindergartens in Austria and Japan and infant classes in Ireland have all been established with the goal of preparing children for primary school and to promote their social development. This partly explains why these facilities were originally established as morning classes only, though in Austria and also in Japan – in response to demand – increasingly and gradually extending into the afternoon. In all three countries, over 95% of all children in the age group 5-6 attend such groups or classes.

In addition, childcare is increasingly provided to help parents in squaring their work and care commitments, reflecting in turn concerns about gender equity and economic performance. Childcare for children under age 3 and after-school care for children age 6 to 9 (or 10 or 12) in particular have predominantly developed in response to labour market aspirations of women with the aim of facilitating maternal employment and labour market reintegration.

For Japan, to foster child well-being and to facilitate parents having as many children as they wish are also important objectives that are closely related to the previous one. In this country, childcare policy initiatives since the beginning of the 1990s are largely discussed and implemented under the umbrella of policies to cope with the declining birth rate, and the lack of sufficient childcare has been identified as one of the key policy levers in reversing this trend (*e.g.* MHW, 1998).

5.2. Parental leave models and take-up

Some parents will want to care for their young children themselves regardless of other childcare options. Other parents will prefer to work, perhaps only part-time, or would prefer to do so if better labour market and childcare opportunities were available. Parental leave schemes give working parents an opportunity to care for their children themselves during the first period after childbirth (Chapter 2), and thus co-determine parental labour market behaviour as well as the demand for (and also the supply of) childcare services for very young children.

All three countries provide for *maternity* leave around childbirth, with similar eligibility criteria and payment duration but different payment rates.[1] Subsequent to maternity leave, during much of which work is prohibited, all three countries provide for some form of *parental* leave. These schemes differ widely between countries in terms of eligibility, duration and benefit levels (Chapter 2 and Background Annex to the Review).

Parental leave policies have been established longest in Austria, where such leave was introduced in the 1960s for insured (*i.e.* working) mothers and in 1990 for insured fathers (originally only for those fathers whose spouse was entitled to take such leave). Since then, there have been numerous reforms, cumulating in a complete overhaul of the system in early 2002, when parental leave and benefit payment became dissociated and leave benefit was replaced by a universal Childcare Benefit. The overall system is now more generous in terms of population coverage, duration and payment rates than ever before (see Box 5.1 for a detailed overview of the current legislation).

The 2002 reform in Austria was intended to give more parents more choice: 1) by extending payments but also coverage of health and pension insurance to parents who were not entitled to parental leave benefit; and 2) by extending work options for those currently on employment-protected parental leave. As these work options largely remain subject to employer-consent, the impact of the latter part of the reform is likely to be limited. The provision of increased cash transfers for a longer period to more people certainly increases parental choice options by enabling more parents to reduce working hours or not to work at all for a prolonged period of time. But it also influences the work and/or care choice: compared to Ireland and Japan, Austrian policy gives significantly more financial support to those families which choose to have a parent caring full-time for a very young child (Chapter 6).

Parental leave and Childcare Benefit are now two different programmes which impact differently on the financial incentive structure that different groups of parents may face (Box 5.1 considers the different aspects of existing rules in some detail). It is as yet uncertain how the 2002 reform may change labour market behaviour of workers in the event of childbirth. A comprehensive evaluation of the 2002 reform will only be possible upon three years of its introduction. Nevertheless, on the basis of past experience in Austria with changes in the duration of parental leave (in 1990) or the duration of leave payment (in 1996), it is to be expected that the longer period of benefit payment will increase the average length of time that mothers are not in work upon childbirth. Austrian mothers will now be tempted to provide full-time maternal care for the full 30-month period of Childcare Benefit payments, thereby losing the right to return to their previous job. Early analysis of the impact of the new regulation on maternal employment patterns, based on behaviour of mothers who started out on the old paid parental leave regulation and extended their leave in 2002 in line with the transition rules of the new regulation, confirms that this is likely to happen (Lutz, 2003). The same study confirms this effect by finding that among mothers with a child between 18 and 30 months, the proportion working more than marginally has *declined* from over 50% to below 30%. But the study also finds that this in-work rate has *increased* among mothers with a child younger than 18 months, from

Box 5.1. **Childcare benefit and parental leave reform in Austria**

In 2002, the system of parental leave with an associated leave benefit was reformed into two separate schemes: a largely unchanged employment-protected parental leave covering employees with a sufficient work record, and a new Childcare Benefit covering all parents who are entitled to family allowance and whose annual (individual) income is below a newly introduced upper limit. This transformation followed a series of changes over the 1990s. In 1990, the duration of parental leave was increased from one year to two years, and the possibility of part-time work subject to employer consent in combination with a partial leave benefit was introduced, initially during the child's second and third year of life and in 1993 until the fourth birthday. Reform in 1996 meant that while employment-protected leave remained at two years, benefit payments were changed so that payment to one parent ended when the child reached 18 months, with the residual six-month payment period being reserved to the other parent.

Unlike the previous parental leave payment, entitlement to Childcare Benefit is no longer related to current or previous work status nor to whether a parent actually takes care of the child, but only to whether the claimant's income is below EUR 14 600 per annum, equivalent to around two thirds of average earnings of a production employee (APE). This income threshold was introduced both for budgetary reasons and with the aim to give incentives to fathers to reduce working hours. Income refers to the claiming parent's individual income (not household income) and includes earnings as well as all other sources of income (e.g. rent or capital income). If the total income exceeds the annual threshold, the benefit payment is completely withdrawn (i.e. payments are not phased out). It is possible, though, to suspend the benefit payment during months with higher earnings.

Childcare Benefit is payable for one parent until the child is 30 months old, and for another six months for the other parent (depending on the claimant's income). During this period, the entitlement can be alternated twice, with each phase stretching over at least three months. The new benefit is paid at EUR 14.36 per day (around USD 410 per month at the average 2002 exchange rate) which is equivalent to 22% of APE earnings, or 30% of APE earnings when including family allowance and child tax credit. Lone parents and low-income couples can get a supplement of EUR 6.06 per day, raising total financial support during this period to almost 40% of APE earnings, but this supplement has to be paid back as soon as income exceeds a certain level (Chapter 6). The person receiving Childcare Benefit is covered by public health insurance, and the first 18 months of benefit receipt also count as contribution years for a retirement pension.

Box 5.1. **Childcare benefit and parental leave reform in Austria** (cont.)

Parental leave lasts until the child's second birthday. Each parent can postpone three months of the entitlement up to the child's seventh birthday, thereby reducing the initial period. Except for one month, parents are not entitled to take parental leave at the same time but, like Childcare Benefit payment, the entitlement can be alternated twice with a minimum period of three months each. Employers have to be notified of any take-up and changes three months in advance (initial take-up must be notified during the maternity protection period). Programme design of the parental leave period allows for two in-work options while on leave that have no implications for employment protection: participate in marginal employment (with earnings up to USD 284 per month); and, as of 2002, and subject to employer-consent, work full-time for a period of up to 13 weeks per year (for either the same or another employer). The latter option may be attractive to employers looking for replacement workers for staff on short-term leave or who wish to meet periodical or seasonal hikes in demand. However, this work option is also conditional on parents being able to find short-term (thus mostly informal) childcare solutions. Instead, and also subject to employer-consent, employees can arrange employment-protected part-time work with working hours reduced by 40%, until up to the child's fourth birthday (leave periods reduce the maximum duration of this).

Parental leave and Childcare Benefit are now two entirely different programmes with different duration of entitlements and different rules on earnings disregards. As the population covered by the two programmes is not the same, different groups of parents need to account for different aspects of Childcare Benefit and parental leave legislation in their work and/or care choice. In *theory*, all Childcare Benefit claimants are allowed to earn up to the income threshold without benefit loss. As benefit payment is not gradually withdrawn but cut completely at the threshold, programme design means that Childcare Benefit claimants potentially face strong incentives to earn less than 69% of average earnings. Earning more only leads to an increase in net family income when in excess of 91% of APE earnings. To what extent this feature is relevant depends on the characteristics of the Childcare Benefit claimant concerned. Considering work options as allowed by the different regulations, there are essentially three broad groups: 1) claimants not entitled to parental leave; 2) claimants on parental leave with previous earnings below the Childcare Benefit income threshold; and 3) claimants on leave with previous earnings above this threshold.

Considering work options is simplest for Childcare Benefit claimants who are not entitled to parental leave. These claimants can work and earn up to the Childcare Benefit income threshold without benefit loss. However,

Box 5.1. **Childcare benefit and parental leave reform in Austria** *(cont.)*

income-threshold design may not be that relevant for these claimants, as it includes those whose weak labour market attachment, if they worked at all, precluded them from entitlement to employment-protected parental leave when they started claiming Childcare Benefit. The other relevant group of claimants here concerns those whose entitlement to parental leave has expired but who continue to claim Childcare Benefit until the 30th month upon childbirth. If these clients already wish to work, they are certain to ensure that earnings levels will not endanger benefit receipt.

Childcare Benefit claimants on employment-protected leave who are considering working also have to account for parental leave programme rules. All those on parental leave are: 1) allowed to engage in marginal employment (with earnings up to 15% of APE earnings); and 2) entitled to return to work for their original employer after the end of their parental leave up to 24 months under the same employment conditions as before. However, to change employment conditions by, for example, adjusting working hours is *not* an entitlement (see below). In view of the existing parental leave entitlements, two further groups of Childcare Benefit claimants can be distinguished along their work options:

i) Workers on parental leave with previous earnings *below* 69% of APE earnings can choose to engage in marginal employment in which case net income would not be that much lower than before childbirth, but they can also return to their previous employer under the same employment conditions (*e.g.* in terms of hours) at any stage while continuing to receive the Childcare Benefit payment.

ii) Workers on parental leave with previous earnings *above* the Childcare Benefit income-threshold cannot claim the payment if they go back to work for their previous employer under the same employment conditions as before. These workers face strong incentives to reduce working hours and earnings to below 69% of APE earnings, but this can only be achieved when the employer agrees, or when workers give up their parental leave entitlement, and find part-time employment elsewhere. At the same time, given their earnings profile these workers are the most likely to return to full-time employment before the leave entitlement expires, so as not to damage their career prospects.

Austrian parental leave legislation has allowed part-time work for many years, although working part-time is not an entitlement, but conditional on employer-consent. For that reason, the part-time option was only used by 3% of leave takers in the late 1990s (BMUJF, 1999a), and there is no reason to believe that this will have changed significantly with recent benefit reform. Regardless

> **Box 5.1. Childcare benefit and parental leave reform in Austria** *(cont.)*
>
> of their earnings, many workers in Austria (in most cases mothers) on parental leave are reluctant to return to their previous post because they feel that full-time work is not compatible with care commitments until the child goes to kindergarten or primary school. The introduction of Childcare Benefit may well lead these parents to look for part-time employment of substantial hours with another employer, rather than staying on parental leave for the full duration.
>
> Finally, at least theoretically, the Childcare Benefit income threshold effectively gives most fathers (i.e. all those earning above 69% of APE earnings) an incentive to reduce working hours and earnings temporarily, as they otherwise cannot claim payments during the six-month period reserved for the "second parent". However, while empirical evidence shows that Austrian mothers would generally change their work pattern considerably in the aftermath of childbirth, prior to 2002 only 2% of all fathers took leave (Chapter 3), and there are no indications as yet that reform has changed their behaviour. Whilst this may also be related to employers not looking favourably upon a reduction of working hours of male employees, this is largely explained by the fact the many mothers choose to provide full-time care for a longer period.

just under 10% to almost 15%, with the overall trend for the group of mothers with a child younger than 2½ years being a decline in the in-work rate from around 25% to around 20%.

In Japan, unpaid parental leave was introduced in 1992, although already the 1986 Equal Opportunities Law provided for parental leave subject to employer consent while encouraging employers to make such leave available. In 1995, a payment through Employment Insurance worth 25% of previous earnings was introduced, while before that around one third of all employers voluntarily offered some wage compensation (JIL, 1993). Coverage was extended to all companies rather than only those with 30 or more employees, but not to all types of workers (while, in contrast to parental leave, maternity leave is granted to all Japanese workers covered by Health Insurance).[2]

Since 2001, the Japanese regulations provide a comprehensive model for parents with young children. During the period of parental leave, the Employment Insurance Law provides for a ten-months benefit payment at 30% of previous earnings with an additional payment when the leave taker goes back to work.[3] This additional benefit is worth another 10% of previous earnings for each month on leave (raising the total payment rate to 40%), and it is paid as a lump-sum six months after the actual return to work. In addition, the

Childcare and Family Care Leave Act obliges employers to take other measures, such as shortening working hours, until the child reaches age 3, and encourages employers to provide similar rights until age 6 (Chapter 3).

The Irish parental leave system was only introduced in 1998, in response to the 1995 EU Directive on Parental leave requiring the provision of three months parental leave, as distinct from maternity leave, for each male and female worker. Parental leave is unpaid and relatively short, but in contrast to the other two countries it gives the same individual non-transferable entitlement of 14 weeks for each parent. Leave can be taken as a block or, with employer consent, in parts until the child reaches age 5 (see Background Annex).

Compared to the other two countries, mothers' take-up of parental leave in Austria is very high. Almost all eligible mothers take leave, with an average duration of about 65 weeks before the recent reform (Table 5.1). With the new Childcare Benefit, the average duration of parental leave may well increase further, as provisional analysis indicates (Lutz, 2003). In total, Austria spends significantly more on maternity and parental leave payments (which benefits children under the age of 2.5-3) than on childcare services (which predominantly benefits children over age 3).

Table 5.1. **High take-up and long duration of parental leave in Austria**
Maternity and parental leave indicators

	Austria		Ireland	Japan
	2001	Estimates for new scheme	2001	2001
Female employment rate age 15-64, in %	60	..	54	57
Mothers with a child under 3 in work, in %[a]	32	..	45	24
... as above, including mothers on parental leave	72	..	51	29
Proportion of eligible mothers taking parental leave	95	Increase	40	56
Proportion of eligible fathers taking parental leave	2	Increase	5	0.4
Average duration of parental leave taken (estimate), in weeks	65	110	..	30
Maximum duration of leave after childbirth for one parent, in weeks	78	130	22	52
Total benefit for full duration, in hypothetical weeks of full earnings[b]	25.5	38.5	5.6	22.4
Public spending on maternity leave in % of GDP	0.15	No change	0.06	0.10
Public spending on parental leave in % of GDP	0.22	0.45	–	0.01
Leave spending, in percentage of childcare spending[c]	86	140	19	34

a) Estimates for Ireland and Japan based on leave eligibility and take-up.
b) For Austria, this is calculated on the basis of an assumed average income.
c) Spending for maternity and parental leave *versus* spending on childcare for children age 0-6.
Source: National authorities and calculations by the OECD Secretariat.

In Ireland and Japan, mothers' take-up of parental leave is lower than in Austria, and the duration of leave much shorter on average.[4] For this reason, overall spending on leave programmes is low relative to public spending on childcare. As payment rates for parental leave are higher in Japan than monthly Childcare Benefit payments in Austria (about 40% of previous earnings in Japan *versus* a flat-rate payment at 22% of APE earnings in Austria), spending in Japan could be similar or even higher than in Austria if Japanese workers would make widespread use of parental leave – whereas at present about 70% of mothers resign from their job around childbirth (NIPSSR, 2000).[5] Indeed, raising take-up of parental leave among mothers and fathers is an explicit objective in the context of Japan's policy to facilitate having a child (Chapter 4).

5.3. Key childcare indicators

5.3.1. Public spending

Overall public spending on childcare is relatively similar in all three countries in 2002: around one third of a percentage point of GDP in Ireland and Japan, and somewhat higher, at 0.43%, in Austria (Table 5.2). In Ireland, 80% of this amount concerns public spending on infant school classes that are open for children aged 4-6. In Japan, almost one third of the total goes into kindergartens (educational facilities) while the other two thirds are allocated to licensed day care. In Austria, most public spending is on day care, including crèches for children under age 3 and kindergartens for children over age 3. In all three countries, the bulk of public expenditure benefits children aged 3-6 (Box 5.2).

Table 5.2. **High public funding of day care per child enrolled in Austria and Japan**

Childcare spending indicators

	Austria	Ireland	Japan
Spending on formal childcare in % of GDP	0.43	0.32	0.32
Day care only[a]	–	0.07	0.22
Pre-school only[b]	–	0.25	0.10
Spending per child enrolled in USD (PPP) per year	4 050	2 075	3 022
Day care only	–	1 009	4 121
Pre-school only	–	2 947	1 877
Spending per child enrolled in % of GDP per capita	15.0	8.7	11.2
Day care only	–	4.2	15.2
Pre-school only	–	12.3	6.9
Spending per child age 0-6 in % of GDP per capita	6.9	3.8	5.6

a) Nurseries (age 0-5) and playgroups (age 3-5) in Ireland and licensed day care (age 0-6) in Japan.
b) Infant classes in primary schools (age 4-6) in Ireland and kindergartens (age 3-6) in Japan.
Source: National authorities and OECD (2002e).

Box 5.2. **Financing and responsibility of childcare**

In Austria, in the 1970s the responsibility for childcare was devolved to the provinces (which set standards) and the municipalities (which distribute childcare subsidies to providers or provide the necessary services themselves). This structure is reflected in the current childcare funding flows (see Chart 5A.1 in the annex to this chapter). 60-70% of the total funds come from the municipalities, 15-25% from the *Länder* governments and some 15% from parental fees (with considerable variation across provinces). As taxes are only collected on a federal level, local and regional governments receive their income through financial adjustment or equalisation. Direct federal funding for childcare is unusual but possible and has been used as an incentive to increase supply in the 1997-2001 period. Through wage subsidies for childcare personnel and means-tested fee subsidies for parents looking for work, the Public Employment Service also carries a certain share of the costs.

As in Austria, the responsibility to provide adequate day care support in Japan lies predominantly with local governments, and prefectures and the central government also contribute to the overall costs. Central government sets minimum standard regulations, and settles standard running costs and nominal user charges of a place in licensed day care. The difference between that standard and the nominal charge is covered from public sources: 50% by the central government and 25% each by the prefectures and the municipalities (see Chart 5A.2 in the annex). Many municipalities offer additional subsidies to reduce the costs for parents. The overall share of total costs covered by parents is under 30%. The costs of non-licensed day care, unless "recognised" and therefore also subsidised by the municipality, are almost entirely covered by parents (see below). The costs for after-school care are shared between parents (50%), municipalities (33.3%) and central government (16.7%).

The situation in Ireland is very different. A public childcare policy only emerged in the 1990s because of social inclusion concerns. Childcare regulations were introduced in 1996. By the end of the 1990s, shortage of labour became the major economic policy issue, leading to unions, employers and the government, but also NGOs and childcare associations, formulating a more coherent childcare policy in the context of Ireland's inclusive social partnership programmes (see Chapter 3 and further below). A series of new structures are put in place at both the local and the national level, but responsibilities remain somewhat fragmented. County committees are established to promote and develop childcare at the local level. The Department of Justice, Equality and Law Reform (responsible for gender equity) allocates subsidies under the National Development Plan, but other departments also play a role. Nevertheless, day care costs are still predominantly covered by parental fees, except for community childcare and infant classes in schools, which are largely government-funded (Chart 5A.3 in the annex).

Box 5.2. **Financing and responsibility of childcare** *(cont.)*

Accurately estimating total costs of a childcare place in the three countries is hampered by data limitations, while directly available national data for certain types of care are difficult to compare because of the different age distributions underlying these figures. For example, with a relatively high share of children over age 3 (which are "cheaper" because of lower staff-to-child ratios) costs are automatically reduced. On average, in Japan a place in care for a 0-6 year old, including both Kindergarten and day care, is estimated to cost about USD 5 400 (PPP) per year (day care cost alone amount to JPY 80 000 per month or about USD 6 400 (PPP) per year). Including different types of care for children up to the age of 6, costs per place in Austria are also about USD 5 400 (PPP) per year, while in Ireland (including day care and infant classes) this is around USD 4 400 (PPP). The difference between Ireland and the other two countries is largely explained by the greater market share of private commercial providers and lower wages of childcare workers (see Section 5.4.4).

Public spending per child enrolled in any form of childcare is highest in Austria, at the equivalent of 15% of GDP per capita or almost USD 4 000 – adjusted for purchasing power parities, or PPP (Background Annex to the Review) – per year per child (Table 5.2). In relation to GDP per capita, this is identical to the amount spent per child enrolled in a licensed day care centre in Japan. This finding is not surprising given a number of similarities between Austrian and Japanese day care systems *e.g.* in terms of age groups covered, opening hours, or required qualifications and wages for childcare workers (see below). Public spending is much lower, around 4% of GDP per capita or USD 1 000, per child enrolled in a nursery or playgroup in Ireland – as these services are predominantly offered by private providers who do not receive any subsidies for their running costs.

Kindergartens in Japan get lower subsidies per child than day care, which is largely explained by the different purpose of the two systems, the higher age of the children and the shorter opening hours of kindergartens. Irish pre-primary infant classes for children age 4-6, in contrast, receive more public funding per child than Irish nurseries for children age 0-5 despite the fact that the latter are closed in the afternoon.

5.3.2. *Types of childcare*

Childcare services can be classified in several groups: centre-based pre-school care, centre-based out-of-school care (the first sometimes, the latter frequently organised within the education sector), childminders or family day care, play groups and kids groups, in-home care (nannies), and informal care provided by relatives and others.[6] The combination of services offered in each country and the importance of each of these segments differs widely between countries (Table 5.3). This is particularly true for the role of informal non-parental care. There is no difference between the three countries in terms of mandatory school age, which is six years everywhere, but primary school hours are shortest in Austria (4-5 hours per day) and longest and more variable in Japan (6-7 hours).

Centre-based kindergartens for children age 3-6, sometimes 2-6, which serve a dual care and education purpose with a shift towards education during the last year before school, are the predominant type of service in Austria. These are run on either a full-day or a half-day basis and are operated by public or private (mostly non-profit but sometimes commercial) providers. Younger children may either find a place in a full-day centre-based crèche or be cared for in a family-like environment by a childminder who can mind up to four children. Childminders in Austria are in most cases registered with the municipality or a NGO. In addition, there are some privately organised kids groups, run by parents and formally registered by the municipality, catering for children at various ages. Out-of-school hours care is either in the form of care in a special centre for children age 6-10, usually linked to a kindergarten, or through all-day supervision (with lessons and leisure separated or integrated) in primary and junior secondary schools. Informal care by nannies and au-pairs plays a minor though increasing role.

In Ireland, there is an administrative divide into day care and school-based early education. This divide continues although policy documents assert that care and early education cannot be separated. Pre-primary schools (so-called infant classes) for children age 4-6 and some smaller pre-school education programmes targeted at children from disadvantaged backgrounds and with special learning needs (Early Start, Rutland Street Project, pre-schools for traveller children) are under the responsibility of the Department of Education and Science (DES). The Department of Justice, Equality and Law Reform (DJELR) is currently responsible for supports towards the development of all kinds of day care services, which are targeted at children under age 4 or 5. There are two types of such service: centre-based full-day nurseries catering for children age 0-5, and partly home-based, partly centre-based playgroups for children over age 3 run on a sessional basis (i.e. one session of 3.5 hours). Both types are mostly offered by private commercial providers, but some are community-run. Out-of-school hours care is virtually non-existent. "Care gaps" are filled by a large number of usually non-registered childminders who can care for up to three children without any legal requirements and up to six children under certain minimum regulations. Finally, there are home-based parent-toddler groups for children under age 3.

Japan also has a dual system to provide care and education for children in pre-school age: full-day centre-based day care providing care and protecting child welfare for kids age 0-6, and (initially only half-day) centre-based kindergartens

Table 5.3. **Diverse childcare markets**
Characteristics of formal and informal childcare services

	Target age group	Location	Providers[a]	Public subsidies	Opening hours[b]	Number of children
Austria						
Children aged 0-6	–	–	–	–	–	**498 000**
Crèches	0/1-3 years	Centre-based	50% private	Significant	Full day	12 000
Kindergartens	2/3-6 years	Centre-based	25% private	Significant	Half or full day	218 000
Kids groups	Usually 1/2-6 years	Usually centre-based	Private	Minor	Half or full day	About 10-12 000
Out-of-school care	6-10/12 years	Centre-based	40% private	Significant	Afternoon	37 000
All-day schools	6-12 years	School-based	Public (schools)	Significant	Afternoon	About 25-30 000
Childminders	Mostly 0-4 years	Childminder's home	private	Variable	Flexible	13 000
Nannies/au-pairs	Any age	Child's home	Private	None	Flexible	Few
Ireland						
Children aged 0-6	–	–	–	–	–	**320 000**
Nurseries	0/1-5 years	Centre-based	Mostly private	Limited (except for publicly provided)	Full day	About 63 000
Playgroups	3-5/6 years	Centre-/home-based	Mostly private	Limited (except for publicly provided)	Sessional i.e. 3.5 hours	77 000
Infant classes	4-6 years	School-based	Public (schools)	Fully public	Half day	Few
Out-of-school care	School age	Centre-based	Private	Very limited	Afternoon	50-75 000
Childminders	Usually 0-5 years	Child's or childminder's home	Private	None	Flexible	Few
Parent-toddler groups	0-3 years	Home-based	Private	None	Flexible	Few
Japan						
Children aged 0-6	–	–	–	–	–	**7 080 000**
Licensed day-care	0-6 years	Centre-based	43% private	Significant	Full day	1 828 000
Non-licensed day-care	0-6 years	Centre-based	Private	Limited	Full day	221 000
Kindergartens	3-6 years	Centre-based	60% private	Significant	Half day (increasingly with extra hours)	1 753 000
After-schools clubs	6-9/10 years	Centre-based	10% private	Limited	Afternoon	547 000
Childminders	Usually 0-3 years	Childminder's home	Private	Variable	Flexible	About 10 000
Nannies/babysitters	Any age	Child's home	Private	None	Flexible	Few

a) In Austria, private providers are predominantly non-profit; in Ireland either non-profit or commercial; and in Japan always commercial for non-licensed but non-profit for licensed day care. Mandatory school age is 6 years in all three countries.

b) Primary school opening hours: Austria 8:00-12/13:00 (4-5 hours), Ireland around 9:00-14:00 (5 hours), Japan around 8:15-15:15 (7 hours) [excluding juku].

Source: National authorities.

BABIES AND BOSSES: RECONCILING WORK AND FAMILY LIFE – ISBN 92-64-10418-6 – © OECD 2003

providing education and social stimulation for children age 3-6. In addition, there is an explicit distinction between licensed and non-licensed day care centres. Licensed centres, offered by private non-profit or public providers, have to satisfy higher standards (determined by the Child Welfare Law) and receive substantial public funding. Non-licensed commercial day care centres are spreading during the last few years, as they are responding more flexibly to emerging needs. After-school care ("after-school children's clubs") for children age 6-9 is mainly organised by the municipalities, outside the day care system, often using school facilities. Home-based childminding, which in Japan is largely formalised through registration with local authorities, plays only a minor role.

5.3.3. Supply and use of childcare

Apart from differences between individual children, there is no agreement in social and psychological research on the age from which non-parental childcare is having positive long-term effects on child development (Box 5.3), or on the duration of parental care needed during the critical first period after childbirth. In practice, countries tend to provide almost universal childcare for kids in the last two years before mandatory school age, but very limited childcare for children under 2 years of age.

Use of non-parental childcare strongly varies with age. In the age group 3-6 years, about six in seven children are attending some form of childcare or pre-primary education in all three countries (Table 5.4). In Ireland this is predominantly (half-day) pre-school, in Austria it is kindergarten of varying duration, and in Japan it is either full-time day care or – more common at this age – kindergarten of varying duration. At this age, attending quality formal care services is regarded as important irrespective of the mother's work status.

By contrast, use of childcare for children under the age of 3 is low in Japan and Austria with 18% and 13%, respectively, and as low as this in Ireland were only *formal* childcare taken into account.[7] This is lower than the actual in-work rates of mothers with a child at this age – which are about 25% in Japan, 32% in Austria and 45% in Ireland (see Table 5.1). This suggests that *informal* childcare plays an important role for this age group. Comparing employment rates and childcare enrolment rates, and assuming that all those mothers using formal childcare are in work, suggests that among women with a child under 3 years of age who are in work roughly the following proportions rely on informal childcare: over 70% in Ireland, almost 60% in Austria, and around 25% in Japan. Data for Ireland confirm that for this age group informal childminding is more important than formal childcare (Table 5.4).

Longer term trends show that in Japan the proportion of children age 0-4 attending licensed day care or a kindergarten has doubled from 15% in 1980 to 29% in 2001. For the entire age group 0-6, the increase was from 41% to 51%,

Box 5.3. **Child development and care**

A major concern in many OECD countries is child development in the early years (OECD, 2001b). There are a multiplicity of interrelated factors that have a bearing on a child's cognitive, physical, social and emotional development including income, parental employment, parenting behaviour, family stability and childcare services, and it is difficult to identify or separate out the effect of each. Child poverty has been the focus of much of the research in this area and evidence strongly suggests that it has negative implications for a wide range of outcomes, both during childhood and later on in life (Kamerman et al., 2003). More recently, there has been increased interest in the impact of the related factors of maternal employment, parental and non-parental care on child development, which is the focus of this box.

There are some concerns that maternal employment may have negative consequences for child development. However, the evidence is far from conclusive (Kamerman et al., 2003). Recent US findings suggest that there are negative effects where mothers work full-time in the first year of life but positive effects where children are aged over one (Han et al., 2001; Waldfogel et al., 2002). Evidence also suggests that participating in collective care arrangements is generally beneficial to children from the 3rd birthday onwards, with evidence being mixed on the effects on children aged one and two. In a survey of Japanese and international evidence, Amino (2001) finds little evidence of the negative effects of maternal employment and suggests it is a myth that children should be reared solely by their mother when aged under three. He concludes that the quality of parental and non-parental care is the most important determinant of outcomes.

This evidence raises the question of whether the two or three years of parental leave common in Austria is necessary from a child development perspective. On the other hand, the conditions of maternal employment are important insofar as they determine the time parents spend with their children, or parenting behaviour. As such, long hours (Poocock, 2001), non-standard hours (Han, 2002) and low job satisfaction and workplace tensions (Stewart and Barling, 1996) have been found to have a negative impact on child development. Ruhm (2000) finds that part-time working and family-friendly policies that allow for time at home with young children may improve children's cognitive development.

Early childhood education and care (ECEC) programmes are complementary to parental care and are an important aspect of policy that can influence child development. Extensive research from Sweden, France, UK and the US shows the positive impacts such programmes can have on child development, especially for the most disadvantaged (Kamerman et al., 2003). There is a growing recognition of the importance of quality childcare services and, in Japan, the day care system is in the process of becoming more oriented towards child development since the 1999 revision to childcare guidelines, although in recent years emphasis in Japan and Ireland has been on extending the provision of ECEC.

Table 5.4. **Most children over age 3 but few under age 3 in childcare**

Childcare enrollment rates in percentage of the population,
by age and type of childcare, latest available year

	Age 0-3	Age 3-6	Age 0-6	School age[a]
A. By age				
Austria (2001)	13	86	51	13
Ireland (1997)	12	74	44	< 10
Including informal	31	86	59	< 10
Japan (2001)	18	89	54	12

	Day care[b]	Pre-school[c]	Childminding	Other[d]	Total age 0-6
B. By type (age 0-6)					
Austria	46	–	3	2	51
Ireland	20	24	16	Minor	59
Japan	29	25	0.1	Minor	54

a) Out-of-school hours care including Austrian all-day schools.
b) Crèches and kindergartens in Austria, nurseries and play groups in Ireland, day care in Japan.
c) Infant classes in Ireland and kindergartens in Japan.
d) Self-organised kids groups in Austria.

Source: OECD secretariat estimates on the basis of various national sources: Austria: Day Care Statistic 2001/2002, ÖIF Survey 1999, Schools in Austria 2001/2002; Ireland: ESRI Survey on Childcare Arrangements 1997, OECD (2002e); Japan: School Basic Survey, Survey Report on Social Welfare Institutions, Survey by Childrearing Promotion Division.

or 54% if including non-licensed day care. During the same twenty-year period, in Austria the proportion of 0-6 year old children attending formal childcare increased from one third to one half, with a doubling of childcare places for kids under age 3 in the last decade. For Ireland, comparable data on trends is not available.

In the absence of a sufficient supply of formal childcare, parents who want to work full-time frequently have to rely on informal childcare arrangements.[8] In both Austria and Ireland, use of formal day care or nurseries is higher among part-time working women with a child under age 6 (under age 4 in Ireland) than among those working full-time (Table 5.5). In Ireland, more than 50% of those women working full-time rely on a childminder's service, and another 8% on paid relatives, while only one in seven use formal nurseries. In Japan, 15% of all working mothers rely on their grandparents, while 5% of those children use non-licensed day care. Kindergartens in the education system are used more frequently by women who are not in work.

School hours are shorter than day care hours, so parents who wish to work full-time must find additional care arrangements. Around 12-13% of all children at primary school-age in Austria and Japan make use of out-of-school hours (OSH) care institutions (Table 5.4). In addition, in Japan some 25-30% of

Table 5.5. **Working mothers in Ireland rely on informal childcare**

Use of childcare by work status, latest available year

		Working full-time	Working part-time	Not working	Total
Austria (age 0-6)					
Day care	Formal	49	59	28	36
No day care	None/informal	51	41	72	64
Ireland (age 0-4)					
No paid childcare	None/informal	22	47	82	62
Nursery	Formal	14	21	17	17
Childminder	Informal	56	27	1	18
Paid relative	Informal	8	5	0	3
Japan (age 0-6)		Working			
Parent	None	13		68	50
Grandparent	Informal	15		6	9
Licensed day care	Formal	45		7	20
Non-licensed day care	Formal	5		1	2
Kindergarten	Formal	15		17	16
Other/unknown	–	7		1	3

Source: Austria: Microcensus September 1995, special programme on childcare; Ireland: ESRI Survey of Childcare Arrangements 1997 (N = 663); Japan: Oishi (2002) based on Basic Survey on People's Life 1998 (N = 3781).

all pupils in elementary school attend private extra-schooling facilities – *juku* classes (Hirao, 2002; and Chapter 4). In Austria, OSH care includes both those attending a care institution (*Horte*) and those under all-day supervision in a primary school. The latter is likely to increase further in importance, as a recent Federal Law specified that in each of the nine Austrian provinces 10-15% of all schools have to provide such service. The city of Vienna is quite different from the rest of Austria, as 50% of all primary school-age children attend either form of OSH care. In Ireland, OSH care is still virtually non-existent, though arguably needed for children from age 4 onwards. There are some centre-based facilities which have an after-school group to fill the places that become available in the afternoon, and in the context of the recent childcare programme OSH care is also being developed.

Austria and Japan have been quite successful at expanding capacity of OSH care since the mid-1990s. In Japan, the number of places in after-school children's clubs has more than doubled since 1994 in the context of the two Angel Plans. In Austria, one third of the current capacity has been created since 1995 mostly due to the introduction and expansion of all-day supervision in schools. This expansion is partly explained by the use of school facilities and vacant classrooms for this purpose, though Japanese children's clubs also utilise other public facilities. Ireland is among the countries in

BABIES AND BOSSES: RECONCILING WORK AND FAMILY LIFE – ISBN 92-64-10418-6 – © OECD 2003

which schools cannot easily be used for after-school care, because of different bodies being responsible for schools and childcare, while in Japan municipalities are responsible for both.

5.4. Childcare policy concerns

Childcare systems differ greatly between the countries, but in all three the proportion of 3-6 year old children using some type of non-parental childcare is high, while it is relatively low for children under age 3 as well as for those in primary school age. This section discusses policy concerns and policy responses along four critical dimensions which can be seen as the major immediate targets of childcare policy: to increase childcare capacity, to increase equity among parents, to increase user choice, and to increase service quality. Realising these to some extent interrelated targets would implicitly secure achieving the broader objectives of childcare policy: to improve child welfare, to promote child development, and to raise gender equity, female employment, and – as part of a broader work/family strategy – possibly also birth rates (Chapter 4).

5.4.1. Increase capacity

5.4.1.1. Indicators on unmet demand

In Ireland, there is consensus that supply of childcare is insufficient.[9] It is estimated that, by 2010, a total of around 210-220 000 childcare places, formal or informal, will be needed (Government of Ireland, 1999). Given the current number of places in nurseries, playgroups and childminding, this suggests an additional demand for around 76 000 places. Accounting for the number of places that may be created through ongoing programmes (see below), another 40 000 places – about one fifth of today's total supply – will be needed during the next seven years (Table 5.6). Waiting lists also illustrate unmet demand. Currently, there are more than 7 400 children on a waiting list for centre-based formal childcare (ADM, 2002, based on the County Childcare Survey 1999/2000). This is about 4% of the total current capacity of formal and informal childcare, but over 20% of the number currently using such services. Waiting lists are by far longest for babies under one year (75% of current capacity) and shortest for infants over 3 years.

In Austria, the question of unmet demand is contested. There is agreement that day care for children under age 3 and after-school care is currently insufficient in most regions. A 1995 survey identified an extra need of 140 000 places, 70% of which for school-age children (Hammer, 1997). Adjusting for the decline in the size of the child population since 1995 and for the number of childcare places created since then, leaves an unmet demand of about 100 000 places for 2001 – assuming that behaviour and preferences have remained unchanged since the mid-1990s (Table 5.6). A recent 2002

Table 5.6.   **Large supply shortages for children under age 3 and over age 6**
Indicators on unmet childcare demand

	Age 0-3	Age 3-6	Age 0-6	School age[a]
Austria				
Unmet demand reported in 1995	17 900	23 500	41 400	98 100
Places created since then	9 865	14 599	24 464	22 859
Population adjustment factor	0.85	0.92	0.89	1.02
Estimated unmet demand in 2001	5 350	7 021	12 371	77 203
Unmet demand reported in 2002	17 500	25 400	42 900	46 400
Demand in % of current supply	60	10	15	70
Ireland				
Total estimated demand in 2010	–	–	215 000	High unmet demand
Places (to be) created through EOCP[b]	–	–	36 000	
Unmet demand by 2010	–	–	40 000	
Demand in % of current supply	–	–	21	
Children on waiting list for nurseries	3 129	4 313	7 442	
Waiting list in % of current supply	6	3	4	
Japan				
Children on waiting lists	16 965	8 482	25 447	Unknown
Waiting list in % of current supply	3	0.7	1.4	
New Angel Plan (1999) targets	100 000	–	–	108 000
Target for 2004 in % of current supply	17	–	–	28[c]
Zero waiting list initiative (2001) targets	–	–	150 000	–
Target for 2004 in % of current supply	–	–	8	–

a)   Out-of-school hours care including Austrian all-day schools.
b)   Equal Opportunity Childcare Programme.
c)   In Japan, targets for after-school children's clubs have been exceeded by 2002.
Source: OECD Secretariat calculations based on national information.

survey, using the same questions as the 1995 survey, indeed estimates unmet demand for 2002 at 90 000 places, but with a different distribution by age group:[10] for children of primary school-age demand has declined much more than projected, while for children under age 3 and between age 3 and 6 unmet demand has remained unchanged despite an increase in capacity since 1995. This suggests that behaviour and preferences have changed and that with increased supply of childcare for children under age 6 new demand for this group was created. In relation to the number of children in childcare, unmet demand in 2002 corresponds to around 60% of the current capacity for children under age 3, to around 10% of the capacity for children age 3-6, and to around 70% for after-school care (in the latter case assuming that children in such care are younger than 12 years old).

Reducing waiting lists for childcare has been a major policy issue in Japan. Currently, there are over 25 000 children on a waiting list for a licensed day care centre, especially in big cities (80% of the total concerns the five largest urban areas) and for children aged 0-3 (two thirds of the total concern this age group). During the last decade or so, despite the declining number of births, use has increased rapidly (from 1.6 million in 1994 to 1.9 million in the early 2000s) in parallel to an increase in supply. The fact that waiting lists have remained unchanged while use of childcare has increased rapidly suggests that, similar to Austria, preferences and behaviour have changed and that there still is "hidden" unmet demand: Discouraged by the shortage of licensed day care, many parents do not apply for a place and thus are not found on a waiting list (Zhou *et al.*, 2002). Ongoing government initiatives with ambitious targets aim to eliminate waiting lists altogether (see below).

5.4.1.2. *Capacity expansion through existing services*

Countries use a variety of approaches to expand the childcare market. One such approach is to make more public funds available to increase capacity of the existing services. In Austria, creation of new childcare places was supported through an initiative by the federal government, the "Kindergarten Billion". In total, the amount of USD 82 million (1.2 billion Austrian shillings) was spent between 1997 and 2001, supplemented by at least the same amount from the regions – together at least 0.022% of GDP annually. 32 188 places had been created through this scheme, two thirds of which for children aged 3-6. While the initiative foresaw various possibilities, incentives were strongest to create new places.[11]

In Ireland, supply of formal childcare was low until very recently. To increase capacity as well as quality, substantial funding has recently been made available through the Equal Opportunities Childcare Programme 2000-2006 (EOCP), as part of the National Development Plan and largely financed from EU Structural Funds. With a budget of USD 411 million for the period 2000-2006 – roughly 0.059% of GDP annually – it is estimated that some 36 000 places can be created, provided that the success of the programme in its last four years matches the success in the first two years.[12]

In Japan, two five-year plans – the *Angel Plan* (1995-1999) and the *New Angel Plan* (2000-2004) – have set ambitious targets for the improvement of childcare provision, especially for children under age 3 and over age 6 (see Chapter 4). In 2001, the "Zero Waiting List" initiative was launched to eliminate waiting lists through creation of another 150 000 places (by 2004) in day care, childminding or kindergartens. This initiative includes subsidies to setting-up costs as well as operating costs and a support for 5 000 childminders. The target is to increase capacity for children aged 0-6 by 8%. The amount spent under these programmes in FY 2002, almost USD 600 million, corresponds to about 0.015% of GDP.

Comparing the recent initiatives in the three countries and the number of childcare places created through these measures suggests that creation of one place came to about USD 5 800 (PPP) in Austria and around USD 8 500 in the other two countries. This considerable difference is largely explained by the fact that in Ireland and Japan predominantly more expensive places for children under age 3 (Japan) or under age 4 (Ireland) had been created (Box 5.2).

5.4.1.3. *Capacity expansion through privatisation*

In Ireland, the childcare market is dominated by private providers (both small-scale providers and large-scale commercial providers), but considerable investment is being made available to community based, non-profit groups to enable them to develop locally focused childcare facilities at community level. In both Austria and Japan, public provision of childcare plays a dominant role (Table 5.3).

In Austria, commercial providers have long existed, but most of the non-public provision is through well-established non-profit organisations. While private centres receive the same per child subsidy for their running costs, they usually receive lower subsidies for setting-up the centre. Moreover, due to the sharing of responsibilities for childcare between different layers of government, as a consequence of which planning and establishment of a day care centre involves both municipal and provincial officials, knowledge on subsidies available from different sources is not transferable from one region to the other. This makes it difficult to enter the market. Consequently, the market in each region is dominated by a small number of players, and very few providers are active in several regions.

In Japan, during the 1990s there was a gradual shift from public to private provision of licensed day care,[13] although commercial providers were not allowed to run licensed day care until 1997 (private centres could only be run by social welfare organisations). In the late 1990s, a new market-oriented approach to day care was announced, which offers greater choice to consumers and circumvent cumbersome regulations (Boling, 2002). Since then, several smaller policy changes have occurred, such as permitting commercial enterprises to become licensed day care providers,[14] licensing of "subsidiary" day care centres that do not fulfil all the national and local standards provided they are within 30 minutes of a core centre (by the same provider) which has the required facilities (*e.g.* a kitchen); or allowing smaller day care centres with fewer than 30 children. These recent changes have had only limited effects so far, but adopting the language of "choice", "user-friendliness", "privatisation" and "deregulation" is likely to have a longer-term impact on the currently inflexible and expensive licensed childcare market.

Despite this shift in Japanese policy, growing childcare demand in many regions led to the emergence of poorly regulated, unlicensed day care offered by commercial providers. Today, such centres cater for about 10% of all children in formal day care, though quite unevenly spread around the country. The advantage of these commercial non-licensed services is the variety of services they offer, including evening or overnight care in baby hotels or short-term childcare by babysitters. In response to this trend and the quality concerns related to it (see Section 5.4.4), some local governments especially in the Tokyo area, where shortages are most pressing, have started to recognise these centres – thereby gaining some form of influence over the quality of care offered. Such "recognised", though not licensed, commercial centres can receive substantial local government subsidies provided they comply with the establishment and operating standards set by each local government and charge parents no more than the maximum fee set in these standards.

In Ireland, the rapid increase in female employment contributed to the development of a private commercial childcare market. In several respects, the childcare system currently is not unlike the US system with its rather diverse childcare market characterised by high fees for parents (in the absence of comprehensive public funding) and variable quality (because of limited qualification requirements of childcare workers and a large segment of the market not being covered by any regulations) – although, unlike the US, there are very few large-scale providers in Ireland.[15] Critics argue that so far policy change is half-hearted and by itself will not produce any major change in childcare provision in Ireland, and rather expect further marketisation of the childcare sector along the American model (Collins and Wickham, 2001).

5.4.2. Increase equity

5.4.2.1. Priority in access

Access to day care centres (including crèches, kindergartens and after-school *Horte*) varies across Austria. Generally priority is given to children in their last year before school, to children whose siblings are already cared for in the same institution, and to children who do not have any siblings. These reasons are best understood in the context of child development and school readiness. In addition, in several but not all regions social reasons are used as a determinant, though not describing what exactly this term comprises. Dysfunctional families, low income groups and lone parent families would usually fall into this category. Being a dual earner couple does not give priority access to a childcare place.[16] Surprisingly, although receiving similar public subsidies, private childcare providers generally do not have to apply the priority regulations set for public childcare centres.

In Japan, access to licensed day care is restricted to children "whose parents are unable to provide adequate care owing to work or illness or other causes provided for by municipal ordinance". Each local government can determine the criteria for admission and for evaluating children who are "lacking care", as well as the priority for admission. Children from lone parent families are always given priority. Dual earner couples would typically have priority access, and the longer the working hours of both parents the higher they are on the priority list. Single earner couples are usually not entitled to subsidised day care for their children.[17] In contrast to Austria, in Japan private and public licensed providers have to apply the same priority regulations.

Under the Irish Constitution and the 1998 Education Act it is the obligation of the State to provide access to appropriate education, including pre-primary education for children age 4-6. In relation to childcare, there are no established rights to provision. Access to non-subsidised childcare is on a first-come first-served basis. Subsidised community childcare – commonly regarded of very high quality – are generally easier to access for the target group of disadvantaged parents, but they are not restricted to disadvantaged groups only.

5.4.2.2. Parental fees

In Austria and Japan, fee *guidelines* are established on a national (Japan) or regional (Austria) level, but municipalities set the *actual* fees. In both countries, fees are determined in relation to the income of the parents, and fee subsidies are paid directly to the provider. The income level at which no fee has to be paid is higher in Austria, whereas the maximum income level at which still some fee reduction is given is much higher in Japan (Table 5.7). In the latter country, fees are identical for public and private licensed day care centres, a situation which by and large is also found in Austria. In Ireland, most parents do not receive any subsidy, unless they are eligible for (or for some reason lucky enough to get access to) community childcare.

The consequence of these differences is that the parental fee covers the large majority of the total childcare costs in Ireland (though infant classes from age 4 onwards are free of charge), but less than 30% of the total in Japan (50% for kindergartens) and only some 15% across all regions in Austria.[18] The average fee paid is 5% of APE earnings in Austria, 8% of APE in Japan and around 20% of APE in Ireland (Table 5.7). In Austria, prices are roughly proportional to the length of the service. In Ireland and Japan, for a place in a nursery or a day care centre usually the full-day price has to be paid irrespective of the number of hours used. Shorter-term care in sessional playgroups of 3.5 hours (Ireland) or a kindergarten of usually four hours (Japan) is available at significantly lower cost. Use of day care by number of hours reflects these differences (see Section 5.4.3).

In Austria, the fee structure does not reflect the higher costs for babies and toddlers compared to infants over age 3 caused by different child-to-staff ratios. Hence, there is implicit cross-subsidising from parents with older children to

Table 5.7. **Considerable fee subsidies in Austria and Japan**[a]

Parental fee indicators

	Austria	Ireland	Japan
Nature of public childcare fee subsidy	Municipal subsidy on prescribed fee, based on family income and family size, paid directly to the provider (varies by region)	No direct subsidy, but limited availability of community childcare at very low fee for the most disadvantaged groups	Subsidy on prescribed fee based on family income, family size and number of kids in daycare, paid directly to the provider (varies by municipality)
Level of income at which childcare is (almost) free of charge	Around 50% of APE (varies by region)[b]	Eligible for community childcare	Eligible for social assistance; very low fee at 50% of APE
Level of income beyond which the full childcare fee has to be paid	Around 115% of APE (varies by region)	Most childcare is not subsidised	Around 200% of APE (with variation)
Parental fee for full-day childcare without income-related subsidy	Around 13% of APE (varies by region)	28-35% of APE	15-23% of APE
Parental fee for half-day childcare without income-related subsidy	Around 6% APE (varies by region)	10-13% APE[c]	8% of APE[d]
Actual average parental fee paid	5% of APE	20% of APE	8% APE
Parental fee for age group 0-3 relative to the fee for age group 4-6	100%	Around 120%	Around 150-250%
Parental fee for the second child in per cent of the fee for the first child	90-100%	Usually 100%	Usually 50%

Note: APE or "average earnings" refer to the annual earnings of an Average Production Employee (APE) in the manufacturing sector. In 2002, these were USD 22 543 (EUR 23 963) in Austria, USD 23 829 (EUR 25 330) in Ireland and USD 33 926 (JPY 4 254 270) in Japan (see OECD, 2003f).

a) Both in Austria and in Japan, there are two types of subsidies that are both paid to the provider: 1) a general subsidy which is identical for all children of the same age; and 2) a specific subsidy that relates to the income of the parents and thus can reduce the actual fee to be paid. Information in this table relates only to the second type of subsidy, thus referred to as "fee subsidy".

b) In one Austrian province, half-day kindergarten for children age 3-6 is provided free of charge irrespective of income.

c) This fee relates to sessional services of 3.5 hours; for a half-day in a nursery usually the full-day price applies.

d) This fee relates to kindergartens for children age 3-6; for a half-day in day care usually the full-day price applies.

Source: National and regional authorities and estimates by the OECD Secretariat.

parents with younger children. The situation is quite different in Japan, where some municipalities differentiate the fee between children under age 3 and over age 3, while others even differentiate at a finer grid.[19] The prices for second or third children are barely lower in Austria and Ireland, but much lower – typically 50% for the second child and even lower for the third – in Japan.

Table 5.8. **Low fees for middle-income groups in Japan, and high fees in Ireland**

Parental fee in per cent of net earnings, by income group and family type[a]

	Income[b]	Austria	Ireland	Japan
Lone parent, one child	0.67 APE	8.8	40.9	6.3
Lone parent, two children	0.67 APE	15.6	54.3	7.2
Lone parent, one child	1 APE	13.7	29.9	7.0
Lone parent, two children	1 APE	24.9	38.9	8.1
Couple, one child	1.33 APE	9.8	23.5	7.9
Couple, two children	1.33 APE	18.5	30.9	9.1
Couple, one child	1.67 APE	9.7	19.5	8.6
Couple, two children	1.67 APE	18.2	25.8	10.0

a) General assumption: first child at age 1 and second child, if any, at age 4.
b) Income as a ratio of Average Production Employee (APE) earnings.
Source: OECD Secretariat calculations on the basis of national and regional authorities: Austria: costs of crèche/kindergarten in Vienna region (costs are significantly lower in some other regions, e.g. Lower Austria). Japan: costs of licensed day care in Shinagawa Ward/Metropolitan Tokyo (full costs in other regions can be up to 50% higher). Ireland: costs of childminder in Dublin area for first child, second child in infant class and then three hours childminding.

In Ireland, the price of childcare to parents is thus higher than in Austria and Japan (Table 5.8).[20] For example, for a lone parent living in Dublin with average earnings (i.e. 100% of APE earnings), the cost of childcare for one child is equivalent to 30% of after-tax net income, and it would be another 30% for a second child – unless this person had access to cheaper community childcare. Therefore, childcare costs can be a barrier to work in Ireland (Chapter 6).

At average earnings, childcare fees in Vienna and Shinagawa/Tokyo are less than half and around a quarter, respectively, of the relative burden for Dubliners.[21] The fee structure in Tokyo implies that, throughout the earnings range from 67 to 167% of APE earnings, childcare fees are at a similar proportion of net earnings (Table 5.8). In contrast, due to the lack of any subsidy, relative to net earnings fees decline with income in Dublin (from 40% at 67% APE earnings to 20% at 167% APE earnings), and they peak at 100-115% of APE earnings – the level at which subsidies are phased out – in Vienna.

Fee levels and structures are different for other types of services than those illustrated in Table 5.8. In Japan, except for licensed day care parental fees are fixed and thus unrelated to income. While fees in non-licensed day care can be significantly higher than for licensed day care (depending on whether these centres receive any subsidies), kindergartens and after-school children's clubs are much cheaper. In Austria, fee structures do not differ between crèches, kindergartens and after-school Horte. All-day supervision in schools is cheaper than after-school care, childminding is cheaper than using

148

a centre-based crèche, and self-organised kid's groups are usually more expensive than kindergartens, but in all cases the fee differences are relatively small. In Ireland, parental costs for childminders and centre-based nurseries are rather similar.

5.4.2.3. Inequity among users

Capacity scarcity in licensed day care in Japan raises significant equity issues. Parents who are unlucky enough to be on a waiting list and therefore depend on using non-licensed day care have to pay more, because non-licensed centres are usually not subsidised by municipalities (unless "recognised" by the municipality and therefore receiving a subsidy). At the same time, however, non-licensed day care also fills important supply gaps, better satisfying diverse parental needs in terms of flexibility (*e.g.* location close to home, more flexible hours, availability of extended hours or weekend care), their preference for having their children cared for in smaller groups, or the possibility to use the service also in case the child is sick (Boling, 2002).

Similarly, in Ireland inequity arises between families in the same income group who have access to heavily subsidised community childcare and those who do not. In Austria, inequity between parents mainly arises across different regions, as – in particular – expensive and generally more heavily subsidised childcare for children under age 3 is only available in some areas. The recent introduction of Childcare Benefit could foster such cross-regional inequities, because provinces and municipalities may see the new benefit as a signal that childcare provision is less necessary.

Inequity issues could be addressed by giving money to *users* (parents) rather than to *providers*, which is tantamount to subsidising some but not all parents, if capacity constraints are not fully resolved. In all three countries, some discussion on possible consequences of implementing such policy has started during the last few years (Box 5.4). Such user subsidies can be paid at the same level to all parents or can be related to the user's level of income – as a recent policy initiative in Australia demonstrates (OECD, 2002f). In Japan, the structure of the current fee subsidy system was shown to be quite efficient in terms of work incentives it creates (Oishi, 2002). Some form of relationship between the level of a user subsidy and the level of family income would therefore be desirable.

5.4.3. Increase choice

5.4.3.1. Choice of provider

In all three countries, parents are generally free to select a provider of their choice. This is evidently the case in the commercial Irish childcare market, but equally so for non-licensed day care and kindergartens in Japan

Box 5.4. **Tackling efficiency, equity, choice and quality through user subsidies**

In all three countries, more recently a discussion has started on whether replacing provider subsidies with user subsidies would produce a more efficient childcare market. Especially in the childcare markets in Austria and Japan, which are relying on substantial public funding for setting-up as well as running costs, public and large-scale non-profit providers face limited incentives to keep costs low and to respond quickly to (changing) parental preferences on matters such as opening hours. The same holds for subsidised community-based childcare in Ireland.

In Austria, to increase choice it was proposed to introduce a Childcare Benefit for children age 0-4 (unrelated to the use of childcare) and a Childcare Voucher (partly) bound to the use of formal childcare for children age 4-6 (Schattovits, 2000). In the end, only the first was introduced (and only for children up to age 30/36 months) while the latter was dropped as many considered the current childcare system to be "functional".

The Japanese government currently aims to solve the inequity problem by increasing capacity. This is potentially costly and may lead to, or continue, a situation of inefficient utilisation. The inefficiency argument was used by Japanese researchers proposing to switch to a system of cash subsidies to users, thereby drawing up childcare fees to equilibrium prices (Zhou and Oishi, 2002, cited in Zhou et al., 2002). If paid in the form of a universal benefit not tied to the actual use of childcare (similar to the Austrian Childcare Benefit), however, as was suggested in this proposal, cash payments to all parents would be very costly and would provide strong incentives for one parent in a dual earner couple to stay at home (Chapter 6).

Proposals made by Irish childcare NGOs point in a similar direction: some direct funding to providers to secure capacity building combined with cash payments to parents to secure equity and quality improvements. The same view is held by the National Childminders Association, which would favour childcare payments to parents to bring childminding into the regular economy, together with tax allowances for childminders as an additional incentive for them to register formally.

In this regard, the income-tested Australian Childcare Benefit (OECD, 2002f), which is partly related to parents' work status, could be an avenue for reform. It obviously gives parents the right to choose the provider and service they want, and as Childcare Benefit is only paid at maximum to licensed centres, all providers have a vested interest in maintaining and improving quality standards and attract clients. The Australian quality system includes a peer review where the emphasis is on improvement of quality (relationship with and respect for

Box 5.4. **Tackling efficiency, equity, choice and quality through user subsidies** (cont.)

children, partnerships with families, staff interactions, planning and evaluation, learning and development, protective care, managing to support quality and health and safety aspects), while local authority inspectors also assure Health and Safety standards of facilities. The Australian system includes family-day care and could, for example, allow for bringing the Irish childminder profession into the formal sector.

and for all day care run by private providers in Austria. For licensed day care in Japan and publicly provided day care in Austria, parents submit an application to the municipality while indicating the centre of their choice: municipal authorities try to adhere to such preferences, but this is not always possible.[22] Due to capacity shortages in some regions of Austria, Ireland and Japan provider choice can be very limited in practice – not least because parents generally prefer to send their children to a day care centre next door (which may well have long waiting lists) to ensure integration in the immediate neighbourhood and to avoid long commuting hours.

One way to increase the choice parents have is to give money to them directly, rather than to the provider. Such a strategy has various advantages: it would increase the choice to parents in terms of what provider to choose and what type of care (centre-based or home-based, full-time or part-time, out-of-school hours care, etc.), and it does not favour one particular provider over another. Such a move also increases cost-consciousness and efficiency among providers and promotes quality when payments are conditional on children being in quality-licensed facilities (again Box 5.4).

In rural areas problems (can) arise due to low population densities and scattered populations. Under such circumstances, standard centre-based childcare is often unsuitable. Small service entities would result in high staff costs, long distances would make the use of the service unattractive to many, thus unavoidably leading to shortages of appropriate services. Under these conditions, non-standard childcare will be more effective and economically more efficient. The Austrian region of Lower Austria, with its well-developed system of childminders and two new and very flexible childcare schemes – the "flying nannies" and the "mobile mummies" – appears to be a model of good practice that could be adopted by other remote rural areas. The two new schemes are designed to provide care otherwise unavailable in such areas and to guarantee streamlined care for children at all ages, and are thus targeted at children aged 0-10.[23]

5.4.3.2. Flexibility of services

With changing employment patterns, the demand for childcare services at hitherto unusual times (e.g. on Saturday) or for longer and later hours or for temporary care is increasing. Regulated childcare markets are slow in reacting to such changes in demand structures. There are large differences in this respect both between countries and between municipalities within each country. Typically, standard full-day operating hours in a day care centre or nursery are from 9am to 6pm in Ireland, from 8am to 6pm in Austria, and from 7am to 6pm in Japan.

Service flexibility is very diverse across Austria. For example, throughout the country two in four kindergartens offer continuous full-day service, one in four closes at noon, and the remaining fourth offers morning and afternoon sessions but closes over lunch. The proportion of kindergartens offering continuous full-day service is less than 20% in three of the nine provinces, 50-70% in five others, but as high as 98% in Vienna. The latter province, therefore, makes it easier for mothers to work full-time. This is reflected in higher activity rates among women with a child under age 15 – at 74% in Vienna compared to 66% elsewhere – and a significantly lower proportion of this group of mothers working part-time – 38% in Vienna compared to 56% in the rest of Austria (AK, 2001).

In Japan, operating hours of day care centres are longest, and a much larger proportion of children than in the other two countries stays in the centre for a whole day.[24] Nevertheless, extending hours into the evening, into the night and into the weekend is an important target of the New Angel Plan. Today, for example, over 50% of all licensed day care centres close after 6pm, and 40% offer extended hours care with operating hours exceeding 11 hours per day. Private licensed centres are those which react more flexibly to these user needs – both for reasons of competitiveness and because of their lower wage costs. Similarly, today some 80% of all kindergartens offer afternoon extensions, though usually only for another four hours i.e. still shorter than day care operating hours. Nevertheless, this has also contributed to the blurring of boundaries between day care and kindergarten.

Supply shortages often occur during school holidays.[25] In Japan, existing out-of-school hours services usually operate throughout the year, including school holidays. This is also often the case for after-school Horte in Austria, but not for all-day supervision in schools, which is tied to school schedules. While recent developments in Austria have enabled many more children of primary school age to be in school during the afternoons, demand during school holidays has to be filled through informal arrangements. In Ireland, many of the rare after-school care facilities close over the summer.

One other problem in Ireland is the lack of part-time places in formal childcare, because it is more expensive per hour than full-time care. Part-time care generally is offered as sessional service, which is limited to no more than 3.5 hours, usually from 9:00-12:30.[26] As a result, non-working mothers predominantly use sessional nurseries or playgroups, whereas working mothers tend to rely on (non-regulated) childminding. If at all, more expensive providers offer long part-time childcare service of six hours, thus making part-time places very expensive.

Across countries, significant differences exist in terms of adjusting hours to parental needs. In Austria, (usually) every child "counts" as one child when determining group size,[27] thus giving parents unlimited possibility to change between different hours of care at very short notice. This approach increases parental choice, but renders the system more costly and less efficient. In Ireland, on the contrary, providers have to respect the child-to-staff ratio at any moment during the day and therefore try to fill their groups as much as possible. Consequently, it is very difficult to switch from a part-time place to full-time care, and *vice versa*. The situation in Japan is similar.

Temporary "emergency" day care for a parent or guardian temporarily unable to care for the child due to illness or other reasons is offered by 15% of all licensed day care centres in Japan. In some Austrian municipalities, such as Vienna, there is a network of temporary nurses who can come to the child's home. In all three countries, but especially in Austria, some form of special nursery leave to care for a sick child has been introduced (Background Annex to the Review).

5.4.4. Increase quality

5.4.4.1. Regulatory frameworks

The quality of childcare services is crucial for child development (Box 5.3). Quality issues differ across countries, and are of particular concern in Ireland where the role of the informal sector is largest (Box 5.5).

In Austria, there are nine different childcare standards with provincial differences reflecting the devolved nature of responsibility for this policy field. The only exception to this is the uniform qualification required for childcare workers (see below). In Japan, minimum standards in terms of child-to-staff ratios, floor space, etc., are determined nationally, but municipalities often set their own higher standards. The more recent Irish childcare regulations are applicable across the whole country.

Child-to-staff ratios are lowest in Ireland. In Japan, they are as low as in Ireland for children under age 3 but much higher than in the other two countries for children over age 3 (Table 5.9). The large difference in child-to-staff ratios by age group in combination with the fact that parental fees do not fully

Box 5.5. **Approaching quality: The example of the Irish National Childcare Strategy**

In the Irish National Childcare Strategy (in line with the work of the European Commission Network on Childcare) quality is defined as a dynamic, continuous open-ended process that should be subject to regular review. The White Paper on Early Childhood Education (National Forum Secretariat, 1998), defines five key areas of quality indicators: 1) *Child indicators:* developmentally appropriate programmes, child progress assessments, programme assessment, size of the group; 2) *Staff indicators:* appropriately trained staff, appropriate pay and conditions, continuity of care, child-to-staff ratios; 3) *Physical environmental indicators:* health and safety standards, quality of space, physical resources; 4) *Social indicators:* affordability, accessibility, parental and community involvement; and 5) *National indicators:* national policy provision for regulation, provision, supervision, co-ordination of responsibility for services.

The White Paper on Early Childhood Education raises a number of important and universal concerns in respect of the concept of quality. It recognises that quality means different things to different people and can be defined by children, parents or care workers/teachers. It also recognises that no one standard of quality can exist for all children in all types of services. Instead, quality should be conceptualised as a set of core criteria to which services can progress and against which their progress can be measured. These include tangible criteria, such as child-to-staff ratios, as well as non-tangible criteria, such as staff-child interaction (Corrigan, 2002).

One of the measures proposed in the White Paper concerns the development of minimum standards for some of the areas that are not covered by childcare regulations. Meeting these standards should be obligatory for those receiving State funding. Non-state funded providers may voluntarily adopt these standards and apply for a Quality in Education Mark. This should lead to an increased recognition of the need for quality standards both to improve services and to guide parents in their choice.

reflect these differences, contribute to capacity constraints for some age groups. Commercial providers in Ireland and local governments in Austria and Japan often refrain from providing childcare places for children under age 3, let alone under age 1. This contributes to care for such children often being provided through the informal (and therefore non-regulated) sector, particularly so in Ireland. Waiting lists also suggest that unmet demand is larger for children under the age of 3.

154

Table 5.9. **Largest cross-country differences are found in regulations on after-school care**

Indicators on group-size by type of care

	Austria	Ireland	Japan
Day care, crèche, nursery	Varies by region. For Vienna, the region with the largest number of children in day care: at least one room plus wardrobe and toilet per group, 3 m² per child, and a playground for the entire facility	Health and safety regulations (only since 1996); 2.32 m² per full-time child (2 m² for sessional attendance); up to 20 kids per group; at least two carers present at any moment of the day	Nursery room with 1.98 m² per child (1.65 m² if under age 2) plus crawling room (age 0-2) or outdoor play area (age 3-6) of 3.3 m² per child, and a kitchen; two carers per centre, plus a temporary doctor and a cook
Child-to-staff ratios	Group size varies by region. Typically around 6:1 (age 0-1), 8:1 (age 1-3) and 14:1 (age 3-6)	3:1 (age 0-1), 6:1 (age 1-3) and 10:1 (age 3-5)	3:1 (age 0-1), 6:1 (age 1-3), 20:1 (age 3-4) and 30:1 (age 4-6)
Pre-primary year in Austria, pre-school in Ireland and kindergarten in Japan	School norms and regulations; class size in pre-primary classes varies and is below 15 pupils	School norms and regulations; class size in infant classes around 25 pupils, but child teacher ratio is 1:30	Regulations (covered by education law) on floor space and outside play areas; minimum pupil/staff ratio is 1:35
Out-of-school care	Generally similar to day care. Again for Vienna: maximum group size of 28 pupils; separate rooms for playing and for preparing homework	No regulations (childcare regulations apply where out-of-school care is provided in a nursery)	Minimum of 1.5 m² per child (no outdoor play area required), but no minimum standard staff ratio
Childminding	Notification at local level; certificate on the adequacy of the location (size and number of rooms); up to four children allowed per childminder	No regulations for up to three children, notification of and inspection by the health board with 4-6 children	Registration for local programmes is voluntary (though can sometimes still receive municipality subsidy), but is required for the national programme

Source: National authorities.

Because of the prevalence of home-based childminding, regulations of this sector are most urgent in Ireland. In this country, resources were made available in 2001 to introduce a voluntary notification and support system aimed at childminders looking after up to three children in their home who are currently not required to notify the Health Boards of their activity and are not subject to inspection under the childcare regulations.[28] The National Childminders Association is also trying to improve the quality of childminding services by establishing a code of good practice.[29] In Japan and Austria, regulations differ between local governments but some standards generally exist (Table 5.9).

The gradual increase in the number of non-licensed day care centres, which operate outside the standard regulations, has raised quality concerns in Japan. Prefectures have a guidance and supervision function and can, ultimately, order the closure of the centre.[30] In the last three years, quality assurance procedures were introduced for licensed day care centres, which could possibly be extended to non-licensed centres. Since 2000, managers of licensed day care centres are required to undertake self-evaluation of the quality of the service they provide, and since 2002 they are evaluated by a third party. The aim is to help operators to grasp actual problems in their operation and make greater efforts to improve quality, but also to enable users to gain a good understanding of the service provided.

5.4.4.2. Qualification of childcare workers

Professionalisation of childcare workers in areas with limited or no regulations is an issue in all three countries. Childcare regulations in Ireland only require "suitable" qualification (Table 5.10); training, therefore, is largely based on voluntary participation. The nine different Irish childcare associations

Table 5.10. **Limited qualification requirements in Ireland**
Staff qualification requirements by type of care

	Austria	Ireland	Japan
Day care, crèche, nursery	Graduation from a five-year special school at upper secondary level or a two-year special training college at post-secondary level (the latter is also open to individuals who pass a special entrance examination)	"Suitable" qualification: no training required but a national certificate after two years of training is available; Level 1 qualification (one year of training) required in Montessori groups	Graduation from a nursery training school/institution (equivalent to junior college) or passed the prefecture's nursery teacher examination
Pre-primary year in Austria, pre-school in Ireland and kindergarten in Japan	Regular primary teacher qualification *i.e.* graduation from a teacher training college (three years of training)	Regular primary teacher qualification *i.e.* graduation from a college of education (three years of training)	Kindergarten teacher license, with three grades of license (junior college, university, graduate school); recently across-ministry co-operation in creating courses that meet day care and kindergarten requirements
Out-of-school care	For "Horte", same as for day care; for all-day schools, qualification as a primary teacher; no qualification for after-school care provided in schools	No qualification required	No qualification required, but often instructors are licensed day care specialist or (kindergarten) teachers
Childminding	No qualification required	No qualification required	No qualification required, but national programme (which covers 50% of costs) requires registration and nursery teacher qualification

Source: National authorities.

encourage training among their members, though still on the basis of different basic standards. Very recently, a "model framework for education, training and professional development in the early childhood care and education sector" has been brought forward.[31]

In contrast to Ireland, professionalisation of the childcare sector in Austria started more than a century ago. Already in 1872, a one-year training course for child carers was established. Today, Austria and Japan have well-developed institutions for the training of new childcare workers. In Austria, graduation is from a special five-year school at upper secondary level (typically at age 15-19), or alternatively from a two-year training college at post-secondary level. In Japan, graduation is from a nursery training school equivalent to junior college. As an alternative, chosen by some 10% of all nursery teachers, a special examination administered by the prefecture has to be passed.

In Japan, due to changing and increasing demand, the strict separation of day care and kindergartens is increasingly blurred. Lately, cross-ministry co-operation has been launched with the aim to create combined facilities that meet both day care and kindergarten requirements. In Ireland, qualifications for teachers of infant classes (which are regular primary school teachers) and childcare workers remain different and separate, although newly accredited courses have emerged that emphasise a combination of care and education.

Across countries, childcare personnel in the public sector earn more than in the private sector. The difference is most pronounced in Japan, where public sector employees are regular workers with seniority-related wages while private centres make more use of non-regular part-time employees with earnings significantly below APE earnings (Table 5.11). After-school care is

Table 5.11. **A dual labour market for childcare workers, especially in Japan**
Average earnings in percentage of APE earnings, by sector

	Austria[a]	Ireland[b]	Japan[c]
Public sector	70-160	70-90	110-190
Private sector	80-120	55-70	85
After-school care	As above	n.a.	66
Non-qualified	55-70	40-50	40-70[d]

a) Data for Austria refer to wage scales (collective minimum wage for private sector) by tenure.
b) Data for Ireland refer to average payment rates (survey estimates).
c) Data for Japan are survey averages, but include information from local governments.
d) Figures refer to non-regular workers (which are often qualified childcare workers).

Source: Estimates based on local authorities, Zhou *et al.* (2002) and Government of Ireland (1999); Local/regional authorities for Austria: Vienna and Lower Austria; Local/regional authorities for Japan: Shinagawa Ward (Tokyo) and Chiba City.

predominantly provided by the municipality, but exclusively on the basis of non-regular work contracts. In Austria, the difference between the private and the public sector is smaller, but as in Japan wages are typically seniority-based. Wages in Ireland are substantially lower than in the other two countries, to which the lower qualification requirements contribute.

5.5. Conclusions

Long parental leave periods are popular with parents in Austria but tend to have a negative effect on labour market skills and work attachment of leave takers, usually mothers. By contrast, the short duration of leave in Ireland forces parents to confront the work/family choice at a very early stage. The Japanese work and family provisions allow for parental leave until the child's first birthday, and reconciliation support (often through adjustment of working hours) until the child is 3 years of age. Nevertheless, as discussed in Chapters 2 and 3, many Japanese women still withdraw from the labour force around childbirth. All three countries face similar childcare capacity shortages, especially for children under age 3 and at primary school age, despite quite different policy approaches.

In Austria, the provision of childcare is a responsibility of the provincial and municipal governments. However, the national government can (as the "Kindergarten billion" initiative exemplified) stimulate and (co-)finance the creation of new childcare places in those areas where support is most needed (*e.g.* children under age 3, longer operating hours in all services). Also, the new focus on all-day supervision in schools, which has successfully reduced capacity concerns among primary school-age children since the mid-1990s, should be continued. In addition, to improve efficiency of the childcare sector, giving subsidies to users (parents) rather than providers could be considered, while current quality levels can be maintained by linking such user subsidies to the use of quality-licensed facilities.

Compared to Ireland and Japan, Austrian policy (leave entitlements and Childcare Benefit payments of prolonged duration) gives significantly more support to those families which choose to have one parent providing full time care when a child is very young. Providing substantial cash transfers for at least 30 months enables parents to reduce working hours and facilitates not working at all, although claimants are allowed to earn up to 69% of APE earnings. However, the majority of Childcare Benefit claimants (initially) is on parental leave, and leave-takers are only entitled to earn up to about 15% of APE earnings, unless their employer agrees otherwise. Alternatively, these parents can give up their employment protection, in which case the Childcare Benefit income threshold gives strong incentives to keep earnings below 69% of APE earnings. In all, Childcare Benefit, certainly in conjunction with the limited work entitlements in leave legislation, gives a clear signal to parents, as it facilitates one parent in couple families to provide full-time care. At the same time, there is a risk that the introduction of Childcare Benefit signals to municipal and provincial governments that it may be less necessary to sustain and/or extend the provision of childcare for children under age 3.

To increase choice for Austrian parents, whilst also addressing concerns on gender equity and future labour supply (Chapters 2 and 4), reform should be considered that makes choosing to work, or choosing to work more hours, a more realistic option. Apart from extending childcare support, one option is to introduce a part-time work entitlement for parents of young children, for example, throughout the period of parental leave or until the child reaches kindergarten age when childcare becomes widely available. The government is currently considering the introduction of the right to part-time work for certain workers until the child's seventh birthday (Österreichische Bundesregierung, 2003). However, employers have so far been reluctant to agree to the introduction of an entitlement to part-time work, and the length of the "proposed" period may well exacerbate existing resistance in view of the associated cost to employers.

Another possibility to increase work options for Austrian parents is to make Childcare Benefit payment rates more flexible by allowing higher payment rates for a shorter duration. To do so with regard to the Childcare Benefit period that is reserved for the "other parent" may help to raise take-up of parental leave among fathers. Furthermore, to promote work options the allowable earnings rules within leave legislation and the Childcare Benefit income threshold should be reformed, reducing the potential risk of concentrating earnings at specific levels. It could also be considered to link part of the Childcare Benefit payment with the use of recognised childcare services. Finally, since Childcare Benefit is paid for at least 30 months while the employment-protected leave period ends upon the child's second birthday, there is a risk that some parents will delay the return to work beyond the point where returning is a protected right. Parents should be made fully aware of this particular design feature.

The Japanese childcare leave regulation is quite innovative as part of the benefit payment depends on the leave taker's actual return to the previous job (for at least six months) upon expiry of leave. However, while entitlement to childcare leave has been progressively broadened during the last decade, data on public spending on that programme suggest that the number of parents actually receiving a childcare leave benefit must be low. To make sure that this scheme is used to its full potential, further efforts could be made to raise the actual take-up of parental leave. A higher take-up could significantly improve the labour market attachment particularly of mothers.

Childcare policy in Japan aims to ensure a sufficient supply of high-quality childcare places to foster child well-being. Growing demand for childcare not met by the existing institutions has led to the emergence of poorly regulated non-licensed day care. The proportion of children cared for in such centres is still low, but the issue is pressing: parental fees for non-licensed day care are generally very high, and quality is considered rather variable. This raises significant equity issues. In response to these concerns, many municipal governments in Japan have started to provide guidance to commercial providers of non-licensed day care – thereby gaining some form of influence over providers.

To raise childcare capacity in Japan, in particular for children under age 3 and over age 6, substantial funding has been made available recently through various government programmes. In addition, since 2000 a new market-oriented approach to childcare is being developed, thereby making it possible for commercial licensed providers to receive the same subsidies as public or non-profit providers. These efforts should be extended. However, and as in Austria, although capacity has increased through these measures, unmet demand continues to exist and waiting lists have not disappeared. One possibility to improve efficiency of the childcare sector is to consider focussing childcare subsidies on parents rather than providers, with such payments being conditional on the use of quality-licensed facilities only.

Demographic trends will also challenge childcare systems, as the working-age population will soon start to decline in both Austria and, most notably, Japan (Chapter 4). The need to mobilise additional female labour supply will therefore become more pressing in future. In part, such demands could be met by making part-time employment opportunities more generally available to mothers (Chapter 3), but it is unlikely that further substantial increases in female employment rates can be achieved without extending childcare capacity.

In Ireland, total costs of providing a childcare place are lower than in the other two countries, but – as there are fewer public subsidies – fees for some parents are too high to make work pay in the short-term (Chapter 6). In addition, the low quality of parts of the informal childcare sector has been raised as a problem of the Irish system. Supply per se does not appear as a constraint, except for after-school care, as the informal market has developed very rapidly. But lack of capacity could soon become a problem: Despite the large increase in employment among younger women there has still been a large pool of women available to provide informal care. With those younger women staying in employment, the supply of informal childminders will decline while the demand for childcare may well continue to increase.

Since 2000, the Irish government has made significant investments in the area of childcare aimed at increasing the supply and (through better training for childcare workers) enhancing the quality of services. At this stage, the government has several options. One is to leave the childcare market as such more or less unchanged and address the issues of child welfare and female employment by targeting additional funding through the Equal Opportunities Childcare Programme on disadvantaged groups – *e.g.* low-skilled low-income groups and lone parents. Another option is to address the issues of service quality and child development more comprehensively, and it is difficult to see how this can be done without additional resources. If the government were to decide that public funding devoted to childcare should further increase, there is a strong case for ensuring that the considerable informal childminding sector should be subject to some basic quality controls in return for being eligible for public subsidies. In such a situation, the introduction of childcare vouchers paid to users would seem particularly useful.

Annex to Chapter 5

Chart 5A.1. **Childcare funding flows in Austria**

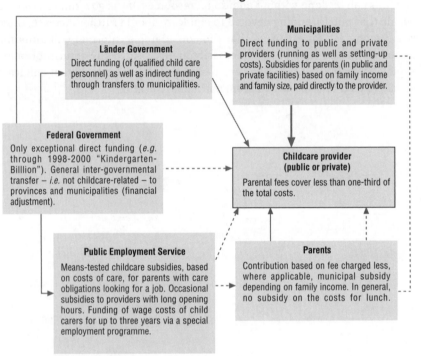

Source: Austrian authorities.

Chart 5A.2. **Childcare funding flows in Ireland**

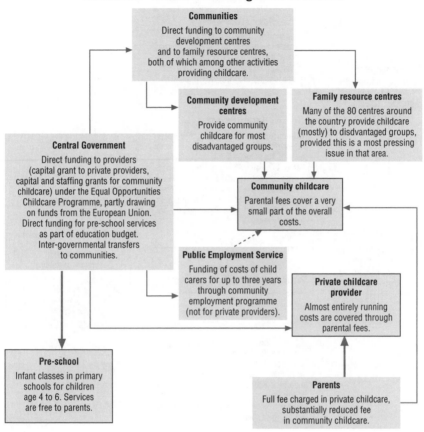

Source: Irish authorities.

Chart 5A.3. **Childcare funding flows in Japan**

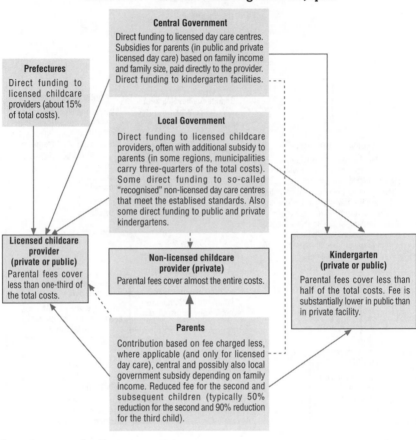

Source: Japanese authorities.

Notes

1. During maternity leave, in Austria full wage payment continues, whereas the benefit paid in that period is 70% of gross earnings in Ireland (up to a maximum of around 50% of APE earnings), and 60% of the average daily standard wage in Japan (Background Annex to the Review).

2. The following groups of Japanese workers are not eligible for child care leave: i) workers who are employed on a day-by-day basis; ii) workers with a fixed-term contract; iii) workers who worked for the same employer for less than one year; iv) workers whose spouse is not in work, or is not working more than two days per week, and can thus take care of the child; and v) workers who are considered "rationally" as not eligible for child care leave such as those working for no more than two days per week.

3. In Japan, similar to Austria, childcare leave and benefit payment during the period of leave is regulated in different pieces of legislation (the Childcare and Family

Care Leave Act and the Employment Insurance Act) with somewhat different criteria for entitlement. Employment Insurance essentially covers workers with a sufficient employment record who work more than 30 hours per week (if being a regular worker) or more than 20 hours (if being a non-regular worker).

4. Among fathers, take-up of parental leave is very low in all three countries, ranging from less than 1% in Japan to 5% in Ireland. Both in Austria and in Japan, raising take-up of men is a policy concern.

5. In Austria, mothers who have no intention to return to their workplace upon expiry of their parental leave would still always claim their childcare benefit payment. In Japan in similar circumstances it is normal to forego the childcare leave payment from the Employment Insurance.

6. Specialised (usually residential) care for reasons related to a child's health or disability or for children under the guardianship of the state are beyond the scope of this study.

7. The number of very young children using childcare in Austria and Ireland is much lower than the target set by the European Council at its meeting in Barcelona in March 2002: by 2010 at least 90% of children between 3 years old and the mandatory school age should be in care or pre-school facilities, while at least 33% of children under 3 years of age are set to be using day care.

8. In many cases, working parents rely on a combination of formal and informal childcare, in which a network of informal carers captures those – possibly even daily – periods which are not covered by formal care. Informal help is also often needed to get over days of a child's sickness, because leave regulations are generally insufficient to cover those periods. This is particularly important for lone parents who work.

9. In Ireland, the social partnership programme *Partnership 2000* (covering the period 1997-1999) was the first agreement committing the government to a range of measures related to early education and childcare (DT, 1997). Out of this process arose the *National Childcare Strategy*, the first concerted attempt to develop a coherent and comprehensive government policy that specifically addressed childcare (Government of Ireland, 1999), and which included several of the recommendations made by the *Commission on the Family*, that was established in response to growing concern on family-stability (Government of Ireland, 1998). The subsequent partnership agreement, the *Programme for Prosperity and Fairness* (covering the period 2000-2002), set forth aims to increase childcare places in both private and community sectors, to protect the well-being of children by appropriate training of childcare workers and by regulation of childcare provision, and to increase out-of-school hours childcare services (DT, 2000).

10. Estimates of unmet childcare demand in Austria in 1995 and 2002 include children who do not have a childcare place as well as those who do, but not for a sufficient number of hours or not the type of place needed. In 2002, additional childcare demand was reported for around 7% of all children under age 6. Of these, over 50% did have a place but not the type or hours needed.

11. In the recent Austrian childcare initiative, financial incentives to extend opening hours were much weaker than those to create new places: A one-off payment was made available conditional on guaranteeing to provide such longer operating hours for a period of at least ten years.

12. The main aims of the Irish Equal Opportunities Childcare Programme 2000-2006, which is bringing a major investment to the childcare sector, are to maintain and increase the number of places and facilities, to improve the delivery structure

through better co-ordination, and to enhance quality. Improving co-ordination is done by putting a series of new structures in place: 33 County/Council Childcare Committees are established to promote, develop and support quality childcare at the local level, the National Co-ordinating Childcare Committee has to oversee all measures under the Childcare Strategy, and the Childcare Directorate of the DJELR is the focal point for the government and responsible for the implementation of the strategy (for more details see Corrigan, 2002).

13. The recent shift from public to private provision of licensed day care in Japan, which is mainly related to the lower wage costs and thus the higher efficiency in private centres, occurs through transformation of public into private centres, through the creation of new private centres in urban areas, and through closing down of public centres in some of the rural areas.

14. By April 2002, *i.e.* two years after commercial enterprises were given the possibility to run licensed day care, 69 licensed day care centres had been set up nationwide under these new conditions (17 by private companies, 7 by non-profit organisations, and the remainder by educational foundations, religious corporations, and individuals) – not a large number, but presumably an important first step.

15. In Ireland, there is considerable inequity between private and community providers in terms of public funding. Commercial private providers can only get capital funds of up to 65% of their start-up costs, while community providers can get capital grants up to 100% of actual costs plus staffing grants. This contributes to explaining why commercial private providers have some difficulty in matching the quality and conditions of community childcare at the same price.

16. In Vienna, dual earner couples and single parents have priority access to all-day supervision in (primary and secondary) schools.

17. Data suggest that among all users of licensed day care in Japan, about one third of the mothers is not in work, while another third has earnings below the income tax threshold (Oishi, 2002).

18. The parental share for day care costs in Japan is much lower than the nominal charge of 43%. Many municipalities set higher standards or pay higher wages or otherwise put much more funds into the operation of licensed childcare, resulting in a situation under which the cost share of parents is closer to 20% (*e.g.* Chiba City) or only 10% (*e.g.* Tokyo or Chiyoda City). Data for Austria refer to 1995 and include only public kindergartens; for the total day care market, the proportion will be slightly higher though not higher than 20%.

19. In Shinagawa Ward in metropolitan Tokyo, for example, the maximum parental fee is USD 458 for a child aged 0-2, USD 180 for a child aged 2-3, and USD 143 for a child aged 3-6.

20. Any comparison of fee levels in relation to household income for different income groups is difficult or somewhat arbitrary, due to large regional differences in all three countries. The assessment presented here rests on information relevant to each country's capital – Vienna, Dublin and Tokyo – thus not necessarily being representative for the whole country but affecting some 20% of the population.

21. In Vienna, full-day childcare fees at average earnings are much higher than the actual average fee paid throughout Austria according to Table 5.8. This is explained by the low average duration of stay in childcare across Austria, which is some five hours per day across the whole country, and by the fact that half-day childcare is free of charge in one of the largest provinces (Lower Austria).

22. Until 1997, in Japan municipal officials allocated children to particular licensed day care centres without necessarily taking parental preferences into account.

23. "Flying nannies" are qualified childcare workers who are employed by one of the three large associations providing childcare in that province. "Mobile mummies" are either childminders or qualified childcare workers or teachers. Both of these schemes, offered in the Austrian province of Lower Austria, were also introduced in response to growing unemployment among teachers and childcare workers.

24. On average, a child spends some 40 hours a week in a licensed day care centre in Japan (MHLW, 2001h), some 28 hours in some type of childcare in Ireland (ICTU, 2002), and some 24 hours in day care in Austria (BMSG, 1999a).

25. School holidays are about 10-12 weeks per year in Japan and somewhat higher than this in Austria and Ireland, with more concentration during the summer in the two European countries.

26. Beyond the 3.5 hours limit for sessional service, day care providers in Ireland would have to run a full-day service with a kitchen, a sleeping room, etc., thus rendering part-time places inefficient. It is noteworthy that, although sessional services are a matter of responsibility for the Department of Health and Children, the length of that service is laid down in the Pre-School Regulations (which themselves are currently under review).

27. In Austria, regulations are not formulated in terms of child-to-staff ratios but in terms of maximum group size.

28. In Ireland, informal childminders caring for more than six children have to respect the childcare regulations, whereas childminders taking care of between four and six children fall under a special category. They have to notify the Health Board and will also be inspected, but the requirements are limited (*e.g.* no restriction in terms of space). About 80% of all childminders care for no more than three children, and most childminders are younger women currently taking care of their own children.

29. Members of the Irish Childminders Association would have to have childminders insurance, a registration form from their family doctor, and fulfil all legal requirements regarding their home. They also encourage tax registration, with the tax burden of a typical childminder being around USD 735 per year plus USD 315 minimum social insurance contributions which would guarantee maternity benefit and secure accumulation of pension rights.

30. In 2002, the former president of a nationwide chain of non-licensed day care centres in Japan was sentenced to a suspended one-year prison term for professional negligence resulting in the death of a four-month old boy. This ruling is considered a landmark event that should raise the pressure on unauthorised childcare services to improve the quality of their facilities and the appropriateness of their staff.

31. The Irish "Model framework for education, training and professional development in the early childhood care and education sector" was published by a sub-group of the National Childcare Co-ordinating Committee in September 2002. It is supported by all national voluntary childcare organisations. At the same time, a new body (the National Qualifications Authority of Ireland) has been established to streamline the qualifications process across all sectors. The Model Framework will contribute to the work of that body when it turns to childcare.

ISBN 92-64-10418-6
Babies and Bosses: Reconciling Work and Family Life
Austria, Ireland and Japan
© OECD 2003

Chapter 6

Tax/benefit Policy: Parental Work and Care Choices

The avowed policy objective in Austria, Ireland and Japan is to "Provide Choice to Parents", but in practice policies and related outcomes differ markedly. Tax/benefit systems co-determine whether it pays for parents to work, work more hours, work few hours or not at all, so as to care for (very young) children on a full-time basis. The very different tax/benefit policies in the three countries under review contribute to significantly different outcomes in parental work and care choices. Low tax burdens in all three countries mean that work pays for most individuals. However, the intricacies of the Japanese benefit system provide incentives to second earners to keep their earnings at relatively low levels. Austrian policy is most generous in support to couple families where one parent chooses to provide full time care for a very young child, while its tax/benefit system favours second earners in couple families when children are older. Irish policy makers are most explicit in their quest to ensure equity between mothers regardless of their employment status, but reducing long-term benefit recipiency among single mothers remains an important policy challenge. This chapter also discusses employment support policies aimed at re-integrating parents into the labour force.

Tax/benefit systems play an important role in shaping the parental choice of hours split between working and caring for young children: they affect whether it pays for parents to work, work more hours, or, alternatively, help parents to care for (young) children on a full-time basis. Of course this choice is being made within the context of parental preferences, labour market opportunities (Chapter 3), and childcare considerations (Chapter 5), but tax/benefit systems can have a significant effect on maternal labour market behaviour.

In each of the three countries, policy rhetoric is to provide parents with choice in allocating their time spent on work and care activities. None of the three countries have an explicit policy objective of getting mothers with young children into work. However, the means of providing choice differs across countries and the policies used do not all have a neutral impact on the relative attractiveness of parental care vis-à-vis paid employment. For potential dual-earner couples, Irish tax/benefit policy comes closest to being neutral on the work/care balance whilst in Japan certain aspects of health and pension insurance regulations are biased in favour of one of the spouses to limit earnings, and thus working hours. Tax/benefit policy in Austria provides significant incentives towards parental care when children are very young, while it is largely neutral in this regard when children are older. In all three countries, the majority of mothers look after their own children when young, but while about 45% of Irish mothers with young children are in work (rather than being formally employed), this is about 30% in Austria and 25% in Japan (even though employment rates are much higher, see Chapter 2).

The Austrian policy stance is to facilitate parental choice in caring and employment decisions, a policy aim that is pursued by supporting families through a system of generous child benefits. Especially in the presence of a young child (generous cash support for 30-36 months, parental leave until the child's second birthday, see Chapter 5), public support to those families that choose to have a parent care full time for a very young child in Austria is generous, certainly in comparison to Ireland and Japan. There is a consensus in Austria about the importance of supporting mothers to care for very young children on a full-time basis. Irish policy makers are keen to ensure equity between mothers who stay at home to care for children and those who go out to work. This a major theme in policy debate in a country where the Constitution holds that no women shall be forced to work out of economic necessity, and many actively emphasise the valuable role that homemakers play, while others, in particular younger people, increasingly feel that being in paid employment is important. The drive to ensure equity between mothers in and out of the labour force is a recurrent theme in policy reform of income tax, child benefit and the treatment of lone parents. While recent social policy reform in Japan has moved towards facilitating mothers being in employment, traditional patterns of caring mothers continue to be generated by existing workplace practices and health and pension insurance regulations that, often reinforced by employer-provided spousal allowances provide financial incentives for married women to limit earnings and, indirectly, working hours.

After a brief summary of the tax/benefit systems in the three countries under review, this chapter will discuss its implications for work decisions. Section 6.2 examines the effect of tax/benefit regimes on the relative financial attractiveness of work *vis-à-vis* care, focussing on incentives for second earners and existing bias in favour of particular working-hours choices. Employment support policies for non-working parents are considered in Section 6.3, covering policy issues specific to lone parents in Section 6.3.2. The chapter concludes by discussing the overall effect of tax/benefit policy on parental work and care choices.

6.1. A concise overview of tax/benefit systems

Tax/benefit regimes in the three countries are very different (a more detailed description of child-related benefits can be found in the Background Annex to the Review). Public social expenditure varies in levels, the extent to which it is universal or targeted at specific groups and its balance in support to working and non-working age populations (Chapter 2). Public revenue systems differ in the relative importance of income tax and social security contributions, the degree of progressivity in income taxation, and the extent to which they are based on the family or the individual.

Central government is responsible for nearly all public spending in Ireland, whereas regional governments have a large role in the other two countries. The proportion of tax revenues given to state and local government gives some idea of their relative spending power (in all three countries they have limited scope to raise other tax revenue). This is lowest in Ireland, where local governments receive 1.8% of total tax revenue compared with Austria where 9.3% is allocated to state government and another 10% to local government, and highest in Japan where local governments receive 25.6% of total allocations (OECD, 2002g).

6.1.1. Public family benefits

In all three countries public spending on family benefits has increased in the last decade, because of increased generosity of general child benefits (in all three countries), and, as in Austria increased generosity of parental leave benefits culminating in a reform extending coverage to those not in employment. In 2001, public spending on family benefits was high in Austria at 2.3% of GDP, lower in Ireland at 1.6% of GDP, compared with 0.3% of GDP in Japan (Background Annex to the Review).

Family benefits in Austria are generally universal and flat rate, except for provincial family benefits, that are generally targeted at low-income families with children below 3-4 years of age. Federal family benefits are largely operated by a separate institutional body – the FLAF (Box 6.1) under the guiding principle that family support is to be identical for each child. As well as providing equal support for children, the Austrian system aims to maintain equity between those with and without children at all levels of income. Interestingly, concern that there was too much inequity at high income levels motivated a Constitutional court ruling in 1998 increasing the level of support for children precisely to reduce this inequity. There are three main benefits for Austrian families: the Family Allowance, with higher payment rates for older children, and the Child Tax Credit are universal benefits for those with dependent children (paid for children under age 19, or 19-26 and in full-time education), whilst the Childcare Benefit is payable to those with very young children (provided individual earnings of one parent are below USD 13 375 annually). In all, the Austrian benefit system provides substantial support to families[1] – for example a family with a one-year old child receives USD 557 per month from these three benefits. The system redistributes resources from those without children to those with children – with the greatest gains to the non-employed, self-employed and civil servant families with children because their contributions to the FLAF are relatively low (Guger, 1998), and those with very young children because benefits for them are particularly high.

The main Irish support for families is the universal non-taxable Child Benefit (paid for children under age 16 or 16-19 and in full time education), which trebled in value between 1997 and 2002, with most of the increase in 2001 and 2002,[2] to USD 111 for the first and second child, bringing it much closer to Austrian levels of support for those with children aged over 3. The increased generosity was enabled by the strong fiscal position. The aim of recent policy reform was to help parents with the cost of caring for children and the government argued that the reform would increase choice for parents, particularly mothers wanting to enter the labour market. The possibility of taxing Child Benefit has only recently entered political discussions; this would target net expenditure more closely on low-income families.

Japanese public benefits for families have recently been reformed too, but nevertheless remain on a very different scale in terms of generosity. Unlike Austria and Ireland where universal benefits are payable to all those with children under age 19 and age 16, respectively (and to parents of older children

172

Box 6.1. **Austria's Family Burden Equalisation Fund (FLAF) and the provision of family support**

In 1949, a special fund fully financed by employer-contributions (in return for wage restraint) was introduced that disbursed family allowances to *employees*. In 1955, the FLAF was formally founded, and payment of family allowance was extended to *all families*. The financing mechanism was again changed in 1967, but employers still finance in excess of 70% of all FLAF spending. Employer financing of the FLAF (equivalent to 4.5% of gross earnings) is generally regarded as part of their social responsibility and is not considered controversial. By contrast there is growing unease with the lack of equity among certain groups of the population: while the self-employed and most groups of public employees pay no contributions and farmers pay reduced contributions, they fully benefit from FLAF-provisions.

FLAF outlays amounted to about EUR 4.5 billion (USD 4.2 billion) in 2002, which covered a range of spending items (free commuting to school, free schoolbooks, family counselling services, advance maintenance payments, and miscellaneous items), but the *Family allowance* (61% of total FLAF expenditure) and the new Childcare Benefit (20%) are the main items. The declining number of children in Austria (Chapter 4) has contributed to a growing surplus of FLAF revenue compared to expenditure, facilitating the introduction of the Childcare Benefit in 2002. In line with the prevailing philosophy that children should receive identical public support, benefits provided by the FLAF are not restricted to payments to workers (such as maternity leave which is operated by the sickness insurance system). This is reflected by the new Childcare Benefit which all families entitled to the family allowance (excluding recent migrants) are eligible for, replacing the previous parental leave benefit for employees.

The *Child Tax credit* is another universal child benefit but funded by the tax authorities. Despite its name, the Child tax credit is a regular cash payment without any reference to tax liability. In fact, the tax authorities disburse the Family allowance and the Child tax credit payment together (in one cheque) once every two months. Nevertheless, there is resistance to integrating these two benefits into one, as it is argued that since raising children affects parental ability to pay tax, parents should also be compensated through the tax system.

in full-time education), the Japanese child allowance has a mild income-test which excludes high-income families from receiving it, is only paid to those with a child under age 6 and is worth USD 40 per month for the first and second child. The benefit is however payable to more families than before the 2000 reform, when only children under 3 were eligible and the income threshold was lower. Reform was intended to improve the situation of low-income families, and 85% of families with children under 6 are eligible for the allowance. It was funded by a cut in dependent child tax deductions and the net effect has been to redistribute income from richer families with older children to poorer families with younger children. The majority of Japanese employers also pay family benefits, although generally only to those in regular employment (Chapter 3) – increasing the income differences between families with a regular worker and those in non-regular employment and/or jobless families.

As well as general family benefits, there are specific lone parent benefits in Ireland and Japan. These payments are most generous in Ireland and account for about 0.6% of GDP (Section 6.3.2). Childcare support to parents (in terms of subsidised user fees) in Austria and Japan is largely income-tested, whereas such support is largely non-existent in Ireland (Chapter 5).

6.1.2. Main characteristics of tax systems

Tax systems generate the main source of revenue for governments and they are generally assessed against general tax policy objectives, as for example in Japan "equity, neutrality and simplicity". It is beyond the scope of this report to assess the functioning of tax systems in the three countries against such general principals. Instead, the discussion here focuses on one particular aspect of tax systems, i.e. how these systems, in conjunction with benefit systems, may affect the individual labour supply decision.

The burden of taxation (sum of income tax and social security contributions)[3] on labour varies from a low of 9.4% as a proportion of GDP in Japan, to 10.9% in Ireland and is highest in Austria at 15.7% (OECD, 2002g) – mirroring the different public social spending levels. Not only the level, but also the structure and progressivity of taxes vary between the three countries. Firstly, income tax burdens are lowest in Japan with limited progression in marginal tax rates: three-quarters of those in work pay income tax, and of these around 80% pay at the minimum 10% rate (Tax Commission, 2002). Austria also has relatively low income tax burdens, but they are more progressive: income tax as a proportion of gross income increases from less than 1% in the first income decile to around 26% in the top decile, with slightly less than 10% at median income (income tax statistic 2001). Compared with the mid-1990s, tax progressivity has increased (Guger, 1996). Irish income tax is even more progressive: rates have been falling (Box 6.2), but 23% of earners still fall into the top rate band of 42% (OECD, 2001).

Secondly, social security contribution (SSC) rules vary, with the highest payments in Austria, relatively high payments in Japan, and the lowest payments in Ireland. For the majority of Austrian employees, SSC are the largest payment to government, and, because of a ceiling on contributions (at

Box 6.2. **Irish tax reform**

In 1980, the Supreme Court ruled that the family-based tax system that generated a "marriage penalty" was unconstitutional. In response, Ireland adopted a system of "income-splitting" whereby family income was aggregated and split equally between partners for income tax purposes in the beginning of the 1980s. Nevertheless, second earners continued to face high effective tax rates because married couples had the same tax band irrespective of whether they had one or two earners, and financial disincentives to work for second earners were therefore not completely eliminated. In a cross-country econometric study, Callan et al. (1999) found that applying individual taxation to the 1987 Irish tax system would substantially increase female participation, whilst applying the Irish regime in other countries would have negative effects. Since then, the huge increase in the labour force participation of married women has led to a significant reduction in their wage elasticity (Callan and Doris, 1999), while recent reforms of the Irish tax system have reduced the effective tax rates on second earners.

Tax reforms since 1997 have improved net returns to work for all. Firstly, tax rates were reduced by 6 percentage points between 1997 and 2000 improving the returns to work. Secondly, since 2000 tax allowances have been replaced by more generous tax credits and as a result 37% of income earners pay no tax compared to 26% in 1997 (DF, 2001). Thirdly, a policy of progressively widening and individualising the standard rate band (the lower of the two Irish tax bands) was initiated in the 2000 Budget, with a view of ensuring that 80% of income earners pat tax at no more than the standard rate. When the policy is fully implemented, all income earners will have their own non-transferable standard rate band – reducing the effective tax rate on second earners. However, because this last reform improved the position of two-earner married couples relative to one-earner married couples (increasing the returns for second earners), it ran into opposition from women who provided care at home. The governemnt subsequently introduced a Home Carer's tax allowance (now a tax credit) for spouses of one-income married couples who work at home caring for children, the aged or handicapped persons (more detail can be found in the Background Annex to the Review).

The combination of more generous tax relief, lower tax rates and wider standard band has substantially reduced average tax rates, with the greatest proportional gains for low-income families. For example, the average tax rate of a married one-earner couple with two children earning EUR 20 000 (USD 18 815) has fallen from 20.7% in 1997 to 4.7% in 2002, whilst a two-earner couple earning EUR 20 000 (USD 18 815) now pays no tax, compared to 15.9% in 1997. At earnings of EUR 40 000 (USD 37 629) the comparative figures are 29.2% in 1997 falling to 15.7% in 2002 for a one-earner couple, and 28.5% down to 13.8% for a two-earner couple (DF, 2001).

164% of APE earnings), they partially counteract the progressivity of income taxes. Considering both SSC and income taxes together, Austrian payments gradually increase from around 13% for employees in the first income decile to around 37% for the top decile.

Fully individualised tax systems, where tax payments of one spouse are independent of the income of the other, are often considered more likely to promote labour supply of second earners in a household than family-based tax systems (Dingledey, 2001). In Austria, and Japan filing is always on an individual basis, while in Ireland married couples are automatically assessed jointly, but they can opt for individual assessment – though tax liability is identical either way. Recent reforms of Irish taxation have reduced financial disincentives associated with systems of joint taxation (Box 6.2). All three tax systems contain some elements that support one-earner families (tax credits in Austria and Ireland) or main-earner families with the dependent spouse having limited earnings at most (chiefly through social security provisions in Japan).

6.2. The implications of tax/benefit systems

Tax/benefit systems affect the financial incentives for parents to seek paid work rather than provide parental care on a full-time basis, and their choice of hours of work. Discussions of associated financial incentives generally focus on mothers' decision to work because they tend to be the main provider of parental care. This is not purely related to traditional values or preferences, it often reflects economic rationality as family income is least affected when the parent with lower earnings reduces his, but usually her hours in work (Chapter 2).

The following sub-sections discuss the effect of tax/benefit systems in 2002 on the immediate financial incentive to work for second earners in couple families, focussing on parents of children not yet 6 years of age (6 years of age being the mandatory school age in all three countries). The analysis is based on tax/benefit equations (OECD, 2003e and 2003f), and thus ignores other possible sources of family income, abstracts from the non-economic value that parents may derive from being in work, and ignores the longer term benefits of staying in the labour force on future earnings prospects. Nevertheless, the analysis illustrates the pressure points ensuing from tax/benefit systems.

6.2.1. Financial incentives for second earners to work

One way of looking at financial incentives for second earners is to assume that their work decision is independent from that of the main earner.[4] For example, Table 6.1 assumes that the main earner has earnings at the level of an Average Production Employee (OECD, 2003f), and then looks at the effects on family income (and taxes and transfers) of different work choices by the

Table 6.1. **In all three countries, total net burdens on couple families are low**

Payments to, and transfers from, government for couple families at different earnings levels, expressed as a proportion of gross parental earnings (2002)

Wage level (first adult – second adult)	Austria				Ireland				Japan			
	100-0	100-33	100-67	100-100	100-0	100-33	100-67	100-100	100-0	100-33	100-67	100-100
1. Gross earnings[a] (USD)												
Transfers (relative to gross earnings)	22 543	30 057	37 571	45 086	23 829	31 772	39 715	47 658	33 926	45 234	56 543	67 851
2. Payments to government												
a) Income tax (%)	9.0	7.6	8.1	10.6	2.4	7.1	9.7	11.4	1.9	3.6	4.4	5.1
b) Social security contributions[b] (%)	18.1	18.1	18.1	18.1	5.0	3.7	3.9	5.0	10.0	10.0	10.0	10.0
3. Family benefits from government[c]												
a) Children aged 1 and 4 (%)	38.1	28.6	22.9	8.1	11.1	8.4	6.7	5.6	2.8	2.1	1.7	0.0
b) Children aged 7 and 9 (%)	16.3	12.2	9.8	8.1	11.1	8.4	6.7	5.6	–	–	–	–
4. Total payments to government less family benefits (2-3)												
a) Children aged 1 and 4 (%)	-11.0	-3.0	3.3	20.5	-3.8	2.5	6.9	10.8	9.1	11.5	12.8	15.1
b) Children aged 7 and 9 (%)	10.8	13.4	16.4	20.5	-3.8	2.5	6.9	10.8	11.9	13.6	14.4	15.1
5. Effective tax rates on second earners[d]												
a) Children aged 1 and 4 (%)		20.4	25.1	52.0		20.5	23.5	25.4		18.0	18.7	18.3
b) Children aged 7 and 9 (%)		20.4	25.1	30.1		20.5	23.5	25.4		18.0	18.7	18.3

Note: A more detailed description and table of payments to and transfers from government is included in the annex to Chapter 6.

a) APE or "average earnings" refer to the annual earnings of an Average Production Employee (APE) in the manufacturing sector. In 2002, these were USD 22 543 (EUR 23 963) in Austria, USD 23 829 (EUR 25 330) in Ireland and USD 33 926 (JPY 4 254 270) in Japan (see OECD, 2003e).

b) At the example earnings levels:

1. Austrian individuals are below the ceiling for social security contributions (164%);

2. Irish social security is lower for two-earner families because below 59% of APE earnings, earnings are exempt from contributions, and on earnings above that level, the first 26% of earnings is exempt;

3. Japanese second earners are just above the exemption threshold (below 31% of APE they do not have to pay health and pension insurance).

c) The Irish Child Benefit increased in April 2002, and the higher rate is taken on a 12 month basis.

d) Effective tax rates are calculated as the difference between the increase in gross earnings, and the increase in net income when a second earner starts work on 33% or 67% of APE earnings, expressed as a proportion of the change in gross earnings.

Source: Calculations based on OECD (2003f).

second earner. One-earner couples (labelled 100-0, signifying that one parent earns at 100% of APE, while the other parent has no earnings) with two children are compared with other couples where the second earner earns one third of the average wage (100-33), two thirds of the average wage (100-67), and where both earn the average wage (100-100). To show the different levels of support for those with young children in Japan and Austria, the modelling compares families with children aged 1 and 4 with families with children aged 7 and 9. The subsequent sections look at how tax/benefit systems may affect the distribution of earnings among parents, and how accounting for childcare costs might affect financial incentives to work. Specific features of tax/benefit systems that affect the financial incentive structure for second earners below one third of APE earnings, are discussed in Section 6.2.2.

Table 6.1 shows the levels of payments to government (in the form of income tax and social security contributions) and the level of family benefits from government as a proportion of gross parental earnings. It clearly illustrates that income tax burdens are lowest in Japan and most progressive in Ireland; social security contributions (SSC) are quite high in Austria and Japan (in Ireland SSC are lower for the example two-earner families than for one-earner families, because of individual earnings exemptions, see the annex to this chapter). Family benefits are highest in Austria and lowest in Japan.

In terms of payment rates, duration and coverage, the Austrian system of cash support to families with a young child is generous, and this influences parents in their work and care decision. The support to families has two effects. First, it makes it financially more likely that families can afford to choose to have one parent caring full time (what economists refer to as the income effect). This is the intended effect of the Childcare Benefit – increasing choice. However, the system also changes the *relative* income position of parents choosing to work. The net increase in family incomes from a second parent working is far less than it would be if Childcare Benefit did not exist. This will, of course, reduce the likelihood of a household choosing to have two earners (and is known as the substitution effect). Both the income effect (increasing the financial ability of families to choose the childcare arrangements that suit them) and the substitution effect (reducing the returns to work) act to reduce labour force participation of second earners in a family. One-earner couple families with a very young child receive cash transfers worth a considerable 38.1% of APE earnings (Childcare Benefit payments account for 22% of APE, Family Allowance and Child Tax Credit are worth about 16% of APE earnings). Similar support for one-earner couple families in Ireland (11.1% of APE earnings) and Japan (2.8% of APE earnings) is much lower (Table 6.1). Compared to Ireland and Japan, the Austrian policy of "providing choice to parents" involves significantly greater support to those families which choose to have a parent caring full time for a very young child.

The Austrian Childcare Benefit is paid to couple families with a young child if income of the claiming parent is less than 69% of APE earnings.[5] If earnings rise above this level, benefit payment is not gradually phased out but withdrawn completely. This is apparent from an examination of effective tax rates on second earners (Table 6.1). A second earner with average earnings in Austria faces an effective tax rate of 52.0% (line 5a) mostly because family benefits are 8.1% of gross earnings (without Childcare Benefit) compared with an effective tax rate on second earners of 25.1% in a 100-67 family, when family benefits (including Childcare Benefit) are worth 22.9% of gross parental earnings. There is no comparable provision in Ireland and Japan, and so effective tax rates are similar for second earners in these countries at earnings above one third of APE earnings (Table 6.1).

Childcare Benefit *in theory* allows for claimants to work up to 69% of average earnings. However, the majority of Childcare Benefit claimants are on parental leave whose earnings' rules restrict earnings to about 15% of APE earnings unless the employer agrees otherwise (Chapter 5). Parents are entitled (subject to due notice) to return to their original employer at any stage, but if parental earnings in the original job are not below 69% of APE earnings, and not above 91% of APE earnings, going back to work does not lead to an increase in net household income (because of the loss of Childcare Benefit). The same financial incentive structure applies when parents are considering giving up their right to return to their previous employer, to work elsewhere. Parents may be hesitant to give up their entitlement to return to work for their previous employer, and given the generosity of support (and childcare constraints, see Chapter 5), it is not surprising that in many couple families with a very young child in Austria, one parent provides full-time care.

With the exception of Austrian families with very young children, financial incentives for second earners on one third or two thirds of APE earnings (line 5) are similar at around 20% in these three countries.[6] The effective tax rates of around 20% are close to those in the countries studied in the initial *Babies and Bosses* review (OECD, 2002f). However, net payments to government (line 4 in Table 6.1) are less than in Australia, and substantially below those in Denmark and the Netherlands. For example, net payments to government for a 100-33 family[7] were 16% of total earnings in Australia, 23.5% in the Netherlands and 35.4% in Denmark. The comparative figures in Austria, Ireland and Japan for those with young children (line 4a) are –4.6%, 2.5% and 11.5% of total earnings respectively and for those with older children (line 4b) are 13.4%, 2.5% and 13.6% respectively.

6.2.1.1. *The distribution of work between parents in couple families*

Tax/benefit systems also potentially affect the distribution of earnings between parents. As such, if net payments for a family with constant gross

Table 6.2.   **The Austrian tax system favours two-earner families**

Average payments to government at different earnings distributions of 133% of APE earnings, expressed as a percentage of gross earnings

Wage level (first earner-second earner)	Austria (%)			Ireland (%)			Japan (%)		
	133-0	100-33	67-67	133-0	100-33	67-67	133-0	100-33	67-67
1. Payments to government									
a) Income tax	12.7	7.6	4.3	6.8	7.1	7.1	3.6	3.6	3.6
b) Social security contributions	18.1	18.1	18.1	5.2	3.7	2.4	10.0	10.0	10.0
2. Family benefits									
a) For children aged 1 and 4	28.6	28.6	28.6	8.4	8.4	8.4	2.1	2.1	2.1
b) For children aged 7 and 9	12.2	12.2	12.2	8.4	8.4	8.4	–	–	–
3. Total payments to government less family benefits (1-2)									
a) For children aged 1 and 4	2.2	–3.0	–6.2	3.6	2.5	1.2	11.4	11.5	11.5
b) For children aged 7 and 9	18.5	13.4	10.2	3.6	2.5	1.2	13.6	13.6	13.6

Source: Calculations based on OECD (2003f).

income varied considerably with the distribution of earnings, this may influence the choices made in allocating paternal and maternal time between work and care-giving. Table 6.2 considers three distributions of income at 133% of APE earnings: *a)* one-earner couples; *b)* two-earner couples where a main earner earns 100% of APE earnings and the second earner earns 33% of APE earnings; and *c)* two-earner couples with earnings split equally between the two (67% of APE earnings each). For each earnings distribution, it shows the level of income tax and social security contributions, and family benefits, as a proportion of gross parental earnings.

The main observation is that the Austrian tax system favours two-earner families. The "breadwinner" family (133-0) pays 12.7% of gross parental earnings in income tax compared with 4.3% for the "equal work" (67-67) family, because of individual taxation (whilst social security contributions are constant across earnings distributions). Meanwhile the Irish system is essentially neutral (the only slight difference being social security contributions because of individual earnings exemptions), and the Japanese system is neutral between one- and two-earner couples at these earnings ranges (see Section 6.2.2.1).

Adding in family benefits (line 2 of Table 6.2) does not affect this picture for Ireland and Japan. As discussed above, however, Austrian policy involves significantly greater support to those families which choose to have a parent caring full time for a very young child compared to Ireland and Japan. Hence, the Austrian system changes its perspective according to the age of children, favouring one-earner or main-earner households where very young children are present, but favouring a more equal distribution of earnings when children are older.

6.2.1.2. The impact of childcare costs

The discussion so far is relevant to the extent that parents have access to unpaid childcare when in work. This is all well and good for exposing the workings of tax/benefit systems. However, childcare costs affect the work and parental care decision by parents. As Chapter 5 explained in detail, in Ireland parental fees for childcare are approximately twice as high as in Austria and Japan. Moreover, while in Austria and Japan parental fees are often income-tested, they are not in Ireland (though the example families considered here are above the threshold for income-tested fees). This section compares a 100-0 family with no childcare costs to 100-33 and 100-67 families with part-time or full-time costs for young children, or after-school costs for older children, based on the costs discussed in Chapter 5.[8] Part-time care is assumed to be for four hours per day – relevant for families where one parent works relatively few hours, or where working hours are flexible and therefore limited non-parental care is needed. In Austria and Japan for families with young children, it is assumed that both children are in daycare, whilst in Ireland 4-year-olds are assumed to be in pre-school (at no financial cost). In all three countries, the costs for full-time childcare assume care lasts from 9am to 6pm involving daycare in Austria and Japan for both children. In Ireland full-time care assumes the 1-year old is in daycare, whilst the 4-year-old is in pre-school for four hours, and with a childminder the rest of the time. These patterns reflect a "typical" form of formal care in each country.

Table 6.3 shows the effect of childcare costs on financial incentives for second earners by expressing net income, as a proportion of APE, before and after childcare costs. The smaller the difference between the net earnings of a one-earner family with no childcare costs and a two-earner family after childcare costs, the more limited the immediate financial return to work.

The costs of part-time care for young children have a similar effect on the financial incentive structure: in all three countries, there is some financial return to work. For example, net earnings after childcare costs for the 100-33 family (line 2) are 15% of APE higher than net earnings of the 100-0 family in Austria, 12% higher in Ireland and 16% higher in Japan.

Compared to part-time care solutions, financial returns for second earners with children in full-time are lower in Austria and especially in Ireland. Full-time childcare costs for parents in Austria are substantial at about 25% of APE earnings, which virtually eliminates net financial gains from work for a second earner at one third of APE earnings (and significantly reduce net returns to work at two thirds of APE earnings). At 39% of APE earnings, Irish full-time childcare costs for two young children mean net earnings of a 100-33 family are *lower* than those of a 100-0 family, and immediate financial returns for a second earner on 67% of APE earnings are significantly reduced. If both children were in

Table 6.3. **Childcare costs significantly reduce financial returns to second earners**

Net income expressed as a percentage of APE earnings, before and after childcare costs

Wage level (first adult – second adult)	Austria (%)				Ireland (%)				Japan (%)			
	100-0	100-33	100-67	100-100	100-0	100-33	100-67	100-100	100-0	100-33	100-67	100-100
Young children (aged 1 and 4)[a]												
1. Before childcare costs	111	137	161	159	104	130	155	178	91	118	145	173
2. part-time childcare costs for both children		126	150	147		116	141	164		107	131	158
3. full time childcare costs for both children		112	136	134		91	116	139		107	131	158
School age children (aged 7 and 9)[b]												
4. Before after school care costs	89	115	139	159	104	130	155	178	88	115	143	170
5. after school costs for both children		103	126	146		102	127	150		112	139	166

Note: It is assumed that parents not in work do not use formal childcare services, although some parents use such services to enhance child development (Chapter 5). In all three countries, full-time childcare is 9-6pm in all three countries, and part-time care lasts 4 hours.

a) In Austria and Japan both children are in childcare whilst in Ireland the older child is in pre-school part-time, which is assumed to be topped up by childminding for the childcare full-time costs. In Japan costs are identical whether a child is in part-time or full-time care, but there is a significant reduction for the second child.

b) In Austria, free text books and free transport or commuting grants for school children are provided (funded by the FLAF). There are no comparable benefits in the other two countries.

Source: OECD Secretariat calculations.

daycare (as opposed to one being in pre-school) these costs would rise to around 50% of APE earnings, further reducing financial incentives to work. Intuitively, this result for Ireland seems contradictory to the huge rise in labour force participation of mothers with young children (Chapter 2). However, in part this is related to the availability of *informal* care, although not all such forms are cheap (Chapter 5). Furthermore, the spiralling house-prices in the 1990s in Ireland, made it difficult for first-time house buyers (many of whom are newly weds or families with young children) to enter the market. This may have increased the necessity of second incomes in families, even if the immediate net returns to work after childcare costs are low.

On the whole, for couple families the immediate financial incentives to second earners being in employment after accounting for full-time childcare costs can be limited. For a family with children aged 1 and 4, assuming that the second earner starts work at two thirds of APE earnings (and thus not being restricted by allowable earnings rules in parental leave legislation – Chapter 5), the net gains from being a two-earner household using childcare rather than a one-earner household are about 25% of APE earnings in Austria, 12% in Ireland and 40% in Japan.

The story for families with school-age children making use of after school care is slightly different. At one end of the spectrum, Irish after-school care costs amount to 28% of APE earnings, and combined with the tax/benefit system means there is no financial incentive for second earners on 33% of APE earnings to start work, though there is some financial return for those on higher earnings. Austrian after-school care costs also notably dampen financial incentives, though they are less than half the Irish level and so the effect is not as large. At the other end of the spectrum, Japanese after-school care costs are relatively low and therefore barely affect financial incentives for second earners. On the other hand, education costs are far higher in Japan than in the other two countries (Chapter 4), and may therefore increase incentives to work for second earners via an income effect.

There are three main observations to be made from this analysis:

- In all three countries, net payments to government are low, so that work *does* pay.

- Compared to Ireland and Japan, Austrian policy involves significantly greater support to those families which choose to have a parent caring full time for a very young child. By contrast, when children are above 3 years of age, the Austrian tax/benefit is most favourable to families with an equal distribution of earnings between parents.

- Although the Irish tax/benefit system maintains financial incentives for second earners, part-time work does *not* pay for those relying on paid childcare.

6.2.2. Low-income families and limited hours employment

Financial incentive effects tend to be most pertinent for low-income families – for whom the difference in net income between working and not working is smallest. Additionally, there are some financial incentive effects arising from the tax/benefit system relevant to low-earners that have not been captured by the discussion above. These are most prevalent in Japan, where health and pension insurance regulations and employer-provided benefits for dependent spouses can provide financial incentives to spouses to keep their earnings below certain (low-level) earnings thresholds. Meanwhile the Irish in-work benefit distorts incentives for low-income working families and Austrian provincial means-tested benefits for those on low-income may also reduce financial incentives to work.

6.2.2.1. Marriage and work in Japan

The income tax schedule, health and pension insurance regulations and remuneration systems for regular employees (Chapter 3) all contain provisions that financially support spouses with no or limited earnings. In fact, the income tax system has two income tax allowances for spouses (see the annex to this chapter for detail), which entitle the primary earner in a couple family to income tax allowances worth a maximum USD 606 (USD 303 after reform to be introduced in 2004) per annum if his/her income is taxed at the standard tax rate of 10% (which concerns about 80% of all taxpayers) and when spousal earnings are below JPY 0.7 million (USD 5 582 or 16% of APE).[9] The system of these spousal tax allowances involves a gradual phasing out of the tax allowance for the primary earner between spousal earnings of JPY 0.7 million (16% of APE) and JPY 1.41 million (33% of APE). In other words, spousal income tax allowances are so designed that additional spousal earnings increase net (after tax) family income (Tax Bureau, Ministry of Finance, 2002), although they may reduce net earnings of the primary earner.

However, the design of Health and Pension insurance regulations as often reinforced by enterprise-provided spousal benefits gives dependent spouses financial incentives to limit their working hours and earnings around specific earnings levels. In this context, two features are particularly relevant:[10]

- Most significantly, below JPY 1.3 million (approximately 31% of APE earnings or about 22 hours weekly at the average female non-regular wage, Chapter 2) spouses generally do not have to pay health and pension insurance contributions (while benefiting from their employed partner's contributions).[11] Above this level, payments are *not* gradually phased in, but are a sizeable lump sum, starting at around USD 1 235 per annum when earnings are about JPY 1.3 million, and increasing with earnings.

● There are employer-provided benefits for "dependent spouses" that are paid by about half of Japanese companies. About 50% of companies that make these payments do so regardless of the spousal earnings. However, the other half pays these spousal benefits subject to the earnings of the spouse, and payments are completely withdrawn (not phased out) at these specified earning levels. On average, enterprise-provided spousal benefits amount to USD 1 005 annually. Of those companies that pay an income-tested benefit for spouses, 76.4% only pay the benefit if spousal earnings are below JPY 1 030 000 (about 24% of APE earnings) and 15.4% only pay the benefit if spousal earnings are below JPY 1.3 million or 31% of APE earnings (MOL, 1997a). Additionally, around 63% of all enterprises pay family benefits for dependent children, bringing average total employer-provided family benefits to USD 1 791 annually (MOL, 1999a). However, the payment of employer-provided child benefit is not generally dependent on spousal earnings, so does not contribute to incentives to limit earnings.

Thus, in contrast to the spousal income tax provisions, design of relevant health and pension insurance regulations – as often reinforced by employer-provided spousal benefits – does not ensure that additional spousal earnings always lead to an increase in net family income. Also, the relevant benefits are worth considerable more than the spousal income tax allowances (the maximum worth of these income tax allowances will be halved with reform in 2004, see the annex to this chapter). Moreover, the earnings threshold in Health and Pension insurance regulations is not the same as the spousal earnings threshold in the income tax schedule, so that spouses in Japan face a complex and distorted financial incentive structure when coming to their labour supply decision.

Chart 6.1 shows the combined effect of these provisions on a couple with two young children assuming the husband earns at the APE earnings level. It demonstrates the very limited incentives families face to increase spousal earnings between 20% and 35% of APE earnings.[12] In this range they lose employer benefits, they start paying social security contributions themselves, and their husband's net earnings fall gradually as dependent spouse income tax allowances are reduced. There are two main points at which incentives are distorted. Firstly, where a wife increases earnings from 20 to 25% of APE earnings, the family faces a marginal effective rate of tax and social security contributions of 71%. This is largely explained by the fact that employers no longer regard the wife as dependent and therefore withdraw the associated benefit. Secondly, the marginal effective rate of tax and social security contributions when earnings are increased from 30 to 35% of APE earnings is even larger at 96%, because this is the point at which the spouse must pay health and pension insurance contributions. The effect would be far smaller, if, as for income tax, a certain amount of earnings were exempt from social security, or contributions were gradually phased in.

Chart 6.1. **Japanese spouses are encouraged to limit their earnings**

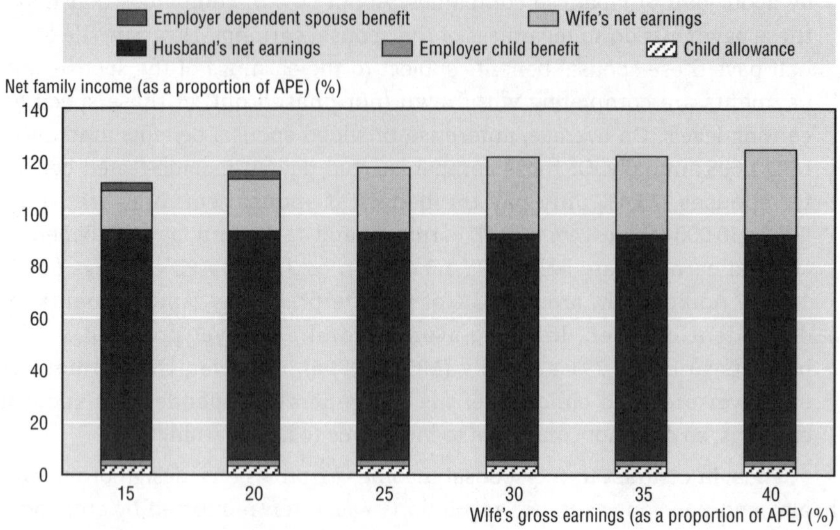

Source: OECD Secretariat calculations.

Although incentives to increase earnings are maintained at higher earnings levels in the Japanese tax/benefit system (Table 6.1), the influence of the health and pension insurance regulations and employer-provided benefits in particular, are relevant in a context where 45% of women are in non-regular (low paid) work (Chapters 2 and 3). Indeed, national studies suggest that married women are deliberately keeping their earnings below the 24% of APE earnings threshold. The earnings distribution of married women peaks at this threshold (Ono and Rebick, 2002; and Nagase, 2002), and around 40% of female non-regular workers adjust their working hours to ensure they and their husbands gain the most from the different benefits for dependent spouses (JIWE, 1995).

Future pension reform may reduce, but not eliminate incentives to limit earnings. Concerns about the coverage of the employee pension system are motivating pension reform for 2004 (MHLW, 2002c), and reform plans include consideration of incentive effects for working spouses. The signal from such reforms may lead to employers considering withdrawing dependent spouse benefits (*Asahi Shimbun*, 2002b), but as these are popular among workers, union resistance will be considerable, if regular employees are not compensated in some other way.

BABIES AND BOSSES: RECONCILING WORK AND FAMILY LIFE – ISBN 92-64-10418-6 – © OECD 2003

6.2.2.2. Ireland: financial support for all low-income families in work

The Irish in-work benefit, the Family Income Supplement (FIS) is one way of helping make work pay, addressing both employment and distributional objectives. The FIS is paid to low-income families with dependent children, where parents work at least 19 hours per week between them. It is a potentially important tool for providing financial incentives for low-skill jobless families to enter work and because of the lower hours limit ensures that it is paid to those who are more than marginally attached to the labour market. However, because entitlement is family-based, it can limit incentives for second earners. A low-income one-earner family may be entitled to the FIS. However, if a second earner started work, even at a low level of income, they may lose entitlement to FIS because total parental earnings will be above the income threshold. Indeed, it is withdrawn at a high rate and therefore provides very limited financial incentives to increase working hours for recipient families (whether the first or second earner). Callan *et al.* (2001) found that around four-fifths of families eligible for the Family Income Supplement face a marginal effective tax rate of 60-70%, and the remainder face marginal tax rates of close to 80%.

However, it is relevant to a relatively small proportion of working families, because it is only paid to those with family income less than around 80% of APE earnings (the exact threshold depends on family size), and there are only 11 570 recipient families (DSCFA, 2002). Moreover, FIS-payments do not seem to reach the population it is intended for: in the mid-1990s estimates suggested that perhaps only one third of eligible families were reached (ESRI, 1997). Policy makers have been keen to increase the awareness of the programme while improving operational procedures. This is likely to have contributed to a reduction of non-take-up.

6.2.2.3. Topping up household income and means-tested benefits in Austria

Working limited hours may be an attractive reconciliation option for mothers, and in Austria it is facilitated by the favourable tax treatment of marginal employees earning up to USD 284 per month (Box 3.3). This option was designed to allow benefit recipients (but also students) with an option to top-up household income.

The financial returns to even marginal employment may, however, be reduced because of the operation of provincial means-tested benefits. Austrian provincial governments provide means-tested housing benefits to those on low income, and family benefits to those with young children. As for the Irish Family Income Supplement, the low-income threshold makes such benefits relevant to relatively few families. Unlike in Ireland, however, Austrian provincial benefits are generally for all low-income families, as opposed to being in-work benefits.

Programme design of family benefits varies across provinces, but nowhere are such benefits paid where children are older than four (provinces finance kindergarten for this age-group). For example, the Viennese family benefit is paid to about 10% of families with children aged 1 to 3 and is worth a maximum USD 144 per child per month (AK, 2002). It is payable in full for couple families with two children (the exact income threshold depends on family size) with earnings below 47% of APE and phased out thereafter up to 71% of APE earnings (housing benefits are payable and withdrawn over a similar income range). Theoretically, the effect of such means-tested benefits is to reduce incentives for low-income families to start work or increase hours of work. However, the Viennese family benefit is withdrawn at a low level, so the effects are relatively limited. For example, where one parent earns 50% of APE earnings, if the other parent starts working the maximum marginal employment, the family loses the equivalent of 3% of APE earnings of Viennese family benefit, but gains a far larger 15% of APE earnings in employment income.

6.3. Promoting employment among non-working parents

Joblessness rates among couple families with children in Austria and Japan are low at 2.5% and 1.1% respectively, and about 14% in Ireland in 1996, although since then the joblessness rate will have declined because of unprecedented employment growth (more recent data is not available). Joblessness among lone parent families is more widespread: 15% in Japan, 19% in Austria, and 55% in Ireland. Austrian and Japanese rates are low in comparison to many OECD countries (OECD, 2002h), but Irish lone parents have a relatively weak labour force attachment. This section considers how tax/benefit policies and active labour market policies assist non-working parents with trying to get (back) into the labour market. This section does not cover all benefits for the unemployed or employment support programmes as they are open to all job-seeker regardless of family status. Instead, the focus is on the general approach of labour market re-integration towards parents and the policy approach towards lone parents.

6.3.1. The general approach towards labour market re-integration

The approach in all three countries is one of support for all jobseekers, generally with limited help specifically for parents. The assistance offered has traditionally been at a very general level, but each country is moving towards providing more individualised, integrated and flexible support. In all three countries, the main employment services are open to all unemployed, often with more assistance (e.g. employment subsidies, training) available to those on unemployment benefit. The Austrian "Returners Programme" (see below) is an exception, as this provides additional support to all parents aiming to return to work, irrespective of their particular non-work or benefit status.

Many social assistance clients are not considered able to work, and tend to receive less systematic access to available labour market help, although those who are job-ready may register themselves with the main support services, or be referred to them. This is more relevant in Ireland than the other two countries, where most social assistance recipients do not have children.[13] (The details on duration and payment of benefits for those out of the labour market are described in the Background Annex to the Review.)

Employment support for Austrian and Japanese jobseekers is largely provided by the public employment service (in Japan known as "Hello Work" offices). The Irish system is less coherent as it involves several players: social welfare offices (benefit registration and administration); the national training and employment authority (FÁS); local employment services contracted by FÁS; regional health boards (that employ the community welfare officers who serve supplementary welfare allowance clients – which is ultimately financed by the DSFA); and 36 local partnerships (in disadvantaged areas). Clients on benefits distributed through the social welfare offices (not including those on supplementary welfare) can approach a Job Facilitator to guide them through the web of available employment services. However, because of the variety of agencies involved, and on occasion, hazy boundaries in responsibilities or information flows that are not mandatory or clear-cut, there is scope for duplication of efforts or gaps in coverage.

In Austria and Ireland, various forms of support are available to those out of work – including interviews to discuss job opportunities, counselling, access to training programmes and social services. In Ireland, improving financial incentives for benefit recipients to start work has been a major pillar of re-integration policy (Box 6.3). In Japan, historically low levels of unemployment meant there was little demand for similar services. Instead the onus has traditionally been on the jobseekers to find work themselves, an approach which has generally been successful – in part because use of the stigma attached to being unemployed and thus the very high self-motivation to look for work immediately. However, with rising unemployment levels there have been recent moves to provide more active assistance with the provision of job consultation and training services.

6.3.1.1. *Support for parents out of work*

In all three countries, recipients of unemployment benefits are expected to look for work, regardless of their family situation. However, there is no hard evidence to suggest that many parents are struck of the register for citing caring responsibilities as a reason to refuse a job-offer in any of the three countries, albeit for different reasons. In Ireland, the sanctioning regime in general is not overly strict (see above). In the Japanese system, where sanctions only happen very rarely, job offers are generally only made if it is

Box 6.3. **Back to work benefits in Ireland**

Along with in-work benefits, back to work benefits can help reduce the poverty trap by decreasing the cost and uncertainty associated with moving into work. Ireland is the only country of the three that provides specific benefits for benefit recipients who move into work. The main support for those entering the labour market is the income-tested Back to Work Allowance – for the first three years of work, recipients keep 75%, 50% and 25% of their social welfare payment. It has helped around 40 000 families (of 80 000 recipients) since its introduction in 1993, and, although there are some problems with dropout in the early phases, nearly three-quarters of former recipients are still in work three years later. Secondary benefits (in particular the free medical card and rent supplement) are also retained for the first three years of work (four years for the self-employed), to support those moving back into work. Although the retention of secondary benefits may ease the move into work, the associated income limit, at 65% of APE biases incentives towards part-time rather than full-time work.

The Back to Education Allowance is based on the same principle whereby benefit recipients who enter second level courses are entitled to an allowance on top of their benefits. However, it is on a much smaller scale than the Back to Work Allowance, with 4 101 recipients in 2001 (DSCFA, 2002), of whom only around 30% have children. Because the Back to Education Allowance is restricted to full-time courses, it is difficult for parents without access to childcare to take advantage of it.

known that the client can accept. If the counsellor is aware that the client has no childcare arrangements, a job-offer *may* not be made. The situation is similar in Austria, where the employment service tries to find a job that is compatible with the childcare arrangement. For Austrian parents who claim UI benefits *in addition* to Childcare Benefit, however, the situation is quite different. In this case, they would have to clarify their childcare situation, and clients who cannot show they have suitable arrangements will *not* be considered eligible for UI.

One of the predominant concerns of parents looking for work is childcare, but employment offices do generally not combine the job-matching function with sufficient care-matching activities. There are two exceptions in Ireland: the Community Employment scheme (discussed in more detail in Section 6.3.2.2) is particularly attractive to parents because childcare is generally provided, and, one local partnership (the Northside Partnership) also combines job-matching and care-matching functions, finding the most suitable childcare option for clients. In general, though, help with respect to childcare from employment services takes the form of information on local childcare services and, in Austria and Ireland, subsidies for childcare fees (in addition to other fee subsidies in Austria).[14] In Ireland these are restricted to mothers in training programmes and there is some concern that subsidies do not match the costs in the regulated childcare sector, and because they are payable to the provider, do not help those relying on informal care (Russell et al., 2002). Employment services in Austria also support the creation of childcare places through direct subsidies to providers, and they subsidise information centres for women, which in turn often help mothers in finding an appropriate childcare arrangement.

Even where childcare provision is nearly universal or free, parents considering work may still face practical issues finding suitable work and establishing a balance between work and care. As such, many mothers wanting to return to work have been out of the labour force for some time and may no longer have appropriate skills, added to which, they would often like to work part-time but the opportunities are not always available. A particular concern in Austria is that 40% of mothers are out of the labour force after finishing paid parental leave and the long period of leave raises issues of how to help these women make the transition back into paid work. In both Austria and Ireland, there is an increasing recognition that there are women in the home who would like to work, and these have become a new target group for employment support.

The Austrian public employment service supported 10 000 women returners in 2002 through information events, guidance in association with other counselling services, skills training and childcare subsidies, and provide ongoing support once women have entered the labour market. The programme is intended primarily for women out of the labour force with children under the age of 15 who have been out of the labour market for a long time. Women returners are supported through a three-phase process which focuses on the needs of mothers.[15] In the first stage, options and aims are discussed with a case manager and a plan is drawn up. If no suitable job has been found after four weeks, this is followed by more detailed consideration of realistic possibilities – taking into account qualifications and perhaps involving new training, counselling, commuting times, childcare and part-time options. If, after a further two months, job search has not been successful, in a third and final stage lasting three months, the client is expected to adjust expectations in terms of working time and types of job, and look for work across a broader range. At the end of six months, they are subject to the same obligations as other unemployed, though in practice sanctions are – as far as benefit recipients are concerned – rarely applied. The intention is to continue supporting women once they have found work, for example, if they wish to continue upgrading their skills.

There is another, smaller-scale initiative for Austrian women who have spent some time out of the labour market caring for children. The *Family Competence* project is run in some family-advice centres (run by the Ministry for Social Security and Generations) for those caring for children or relatives who want to resume work. Through consultation, it aims to help parents recognize the skills used in the home, increasing their self-confidence and helping them use these abilities effectively in job search.

In Ireland, an estimated 27 000 women currently out of the labour market are considering returning to work (FÁS, 2002a). The Irish Gateway for Women, launched nationally in November 2002, is designed to help these women make the transition to work. As its name suggests, the initiative will provide a gateway to existing resources. In addition, responding to concerns (Russell *et al.*, 2002) that the inflexibility of most training courses makes them inaccessible for those with family responsibilities, it also seeks to provide flexible and local training to meet each individual's needs. It is hoped that up to 1 000 women returners will benefit from FÁS training and job placement in 2003.

6.3.2. Lone parents

Lone parents face particular resource constraints with more limited time than couples available to share between work and caring responsibilities. They also have a relatively high poverty risk, particularly in Ireland – related to low education levels (DSCFA, 2000) and employment rates, and, in Japan (associated with low-paid non-regular work). As a result, lone parents frequently receive specific policy attention, although the intensity of focus and policy approach differs across OECD countries, as they do in the three countries under review. The cross-country differences in policy concern are related to the different labour market outcomes for single parents. In both Austria and Japan, employment rates of single parents are high (also when compared with mothers in couple families). By contrast, employment rates for Irish single parents are half of those in Austria and Japan (Table 6.4).

Table 6.4. **Less than half of Irish lone parents are in work**

	Austria	Ireland	Japan
Employment (2001), %	81	45	83
of whom in part-time (non regular in Japan), %	33	–	50
Income poverty rate (mid-1990s), %	17	24	44
Financial support in 2002, USD (for a lone parent with 2 children aged 4 and 6)			
Maximum lone parent benefit	–	642	378
General family benefits	306	221	80

Source: Employment (Table 2.6), income poverty (Table 2.7), financial support (Background Annex to the Review).

Austria and Japan do not treat lone parents very differently from other jobseekers. Lone parents are generally expected to work, except for when children are very young. As for everyone else, social assistance support may be available, but this is not always easy to get hold of (because of strict means-testing, and in both countries, other relatives are legally obliged to help those in need) nor is it a particularly attractive option, both because of the associated stigma and low payment rates. Irish policy treats lone parents as a very specific group and there is no compulsion to look for work attached to benefit receipt for as long as single parents on benefit have dependent children (up to age 18, but 22 when the "child" is in higher education). There are no specific lone parent benefits in Austria, and there is only a small benefit for Japanese lone mothers worth a maximum USD 378 per month compared with a maximum Irish lone parent benefit of USD 642 monthly.[16]

Only a small minority of lone parents are male, and in Austria they are treated exactly the same as lone mothers. This is also true in Ireland since policy reforms in 1990 and 1997 that integrated various lone parent benefits. Conversely, in Japan central government benefit programmes are only accessible to lone mothers while municipalities may operate specific lone parent programmes open to single parents of both sexes.

6.3.2.1. *Austrian and Japanese lone parents need to work*

The primary sources of lone parent income are earnings and/or public income support (maintenance support is mostly paid only for children, and cannot be relied on in Ireland and Japan – see Box 6.4). The overall policy stance towards Austrian (at least where children are older than 3) and Japanese lone parents is clearly one that expects them to work: financial support is low and lone parents are not treated very differently from other parents. If anything, lone parents are given priority over other parents: in terms of access to formal childcare centres and support from public employment services, which is slightly higher than for other parents. With regard to the latter, Austrian public employment services are legally obliged[17] to find them either work or training within four weeks of claiming both Childcare Benefit and unemployment benefit, and non-working Japanese lone mothers may receive information and counselling or be eligible for wage subsidies.

Austrian lone parents with a child under 2½ years old will, as other parents, be eligible for the Childcare Benefit and a potential low-income supplement in the form of a loan. Along with the family allowance and child tax credit, maximum support from central government for a child under the age of 2½ amounts to USD 728 monthly (which may be bolstered by support from provincial governments). The design of the Childcare Benefit is such that it may be most financially worthwhile to top up this income with marginal or

> ## Box 6.4. **Lone parent maintenance support**
>
> Austrian lone parents are far more likely to be in receipt of maintenance payment than their Irish and Japanese counterparts. Previously married parties have a legal obligation to pay maintenance, and in the case of default, advance payments may be granted by the FLAF. AK (2001) reports that around four-fifths of lone mothers in Vienna receive maintenance from the absent parent, and among non-receivers, one third get an advance payment from the FLAF. In 1998, the FLAF paid advance maintenance for 36 546 children in Austria (BMUJF, 1999).
>
> In Ireland and Japan, the main responsibility for pursuing maintenance lies with the lone parent. The state provides some incentive to pursue maintenance through income disregards in benefit payments in Ireland and Japan (50% and 20% of maintenance respectively is disregarded in the calculation of means-tested benefit payments). Beyond this, Irish and Japanese state involvement in assisting with maintenance claims is limited. Ireland has a national maintenance recovery unit which was recently expanded and is responsible for determining liable relatives' contribution levels, reviews and monitors payments and pursues those who do not pay. Nevertheless, only about 10% of absent parents are actively pursued: others are not either because of a lack of information, or because they are not expected to be able to pay. In Japan, the courts can enforce maintenance payment, but this is a time-consuming exercise. Moreover, the claimant has to file for each payment individually. Under Justice Ministry reform proposals, child support would be automatically deducted at source from the absent spouses' monthly salaries for an agreed period of time.
>
> The difficult procedures and the probability that absent parent may not be able to give financial support result in a relatively small proportion of lone parents receiving maintenance in Ireland and Japan. A government of Ireland report (2000) estimated that 3.5% of lone parent benefit recipients received maintenance and concluded that department efforts were "ineffective and of little deterrent value for liable relatives to meet their commitments". Japanese survey evidence shows that around one fifth of divorced lone-mother families receive maintenance payment (MHLW, 2001b).

part-time work and keep earnings below 69% of APE earnings, as opposed to earning slightly more than this threshold. There is the possibility of receiving both Childcare Benefit and unemployment insurance but this is not a long term option for relying on benefit income – the client has to show that childcare responsibilities do not deter him or her from being in work or searching for work immediately. For those with older children, central government benefits fall to USD 147 for a family with one child or USD 306 for two children (for both lone parent and couple families), and because lone parents are essentially treated the same as couple families (for example, tax credits are the same as for single-earner couples), they are compelled by economic necessity to find full-time work. Therefore, the structure of financial support enables Austrian lone parents to work part-time until their child is 2½ years old, but after that they have little option but to work full-time to have a sufficient income.

Unlike in Austria, there is a specific Japanese means-tested lone mother benefit for those with children up to age 18. However its maximum value is USD 378 monthly (this may be topped up by small support from municipalities), and so Japanese lone parents, without financial support from elsewhere, face the same financial need to find full-time work, irrespective of the age of the child.

6.3.2.2. Irish lone parents' main source of income is from benefits

The situation in Ireland is very different: the explicit Irish priority (Government of Ireland, 1998) is to ensure adequate income support for lone parent families. Hence, Ireland has a specific lone parent benefit, in combination with high earnings disregards without loss of benefit (see below), and extended duration (until children are 18 years old, or 22 if they enrol in tertiary education), spending on this programme amounts to about 0.6% of GDP. For most Irish lone parents, social welfare is their principle or only source of income (DSCFA, 2000).

The Irish One Parent Family Payment (OPFP) is far more generous than its Japanese counterpart: with maximum support for a lone parent with two children worth USD 642 monthly. As well as this, some lone parents may receive a partial UI payment, so that out-of-work income (including Child Benefit, OPFP and UI) can be as high as 53% of APE (just over USD 1 050 monthly). There is then not the same economic necessity to work as in the other two countries (although financial incentives to work are maintained because the OPFP is also paid to those in work on low earnings). On top of which there is no compulsion to look for work: a government review (DSCFA, 2000) concluded that the introduction of a work test and/or time limited benefit was not practical with the existing lack of affordable childcare and insufficient training, education and employment support. The review recommended that this position should be re-considered as the necessary infrastructure develops. As a result, there is an expectation that lone parents can depend on benefit and nearly half of OPFP payments last more than 8 years (DSCFA, 2000). Government efforts to encourage employment have however been stepped up in recent years and there is some evidence to suggest the culture of dependency is changing. Lone parent employment rates have increased (Chapter 2) and 67% of those with children aged 5-14, compared with 33% of those with children aged 15 and over, are in work (CSO, 2002). It is, however, difficult to assess to what extent this is related to policy encouragement or strong labour demand and changing cohort behaviour.

The main measure introduced in order to encourage lone parents into work is a generous earnings disregard to the OPFP: those with earnings up to 30% of APE earnings may be entitled to the maximum OPFP payment (provided they satisfy other means-tests). Earnings disregards are policy measures that aim to ease the transition off benefit into employment. There is a risk, however, that instead of providing a route off benefit, beneficiaries become content with an intermediate position, combining some benefit and some earnings on a long term basis. Chart 6.2 shows how, as earnings from work increase, net income changes. It assumes the lone parent is entitled to UI to show the maximum level support from government (the results are similar, though net income slightly lower, if there is no UI entitlement) and does not include possible Family Income Supplement payment.[18]

Chart 6.2. **Topping up benefit income with earnings**

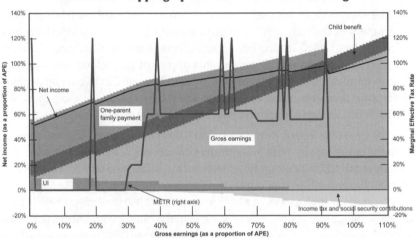

Note: Does not include possible Family Income Supplement payment.
Source: OECD calculations based on OECD (2003e).

There are clearly several spikes in the marginal effective tax rate (METR) schedule corresponding to drops in UI and OPFP payments and the end of income tax and social security exemptions. Most notable however is the fact that METRs (measured on the right axis) are consistently around 60% for those on earnings between 35% and 90% of APE earnings. This is largely because of the withdrawal of OPFP (and reinforced by the withdrawal of UI and the increase in income tax and social security payments), and provides very limited incentives for lone parents to move into regular or full-time employment. This bias in favour of part-time work is reinforced by secondary benefit eligibility, though the thresholds are slightly different. Firstly, the Rent Supplement (paid to 9 000 of the 77 142 OPFP recipients; DSCFA, 2002), is not payable to full-time workers. Secondly, free medical coverage is only available for those with earnings below half of APE earnings.

Evidence on the earnings of OPFP recipients reflects these incentive effects: only 17% of OPFP recipients earn more than the earnings disregard of 30% of APE earnings (DSCFA, 2000). The main effect of the disregard is to enable lone parents to top up their benefit income with small earnings as opposed to encouraging them to move off benefit into regular employment. Though the earnings disregard has had some positive employment effect, it does not seem to have changed the expectation that lone parents can rely on a significant level of benefit income, and many still do. This means that full advantage of the booming Irish economy has not been taken as in other countries (e.g. Canada, the United States) which have been able to dramatically increase the number of lone parents in full-time work.

The final point to make regarding OPFP is that, from an administrative point of view, there is some concern of fraudulent claims – either where recipients are working in the informal sector, or are actually cohabiting. As such, in 1999, the External Control Unit (which detects fraud on various benefit schemes) dealt with more than 1 500 OPFP suspected fraud cases and terminated or reduced the payment in over half of them (DSCFA, 2000).

The other strand of Irish labour market re-integration policy encouraging lone parent employment is an increasingly proactive information policy aiming to raise awareness of work options. However, these have met with limited success for two main reasons. First, there is a lack of policy coherence between Departments, and between national and local offices, with scope for greater integration, coverage and accessibility (NESF, 2001). Second, there is no compulsion for lone parents to take part in active labour market programmes. Indeed, lone parents' participation in these programmes is mainly restricted to the Community Employment scheme,[19] which appeals because it is locally based, flexible (and mostly part-time), generally provides childcare and it allows for the retention of secondary benefits and OPFP (as well as the USD 24 a week paid for participation). However, only around 15% of lone parents (Deloitte and Touche, 1998) move into employment after participation. Because of its disappointing performance (certainly in view of the booming economy in the late 1990s) the number of CE placements is being gradually reduced (from a high of 41 000 in 1998 to under 25 000 in 2003), and will be replaced by the Social Economy scheme. For this or any other programme to be effective in improving participants' job prospects, it is important that it has a far stronger link to the labour market than the CE scheme (Denny et al., 2000).

6.4. Conclusions

The avowed policy intention in all three countries to support parents in their work and care choice is reflected in existing tax/benefit policies, to a considerable extent. Low tax burdens across the three countries do make work pay. They also make it easier financially to choose to have one earner, although second earner incentives are *generally* maintained by second earners facing overall low effective tax rates. In each country, however, there are elements of existing policy that affect the work and care choice that parents make. The Irish tax/benefit system is the most consistent for couple families: at most earnings levels, and irrespective of the age of the children, it is largely neutral on the work and care balance chosen by parents. The same is not entirely true in the other two countries – the Austrian regime favours second earners (usually mothers) with older children working, but it provides very strong incentives to mothers with very young children to limit their earnings and/or provide full-time parental care. The Japanese health and pension system as reinforced by design of employer-provided spousal allowances provides incentives for married women, to limit their earnings around specific (low) earnings levels.

The design of the Austrian Childcare Benefit and parental leave regulations were discussed more fully in Chapter 5. Clearly, the Austrian policy of "providing choice to parents" involves significantly greater support to those families which choose to have a parent caring full time for a very young child than in Ireland and Japan. Recent reform made it financially more likely that families can afford to choose to have one parent caring full time for a very young child, while the relative income position of families with a young child also changed to reduce the likelihood of such a household choosing to have two earners. The system should be reformed to make choosing work for such families a more realistic option (as outlined in the conclusions to Chapter 5) Japanese plans to reform pension insurance in 2004 should reduce the bias in favour of dependent spouses, but this bias is unlikely to be eliminated completely without further changes, in particular to health insurance regulations and employer-provided benefits. Added to which, any change in incentive structures would only have a real effect if there was a simultaneous change in workplace culture providing better labour market opportunities to working mothers (Chapter 3).

Ireland is the only country of the three to have an in-work benefit. The Family Income Supplement is a useful tool for providing financial incentives for parents to enter regular employment (because it is conditional on them working at least 19 hours per week). However, there are some issues surrounding awareness and take-up which need to be addressed to ensure it reaches all eligible families. With lone parent employment rates around half those in the other two countries, this benefit could also be better promoted amongst this

198

group as a route into regular employment. As such, current policy attempts to encourage lone parents into work through earnings disregards in benefits provides financial incentives to top-up benefit income with small earnings as opposed to becoming more closely attached to the labour market. Shifting the policy emphasis for lone parents from earnings disregards in the One Parent Family Payment to the in-work benefit could be part of a strategy to ensure they do not rely on benefit income for long periods of time.

But reducing the expectation of long-term benefit recipiency among new clients of One Parent Family Payment, and a more forceful assistance in employment support policy are needed to change labour market behaviour among many OPFP-clients. There is a need for earlier intervention in Ireland of a more active nature towards OPFP-clients with very young children, including childcare support, while for the existing long-term clientele comprehensive measures to upgrade skills are likely to be necessary. For this to work effectively there would need to be a requirement for lone parents to take advantage of the opportunities open to them, and made available through the increased resources provided by society to help them in this way. A system of mutual obligations should be embraced and enforced. The trend in other countries which have had similarly long duration of lone parent payments as Ireland, has been to combine an expansion of labour market and social support with a greater focus on the duty of lone parents to prepare themselves for employment, and indeed to work, even when their children are still at school. Irish social policy should move in the same direction; it is not in anyone's interest to tolerate passive benefit receipt over many years.

On another angle, labour market policy can complement tax/benefit regimes by helping non-working parents to make the transition into employment. In Austria and Japan, labour market policy is mainly the responsibility of the public employment authorities, whilst there are several actors involved in Ireland and therefore scope for duplication or gaps in coverage. These shortcomings (which may become more apparent with the changing economic fortunes) could be reduced by a clearer definition in the roles of individual players, and perhaps a stronger administrative incentive structure for coordination between them – for example, by enabling social welfare offices to buy services from FÁS.

In Ireland and Japan, programmes specifically for parents are relatively new and may be more successful than existing general initiatives that do not meet parental needs. Various design features could help promote the participation of parents including combining job- and care-matching facilities, and ensuring programmes are sufficiently flexible. To maximise participation, it is important that awareness is raised about these new schemes, and that processes and associated benefits are transparent to those considering taking part. Moreover, schemes need to be closely linked to the labour market so that they do improve job prospects and a significant proportion move into regular employment upon completion. While this generally also applies to Austrian policy, the "Returners Programme" seems to be a successful example that combines many of the necessary design features.

Of course, tax/benefit systems and labour market policy must not be viewed in isolation when considering work decisions. While the Irish tax/benefit system largely supports the work/care choice, this is countered by expensive childcare for those without access to other arrangements, to the extent that it may not be financially worthwhile for second earners to work. This could act as a barrier to further increases in maternal employment rates as informal childcare options become more restricted. Full-time childcare costs are also high in Austria and this, combined with the design of the Childcare Benefit, means that there may be limited or no immediate financial returns to work for low-earning mothers. Childcare costs for parents in Japan are not as large and so have a smaller negative effect on financial incentives. On the other hand, longer-term earnings prospects may encourage parents to work despite limited immediate financial returns. And, ultimately, it is not just financial factors that motivate people to work – available job opportunities and benefits in terms of self-esteem and social contact also play their part.

BABIES AND BOSSES: RECONCILING WORK AND FAMILY LIFE – ISBN 92-64-10418-6 – © OECD 2003

Annex to Chapter 6

Financial returns for second earners

Table 6A.1 presents the detailed information underlying Table 6.1.

Additional information

Income tax (lines 2 to 8). Income tax relief operates solely through tax allowances in Japan, through tax credits in Ireland, and a mixture of the two in Austria. In all three countries there is an element of family-based tax relief (the Japanese tax allowance – in line 2, and Austrian and Irish tax credits – in line 6, for married or head of family), but it is relatively small in Austria. Earned income is taxed on an individual basis in Austria and Japan, whilst Irish families are usually assessed jointly, but can opt for separate assessment (the calculations assume joint assessment). Japan is the only country of the three to have state and local income taxes, the latter varies slightly depending on city size.

Social security contributions (line 9). There is a low-earnings exemption in Austria and Ireland (15% and 59% of APE respectively), and an exemption for low-earning Japanese spouses at 1.3 million yen per annum (equivalent to earnings below 31% of APE) married to workers contributing to employee pension and health insurance. Above these earnings levels, Austrian and Japanese earners pay SSC with respect to all their earnings, whilst in Ireland 26% of APE is exempt. Contributions are subject to a ceiling in Austria – for all contributions (at 164% of APE), and, Ireland – for pension contributions (at 153% of APE), but not in Japan.

Payments for families (line 11). There are various government cash transfers for children in Austria which are added together in line 11: Child Tax Credit (which is paid with family allowance and not related to income tax assessment), Family Allowance and Childcare Benefit. In the other two countries there is one main benefit for those with dependent children included here: Child Benefit in Ireland and Child Allowance in Japan. All the example Japanese families with young children receive the Child Allowance because they are below the earnings threshold (see Background Annex to the Review).

Table 6A.1. **Financial returns for second earners on three levels of earnings**

Detailed payments to and transfers from government at different earnings levels, expressed as a proportion of gross earnings

Wage level (first adult-second adult)	Austria				Ireland				Japan			
	100-0	100-33	100-67	100-100	100-0	100-33	100-67	100-100	100-0	100-33	100-67	100-100
1. Gross wage earnings (USD)	22 543	30 057	37 571	45 086	23 829	31 772	39 715	47 658	33 926	45 234	56 543	67 851
2. Standard tax allowances (%)												
Basic allowance	0.3	0.4	0.3	0.3	–	–	–	–	8.9	13.4	10.7	8.9
Married or head of family	–	–	–	–	–	–	–	–	17.9	–	–	–
Dependent children	–	–	–	–	–	–	–	–	17.9	13.4	10.7	8.9
Deduction for social security contributions and income taxes	18.1	18.1	18.1	18.1	–	–	–	–	10.0	10.0	10.0	10.0
Work-related expenses	0.6	0.8	0.7	0.6	–	–	–	–	32.7	36.0	34.2	32.7
Other	4.6	5.9	5.1	4.6	–	–	–	–	–	–	–	–
Total	23.4	25.1	24.1	23.4	–	–	–	–	87.4	72.8	65.6	60.6
3. Tax credits or cash transfers included in taxable income (%)	–	–	–	–	–	–	–	–	–	–	–	–
4. Central government taxable income (1 – 2 + 3) (%)	76.6	74.9	75.9	76.6	100.0	100.0	100.0	100.0	12.6	27.2	34.4	39.4
5. Central government income tax liability (excl. of tax credits) (%)	15.7	12.8	14.2	15.7	20.0	20.0	20.0	20.0	1.0	2.2	2.8	3.2
6. Tax credits (%)												
Basic credit	3.7	5.6	4.4	3.7	12.0	9.0	7.2	6.0	–	–	–	–
Married or head of family	1.5	0.0	0.0	0.0	3.0	–	–	–	–	–	–	–
Children	a	a	a	a	–	–	–	–	–	–	–	–
Other	1.4	2.2	1.7	1.4	2.6	3.9	3.1	2.6	–	–	–	–
Total	6.7	7.7	6.2	5.1	17.6	12.9	10.3	8.6	–	–	–	–
7. Central government income tax finally paid (5 – 6) (%)	9.0	7.6	8.1	10.6	2.4	7.1	9.7	11.4	1.0	2.2	2.8	3.2
8. State and local taxes (%)	–	–	–	–	–	–	–	–	0.9	1.4	1.7	1.9

Table 6A.1. **Financial returns for second earners on three levels of earnings** (cont.)

Detailed payments to and transfers from government at different earnings levels, expressed as a proportion of gross earnings

Wage level (first adult-second adult)	Austria				Ireland				Japan			
	100-0	100-33	100-67	100-100	100-0	100-33	100-67	100-100	100-0	100-33	100-67	100-100
9. Employees' compulsory social security contributions (%)	18.1	18.1	18.1	18.1	5.0	3.7	3.9	5.0	10.0	10.0	10.0	10.0
10. Total payments to general government (7 + 8 + 9) (%)	27.1	25.6	26.1	28.6	7.3	10.8	13.6	16.4	11.9	13.6	14.4	15.1
11. Cash transfers from general government (%)												
Children aged 1 and 4	38.1	28.6	22.9	8.1	11.1	8.4	6.7	5.6	2.8	2.1	1.7	0.0
Children aged 7 and 9	16.3	12.2	9.8	8.1	11.1	8.4	6.7	5.6	–	–	–	–
12. Take-home pay (1 – 10 + 11) (%)												
Children aged 1 and 4	111.0	103.0	96.7	79.5	103.8	97.5	93.1	89.2	90.9	88.5	87.2	84.9
Children aged 7 and 9	89.2	86.6	83.6	79.5	103.8	97.5	93.1	89.2	88.1	86.4	85.6	84.9
13. Employer's wage dependent contributions and taxes (%)												
Employer's social security contributions	21.7	21.7	21.7	21.7	10.8	10.2	9.9	10.8	10.5	10.5	10.5	10.5
Pay-roll taxes	7.5	7.5	7.5	7.5	–	–	–	–	–	–	–	–
Total	29.2	29.2	29.2	29.2	10.8	10.2	9.9	10.8	10.5	10.5	10.5	10.5

Note: The Irish Home Carer's Tax Credit is included in the 'married or head of family' tax credit in line 6.

a) The Austrian Child Tax Credit is paid with the Family Allowance, and not related to income tax assessment, so is included in line 11 and not line 6. Line 11 includes the Irish Child Benefit rate as of April 2002, taken on a 12 month basis.

Source: Calculations based on OECD (2003f).

The reform of Japanese income tax allowances for dependent spouses

There are currently two different income tax allowances for dependent spouses in Japan. Firstly, where annual spousal earnings are below JPY 1.03 million (USD 8 214), the main earner is eligible for an income tax allowance of JPY 380 000 (USD 3 030). When earnings exceed this limit, this allowance is stopped completely. Secondly, a "special" income tax allowance is available where spousal earnings are below JPY 1.41 million (USD 11 244). This second allowance is a maximum JPY 380 000 (USD 3 030) where spousal earnings are below JPY 0.7 million (USD 5 582), and phased out thereafter. The combined effect of these two tax allowances is to have a gradual phasing out between spousal earnings of JPY 0.7 million (USD 5 582) and JPY 1.41 million (USD 11 244) – as shown in Chart 6A.1. An employed partner facing an income tax rate of 10% (this concerns about 80% of all taxpayers) is entitled to income tax allowances worth a maximum USD 606 per annum, when spousal earnings are below JPY 0.7 million (or USD 5 582).

Chart 6A.1. **Japanese income tax allowances for dependent spouses**

Value (in thousand yens)

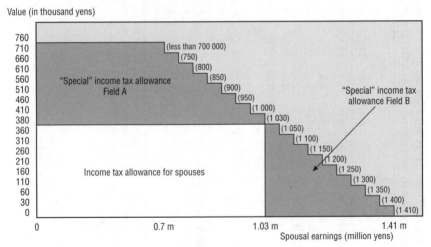

Spousal earnings (million yens)

Source: Japanese authorities.

The special income tax allowance was introduced specifically to overcome distorted financial incentive effects for second earners in families: without it, an increase of annual spousal earnings from, for example, JPY 1.0 million to JPY 1.05 million would generate a decline in overall household income (Tax Bureau, Ministry of Finance, 2002). In view of changing spousal work patterns, income tax reform to be introduced in 2004 will abolish part of the special income tax allowance scheme (Field A in Chart 6A.1), but above the JPY 1.03 million threshold the special tax allowance will continue to be gradually phased out, thereby ensuring that work pays for second earners.

Notes

1. The nature of Austrian family support is also illustrated by equivalence elasticities, which show the high increase in payment rates for an additional household member compared to payments to a single person. For a couple on social assistance, the equivalence elasticity of one child is 0.79 in Austria, compared to 0.38 in Ireland and Japan (Background Annex to the Review). Austrian equivalence elasticities for the presence of additional children in the household are also high when compared to other countries, *e.g.* 0.62 in the Czech republic, 0.39 in Germany and 0.07 in the Netherlands (Adema *et al.*, 2003).

2. The Irish universal Child Benefit was increased by over 50% in Budget 2001 and a further 37% in Budget 2002. A final increase planned for 2003 has now been postponed to 2004 and 2005 because of budgetary pressures.

3. In line with international conventions (OECD, 2002g) the use of the word "tax" refers to both income tax (or any other tax item) *and* social security contributions. If an item solely refers to "income tax", it is specifically identified as such in the discussion.

4. Secretariat simulations of financial incentives at different earnings levels show that the effect of tax/benefit systems for second earners is fairly similar whatever the partner's earning level in Japan, and for those with above APE in Austria and Ireland. The provision of income and/or means-tested benefits may provide some disincentives, especially to second earners in low-income families (see Sections 6.2.2.2 and 6.2.2.3).

5. The threshold for entitlement to the Austrian Childcare Benefit is related to taxable income before deducting special expenses (as opposed to gross earnings), and is slightly different for self-employees and employees. At most, gross earnings (for an employee with a tax-free income of 2%) can be 69% of APE earnings while still receiving the Childcare Benefit payments.

6. In a 22-country study, Bradshaw and Finch (2002) find that Austrian, Irish, and Japanese marginal tax rates before housing and services costs are about average for the 22 countries at various family (with two children) earnings levels in the range of 50 to 140% of average male earnings. Broadly speaking this suggests that tax/benefit systems do not have unusually large distortionary effects on the choice of working hours in these earnings ranges. This study, which was completed prior to the introduction of Childcare Benefit in Austria, therefore broadly confirms the findings in Tables 6.1 and 6.3.

7. The calculations of net payments by couple families to government at different earnings levels in the first *Babies and Bosses* review did not cover children of the same age, but while abstracting from childcare support, Australian, Danish and Netherlands systems are not wildly more generous to families with very young children.

8. Estimates of the costs of childcare refer to the average user fees in the capital of each country.

9. Japanese income tax allowances for dependent spouses are worth more, for employed partners who pay tax at higher rates.

10. Two other (less significant) features further reinforce the financial disincentive effects of health and pension insurance regulations: individuals: a) start paying income tax on earnings above 24% of APE; and b) may pay employment insurance when they work more than 20 hours a week.

11. In general, low-income spouses in Japan pay contributions to Health Insurance and Health and Welfare Pension in proportion to their earnings, if they work more than three-quarters of the working hours of ordinary workers. Those who do not work that many hours, but nevertheless earn more than JPY 1.3 million per annum do have to pay contributions to the "National Pension" insurance proportional to their earnings.

12. The exact marginal effective tax rates faced by Japanese families as spousal earnings increase will vary between families depending on the generosity of employer benefits and the level at which they are withdrawn, the husband's earnings – and therefore the rate at which the husband pays income tax.

13. In Japan, social assistance recipients mainly are elderly or disabled persons (MHW, 1999) whilst in Austria the proportion of families with children among social assistance clients is somewhat higher. For example, in Vienna 3 354 households receiving social assistance had children, out of a total 12 349 recipient households in December 2001.

14. In 2001, employment services' spending on childcare subsidies was EUR 1.7 million in Ireland and EUR 8.4 million in Austria (concerning 9 678 women and 189 men).

15. In Austria, there is a three-phase process for all unemployment benefit recipients, not dissimilar as the set-up of the women returner's programme. The initial phase of the women's returner programme provides more intensive support to clients than contained in the general set-up for unemployment-benefit recipients.

16. Net replacement rates (income net of taxes and benefits when out of work expressed as a proportion of net income in work) for lone parents with two children aged 4 and 6, starting work on two thirds of APE earnings are 74% in Austria, 60% in Ireland and 72% in Japan for UI recipients (OECD, 2003d), and are similar for social assistance recipients. The low Irish NRR reflects the fact that even in work at two thirds of APE, an Irish lone parent is eligible for a considerable lone parent benefit payment (see Chart 6.2) whilst this is not the case in the other two countries.

17. Interestingly this legal obligation on the Austrian public employment services to find work or training for lone parents within four weeks of claiming both Childcare Benefit and unemployment benefit does not apply to other non-working parents, although the public employment services are also expected to find them work or training within four weeks.

18. At low levels of earnings, Irish lone parents are likely to work less than 19 hours and therefore not be entitled to the Family Income Supplement. At higher levels of earnings, they may fulfil the hour conditions, but Family Income Supplement payments would be small because both OPFP and income is taken into account in calculating the amount of FIS.

19. 96% of lone parents on work schemes are in the Community Employment scheme (NESF, 2001). In April 2000, there were 10 000 lone parents participating in CE (DSCFA, 2000).

References

ABE, A. (2002), "Effects of Child-related Benefits in Japan", paper for International Workshop on Low Fertility and Social Policies, 19-22 November, National Institute for Population and Social Security Research, Tokyo.

ADEMA, W. (2001), "Net Social Expenditure, 2nd Edition", Labour Market and Social Policy Occasional Papers, No. 52, OECD, Paris (available in Japanese from *www.ipss.go.jp*).

ADEMA, W., GRAY, D. and KAHL, S. (2003), "Social Assistance in Germany", Labour Market and Social Policy Occasional Papers, No. 58, OECD, Paris.

ADM (2002), *The National Summary of the County Childcare Census 1999/2000*, Area Development Management Limited, Dublin.

AHN, N. and MIRA, P. (2002), "A Note on the Changing Relationship between Fertility and Female Employment Rates in Developed Countries", *Journal of Population Economics*, Vol. 15, pp. 667-682.

AK (2001), *Alleinerzieherinnen in Wien* [Lone Mothers in Vienna], Arbeiterkammer, Vienna.

AK (2001a), *Wirtschafts- und sozialstatistisches Taschenbuch 2001* (Economic and Social Statistics 2001), Arbeiterkammer, Vienna.

AK (2002), *Sozialleistungen im Überblick* (Survey of Social Benefits), ÖGB Verlag, Vienna.

AMINO, T. (2001), *Study on the Effects of Day Care on the Development of Children: Longitudinal Study on the Effect of Infant Day Care*, Sophia University, Japan.

ANTECOL, H. (2000), "An Examination of Cross-country Differences in the Gender Gap in Labour Force Participation Rates", *Labour Economics*, Vol. 7, pp. 409-426.

ARAKI, T. (1999), "1999 Revisions of Employment Security Law and Worker Dispatching Law: Drastic Reforms of Japanese Labor Market Regulations", *Japan Labor Bulletin*, Vol. 38, No. 9, Japan Institute of Labour, Tokyo.

ARAKI, T. (2002), "Re-examining the Role of Labor Unions in the era of the Diversified Workforce", *Japan Labor Bulletin*, Vol. 41, No. 5, Japan Institute of Labour, Tokyo, pp. 6-14.

The Asahi Shimbun (2002), "Overtime Without Pay Still Business as Usual", 3 December.

The Asahi Shimbun (2002a), "Baby Dearth Pushes State to Matchmaking", 19 November.

The Asahi Shimbun (2002b), "Taxpayers at Odds Over Scrapping Spousal Deductions", 6 December.

The Asahi Shimbun (2003), "Analysis: Arrest Regarded as Warning Against Unpaid Overtime", 5 February.

ATOH, M. (2000), "The Coming of a Hyper-aged and Depopulating Society and Population Policies: The Case of Japan", National Institute of Population and Social Security Research, Tokyo.

ATOH, M. (2001), "Very Low Fertility in Japan and Value Change Hypotheses", *Review of Population and Social Policy,* No. 10, pp. 1-21.

BARRETT, A. and CALLAN, T. (eds.), DORIS, A., O'NEILL, D., RUSSELL, H., SWEETMAN, O. and McBRIDE, J. (2000), *How Unequal: Men and Women in the Irish Labour Market,* Economic and Social Research Institute, Dublin.

BECKER, G. (1981), *A Treatise on the Family,* Harvard University Press.

BLANCHET, D. and EKERT-JAFFE, O. (1994), "The Demographic Impact of Fertility Benefits: Evidence from a micro-model and from macro-data", in J. Ermisch and N. Ogawa (eds.), *The Family, the Market and the State in Ageing Societies,* Clarendon Press, Oxford.

BLAU, D. (2002), "An Economic Perspective on Child Care Policy", paper for International Workshop on Low Fertility and Social Policies, 19-22 November at the National Institute for Population and Social Security Research, Tokyo.

BMF (2002), *Austrian Tax Book 2002,* Federal Ministry of Finance, Vienna.

BMUJF (1999), *Österreichischer Familienbericht 1999, Band I* (Austrian Family Report 1999, Part I), Bundesministerium für Umwelt, Jugend und Famile, Vienna.

BMUJF (1999a), *Österreichischer Familienbericht 1999, Band II: Familen- and Arbeitswelt* (Austrian Family Report 1999, Part II: Family and Work), Bundesministerium für Umwelt, Jugend und Famile, Vienna.

BMWA (2002), *Beschäftigung und Einkommen von Frauen und Männern* (Employment and Earnings of Women and Men), Bundesministerium für Wirtschaft und Arbeit, Vienna.

BMSG/BMBWK (2002), *Geschlechstsspezifische Disparitäten* (Gender-specific Disparities), Bundesministerium für soziale Sicherheit und Genrationen and Bundesministerium für Bildung, Wissenschaft und Kultur, Vienna.

BOLING, P. (2002), "Family Support Policies in Japan", memo prepared for seminar on working mothers in Japan at Yale University, 22 July.

BONGAARTS, J. (2002), "The End of the Fertility Transition in the Developed World", *Population and Development Review,* Vol. 28(3), pp. 419-443.

BONGAARTS, J. and FEENEY, G. (1998), "On the Quantum and Tempo of Fertility", *Population and Development Review,* Vol. 24(2), pp. 271-291.

BOOCOCK, S.S. (1995), "Early Childhood Programs in Other Nations: Goals and Outcomes", *The Future of Children,* Vol. 5, No. 3, pp. 95-114.

BRADSHAW, J. and FINCH, N. (2002), *A Comparison of Child Benefit Packages in 22 Countries,* Research Report No. 174, Department for Work and Pensions, London.

BREWSTER, K.L. and RINDFUSS, R.R. (2000), "Fertility and Women's Employment in Industrialized Nations", *Annual Review of Sociology,* Vol. 26, pp. 271-296.

BUBER, I. (2001), "The Effect of the Completion of Education on Entry into Motherhood in Austria. Or: The real educational catch-up effect", paper presented at the 15th Annual Conference of the European Society for Population Economics, 14-16 June, Athens.

CALLAN, T. and DORIS, A. (1999), "Labour Supply Responses", *The Impact of the Minimum Wage in Ireland,* Final Report of the Interdepartmental Group of Implementation of Minimum Wage, Dublin.

CALLAN, T., DEX, S., SMITH, N. and VLASBLOM, J.D. (1999), "Taxation of Spouses: A Cross-Country Study of the Effects on Married Women's Labour Supply", August, Centre for Labour Market and Social Research Working Paper 99-02, University of Aarhus, Denmark.

CALLAN, T. and KEENEY, M. (2002), "Taxes, Benefits and the Financial Incentive to Work: Evolution and Policy Impacts", *Impact Evaluation of the European Employment Strategy in Ireland*, Department of Enterprise, Trade and Employment, Dublin.

CALLAN, T., NOLAN,B., O'NEILL, D. and SWEETMAN, O. (1998), *Female Labour Supply and Income Inequality in Ireland*, National University of Ireland Maynooth, Economics Department Working Papers Series, No. 79/06/98.

CALLAN, T., KEENEY, M., NOLAN, B. and WALSH, J. (2001), *Reforming Tax and Welfare*, October 2001, Policy Research Series No. 42, Economic and Social Research Institute, Dublin.

CASTLES, F.G. (2002), "The World Turned Upside Down: Below-replacement fertility, changing preferences and family-friendly public policy in 21 OECD countries", mimeo, University of Edinburgh.

CHESNAIS, J.C. (1998), "Below-Replacement Fertility in the European Union (EU-15): Facts and Policies, 1960-1997", *Review of Population and Social Policy*, No.7, pp. 83-101.

COLLINS, G. and WICKHAM, J. (2001), "What Childcare Crisis? Irish mothers entering the labour force", Report for the Employment Research Centre Labour Market Observatory, 10 May, Trinity College Dublin.

CORRIGAN, C. (2002), "OECD Thematic Review of Early Childhood Education and Care, Background Report", October, prepared for The Department for Education and Science, Dublin.

CSO (2000), *Quarterly National Household Survey*, Central Statistical Office, Dublin.

CSO (2002), *Quarterly National Household Survey*, Central Statistical Office, Dublin.

DALY, M. and CLAVERO, S. (2002), *Contemporary Family Policy: A comparative review of Ireland, France, Germany, Sweden and the UK*, Institute of Public Administration, Dublin.

DATTA GUPTA, N. and SMITH, N. (2002), "Children and Career Interruptions: the Family Gap in Denmark", *Economica*, Vol. 69, No. 4.

DATTA GUPTA, N., OAXACA, R. and SMITH, N. (2001), "Swimming Upstream, Floating Downstream – Trends in the US and Danish Gender wage gaps", Centre for Labour Market and Social Research, Working Paper 01-06, University of Aarhus, Denmark.

DELOITTE and TOUCHE (1998), *Review of Community Employment Programme*, Final Report for the Department of Enterprise, Trade and Employment, September, Dublin.

DEMENY, P. (1997), "Replacement-Level Fertility: The Implausible Endpoint of the Demographic Transition", in G.W. Jones (ed.), *The Continuing Demographic Transition*, Clarendon Press, Oxford, pp. 94-110.

DENNY, K., HARMON, C. and O'CONNELL, P.J. (2000), *Investing in People*, Policy Research Series No. 38, Economic and Social Research Institute, Dublin.

DETE (2001), *Protection of Employees (Part-time Work) Act, 2001*, No. 45, Department of Enterprise, Trade and Employment, Dublin.

DF (1999), *Budget 2000*, December, Department of Finance, Dublin.

DF (2001), *Budget 2002*, December, Department of Finance, Dublin.

DF (2002), *Economic Review and Outlook 2002*, Department of Finance, Dublin.

DF (2002a), *Budget 2003*, December, Department of Finance, Dublin.

DINGELDEY, I. (2001), "European Tax Systems and Their Impact on Family Employment Patterns", *Journal of Social Policy*, Vol. 30, No. 4.

DJELR (2002), *Report of the Working Group on the Review of the Parental Leave Act 1998*, April, Department of Justice, Equality and Law Reform, Dublin.

DSCFA (2000), *Review of the One-Parent Family Payment*, September, Department of Social, Community and Family Affairs, Dublin.

DSCFA (2001), *Social Welfare Rates of Payment 2002*, December, Department of Social, Community and Family Affairs, Dublin.

DSCFA (2002), *Statistical Information on Social Welfare Services 2001*, Department of Social, Community and Family Affairs, Dublin.

DT (1997), *Partnership 2000*, December, Department of the Taoiseach, Dublin.

DT (2000), *Programme for Prosperity and Fairness*, December, Department of the Taoiseach, Dublin.

DT (2003), *Sustaining Progress*, February, Department of the Taoiseach, Dublin.

EASTERLIN, R. (1980), *Birth and Fortune: The Impact of Numbers on Personal Welfare*, Basic Books, New york (2nd edition, University of Chicago Press, Chicago, 1987).

ECATT (2000), *Benchmarking Progress on New Ways of Working and New Forms of Business across Europe*, August, Electronic Commerce and Telework Trends (funded by the European Commission).

EDIN, P.A. and GUSTAVSSON, M. (2001), "Time out of Work and Skill Depreciation", mimeo, Uppsala University.

EFILWC (2001), *Third European Survey on Working Conditions 2000*, European Foundation for the Improvement of Living and Working Conditions, Dublin.

EIRO (2002), *Annual Review 2001*, European Industrial Relations Observatory, Dublin.

EKERT, O. (1986), "Effets et limites des aides financiers aux familles: une expérience et un modèle", *Population*, Vol. 2, pp. 327-348.

ENGELHARDT, H., KÖGEL, T. and PRSKAWETZ, A. (2001), "Fertility and Female Employment Reconsidered: A macro-level time series analysis", MPIDR Working Paper WP 2001-021, Max Planck Institute for Demographic Research, Rostock.

ESPING-ANDERSEN, G. (1999), *Social foundations of postindustrial economies*, Oxford University Press, Oxford.

ESRI (1997), *Income Support and Work Incentives: Ireland and the UK*, Policy Research Series Paper No. 30, The Economic and Social Research Institute, Dublin.

ESRI (1999), "Monitoring Poverty Trends: Results from the 1997 Living in Ireland Survey", Working Paper No. 140, The Economic and Social Research Institute, Dublin.

ESRI (2002), "Monitoring Poverty Trends: Results from the 2000 Living in Ireland Survey", Policy Research Series No. 45, The Economic and Social Research Institute, Dublin.

EUROPEAN COMMISSION (2001), "Family and Social Situation", *Eurobarometer 56* (EB56.2), Commission of the European Union, Brussels.

EUROSTAT (1999), NewCronos Database, Population scenarios (revision 1999), Luxembourg.

EUROSTAT (1999a), *Household Budget Survey*, Luxembourg.

EUROSTAT (2001), *European Labour Force Survey*, Luxembourg.

EUROSTAT (2002), Demographic data, NewCronos database, Luxembourg.

FAHEY, T. and RUSSELL, H. (2001), "Family Formation in Ireland Trends, Data Needs and Implications", Policy Research Series No. 43, Economic and Social Research Institute, Dublin.

FÁS (2002), *The Irish Labour Market Review 2002*, Training and Employment Authority, Dublin.

FÁS (2002a), FÁS Initiative "Gateway for Women" launched by Minister for Labour Affairs, Mr. Frank Fahey, T.D., press release 19 November 2002, *www.fas.ie*

FINE-DAVIS, M., FAGNANI, J., GIOVANNINI, D., HOJGAARD, L. and CLARK, H. (2002), *Fathers and Mothers: Dilemmas of the Work-Life Balance*, University of Dublin.

FISHER, H. (2000), *Investing in People – Family-friendly arrangements in small and medium sized enterprises*, The Equality Authority, Dublin.

FÖRSTER, M. (2000), "Trends and Driving Factors in Income Distribution and Poverty in the OECD area", Labour Market and Social Policy Occasional Paper Series, No. 42, OECD, Paris.

FÖRSTER, M., REDL, J., TENSCHERT, U. and TILL, M. (2001), "Dimensions of Poverty in Austria in the late 1990s", *Eurosocial Reports*, Vol. 69/01, European Centre for Social Welfare Policy and Research, Vienna.

FREIJKA, T., CALOT, G., SARDON, J.P. and CONFESSON, A. (2001), "Cohort Childlessness and Parity in Low-fertility Countries", paper presented at the European Population Conference 2001, 7-9 June, Helsinki.

FUJIKI, H., KURODA, S. and TACHIBANAKI, T. (2001), "Structural Issues in the Japanese Labor Market: An Era of Variety, Equity, and Efficiency or an Era of Bipolarization?", *Monetary and Economic Studies (Special Edition)*, February, pp. 177-205.

GAUTHIER, A.H. (2001), "The Impact of Public Policies on Families and Demographic Behaviour", paper presented at the ESF/EURESCO conference "The second demographic transition in Europe", Bad Herrenhalb, 23-28 June.

GAUTHIER, A.H. (1996), *The State and the Family; A Comparative Analysis of Family Policies in Industrialized Countries*, Clarendon Press, Oxford.

GAUTHIER, A.H. and HATZIUS, J. (1997), "Family Benefits and Fertility: an econometric analysis", *Population Studies*, Vol. 51(3), pp. 295-306.

GISSER, R., HOLZER, W., MÜNZ, R. and NEBENFÜHR, E. (1995), *Familie und Familienpolitik in Österreich. Wissen, Einstellungen, offene Wünsche, internationaler Vergleich* [Family and Family Policy in Austria], Institute for Demography, Vienna.

GOLDSTEIN, J., LUTZ, W. and TESTA, M.R. (2002), "The Emergence of Sub-replacement Family Size Ideals in Europe", Institute for Demography, Vienna.

GOVERNMENT OF IRELAND (1998), *Strengthening Families for Life: Final Report of the Commission on the Family*, The Stationery Office, Dublin.

GOVERNMENT OF IRELAND (1999), *National Childcare Strategy: Report of the Partnership 2000 Expert Working Group on Childcare*, The Stationery Office, Dublin.

GOVERNMENT OF IRELAND (2000), *Annual Report of the Comptroller and Auditor General and Appropriate Accounts*, Vol. 1, The Stationery Office, Dublin.

GROSS, I. (1995), "Erhebungen über die Zeitverwendung 1981 und 1992" (Survey on Time Use 1981 and 1992), *Statistische Nachrichten*, No. 2, Vienna, pp. 116-121.

GUGER, A. (1996), *Redistribution by the State in Austria*, Austrian Institute of Economic Research (WIFO), Vienna.

GUGER, A. (1998), *Verteilungswirkungen familienpolitisch motivierter Maßnahmen in Österreich* (Distributional Effects of Family-related Instruments in Austria), Austrian Institute of Economic Research (WIFO), Vienna.

GUGER, A. and MUM, D. (1999), *Die Verteilungswirkungen des Familienpakets 1998* (Distributional Effects of the 1998 Family Policy Package), Austrian Institute of Economic Research (WIFO), Vienna.

HAMMER, G. (1997), "Kinderbetreuung – Ausgewählte Hauptergebnisse des Mikrozensus September 1995", *Statistische Nachrichten*, No. 3, Vienna, pp. 168-175.

HAN, W. (2002), "Nonstandard Work Schedules and Child Cognitive Outcomes", paper prepared for the Family and Work Policies Committee of the National Research Council/Institute of Medicine's Board on Children, Youth, and Families, 15 July.

HAN, W., WALDFOGEL, J. and BROOKS-GUNN, J. (2001), "The Effects of Early Maternal Employment on Later Cognitive and Behavioural Outcomes", *Journal of Marriage and the Family*, Vol. 63, No. 2, pp. 336-354.

HANIKA, A (2001), "Bevölkerungsvorausschätzung 2001-2050 für Österreich und die Bundesländer" (Population Projection 2001-2050 for Austria and its Provinces), *Statistische Nachrichten*, No. 9, Vienna, pp. 626-637.

HAUPTVERBAND (various years), *Statistisches Handbuch der österreichischen Sozialversicherung* (Statistical Manual of the Austrian Social Security), Hauptverband der Sozialversicherungsträger, Vienna.

HIRAO, K. (2001), "The Effect of Higher Education on the Rate of Labor-Force Exit for Married Japanese Women", *International Journal of Comparative Sociology*, Vol. 42, No. 5.

HIRAO, K. (2002), "Privatized Education Market and Maternal Employment in Japan", paper prepared for the Workshop of Childcare and Maternal Employment in Japan, Yale University, 22 July.

HIROSIMA, K. (2001), "Decomposing Recent Fertility Decline: How Have Nuptiality and Marital Fertility Affected it in Japan?", paper presented at the IUSSP Seminar on "International Perspectives on Low Fertility: Trends, Theories and Policies", Tokyo, 21-23 March.

HOEM, B. (2000), "Entry into Motherhood in Sweden: the influence of economic factors on the rise and all in fertility, 1986-1997", *Demographic Research*, Vol. 2, Article 4.

IBEC (2000), *Family-Friendly/Work-Life Balance Policies*, Irish Business and Employers Confederation, Dublin, December.

IBEC (2001), *National Survey on conditions of Employment for the Manufacturing and Wholesale Distribution Sectors*, Irish Business and Employers Confederation (survey for IBEC members), Dublin, September.

IBEC (2002), *Women in Management in Irish Business*, Irish Business and Employers Confederation, Dublin, March.

IBEC (2002a), *Human Resources Management Survey 2002*, Irish Business and Employers Confederation, Dublin, July.

ICTU (2002), *Identifying Member's Childcare Needs,* Irish Congress of Trade Unions, Dublin.

ILO (2003), "Laborsta", Database on Labour Statistics, International Labour Organisation, Geneva.

IWASAWA, M. (2001), "Partnership Transition in Contemporary Japan: Prevalence of Childless Non-Cohabiting Couples", paper presented at the IUSSP Conference on "International Perspectives on Low Fertility: Trends, theories, policies", Tokyo, 21-23 March.

The Japan Times (2002), "The Thorny Topic of 'Office Flowers'", 16 December.

JIL (1993), "Working Conditions and the Labour Market", *Japan Labor Bulletin,* Vol. 32, No. 6, Japan Institute of Labour, Tokyo.

JIL (2002), "Working Conditions and the Labour Market", *Japan Labor Bulletin,* Vol. 41, No. 7, Japan Institute of Labour, Tokyo.

JIL (2002a), "Number of Dispatched Workers in FY 2000 Jumps 30% from Previous Year", *Japan Labor Bulletin,* Vol. 41, No. 4, Japan Institute of Labour, Tokyo.

JIL (2002b), *Japan Labor Bulletin,* Vol. 41, No. 6, Japan Institute of Labour, Tokyo.

JIL (2002c), *Japan Labor Bulletin,* Vol. 41, No. 8, Japan Institute of Labour, Tokyo.

JIWE (1995), *Survey on Work,* Japan Institute of Workers' Evolution.

JIWE (2000), *Survey on Female Sougou-shoku Workers' Condition*, Japan Institute of Workers' Evolution.

JIWE (2001), *Survey on Atypical Work,* Japan Institute of Workers' Evolution.

JTUC (2002), *Rengo's Survey on Life 2002,* Japanese Trade Union Confederation.

JTUC (2002a), *The Spring Struggle for a Better Life 2002,* Rengo White Paper, Japanese Trade Union Confederation.

JTUC (2003), *The Spring Struggle for a Better Life 2003,* Rengo White Paper, Japanese Trade Union Confederation.

KAMERMAN, S., NEUMAN, S., WALDFOGEL, J. and BROOKS-GUNN, J. (2003), "Social Policies, Family Types, and Child Outcomes in Selected OECD Countries", OECD Social, Employment and Migration Working Papers, forthcoming.

KATO, H. (2000), "Econometric Analysis on Childbirth, Marriage and Labour Market" [Shussei, Kekkon oyobi Roudou Shijyou no Keiryou Bunseki], *Population Study Vol. 56(1)*, National Institute of Population and Social Security Research, Tokyo.

KAWAGUCHI, A. (2001), "Women's Marriage Premium – Effects of Marriage and Child Birth on Employment and Wage", *Quarterly Journal of Research on Household Economics,* No. 51, Institute for Research on Household Economics, Tokyo.

KAWAGUCHI, A. (2002), "Family-Friendly Policies and Equal Opportunity Policies", *The Japanese Journal of Labour Studies,* No. 503, Japan Institute of Labour, Tokyo.

KEZUKA, K. (2000), "Legal Problems Concerning Part-time Work in Japan", *Japan Labor Bulletin,* Vol. 39, No. 9, Japan Institute of Labour, Tokyo.

KIELY, G. (2000), "Ireland: Low Fertility", Contribution to the European Observatory on Family Matters, Vienna (Focus monitoring 2000: Fertility).

KIERNAN, K. (1999), "Childbearing Outside Marriage in Western Europe", *Population Trends,* Vol. 98, pp. 11-20.

KOHLER, H.P., BILLARI, F. and ORTEGA, J.A. (2001), "Towards a Theory of Lowest-Low Fertility", Working Paper 2001-032, Max Planck Institute for Demographic Research, Rostock.

KOHLER, H.P. and ORTEGA, J.A. (2002), "Tempo-adjusted Period Parity Progression Measures, Fertility Postponement and Completed Cohort Fertility", *Demographic Research*, Vol. 6, Article 6.

KÖGEL, T. (2002), "Did the Association Between Fertility and Female Employment within OECD Countries Really Change its Sign?", Max Planck Institute for Demographic Research, Rostock.

KRAVDAL, Ø. (1996), "How the Local Supply of Day-care Centers Influences Fertility in Norway: A parity-specific approach", *Population Research and Policy Review*, Vol. 15(3), pp. 201-218.

LEHNER, U. and PRAMMER-WALDHÖR, M. (2002), "Wie gut gelingt die erneute Beschäftigungsintegration nach der Elternkarenz?" (How Successful is Work Re-integration after Parental Leave?), *Kurzbericht 1/02*, Synthesis Forschung, Vienna.

LESTHAEGE, R. (2000), "Europe's Demographic Issues: Fertility, household formation and replacement migration", Interuniversity Papers in Demography, WP 2000-6, Vrije Universiteit Brussel.

LESTHAEGE, R. and MOORS, G. (1996), "Living Arrangements, Socio-economic Position and Values among Young Adults: a pattern description of France, West Germany, Belgium and the Netherlands 1990", in D. Coleman (ed.), *Europe's Population in the 1990s*, Oxford University Press, Oxford, pp. 163-221.

LUTZ, H. (2003), "Auswirkungen der Kindergeldregelung auf die Beschäftigung von Frauen mit Kleinkindern", Austrian Institute of Economic Research (WIFO), Vienna.

LUTZ, W. (2000), "Determinants of Low Fertility and Ageing Prospects for Europe", in S. Trnka (ed.), *Family Issues Between Gender and Generations*, Seminar Report, European Observatory of Family Matters, Vienna, pp. 49-65.

MAHON, E., CONLON, C. and DILLON, D. (1998), "Women and Crisis Pregnancy", Report presented to the Department of Health and Children, The Stationery Office, Dublin.

MASON, K., OPPENHEIM, N. TSUYA et M.K. CHOE (eds.) (1998), *The Changing Family in Comparative Perspective: Asia and the US*, East-West Center, Honolulu.

McDONALD, P. (2000), "Gender Equity in Theories of Fertility Transition", *Population and Development Review*, Vol. 26(3), pp. 427-439.

McDONALD, P. (2000a), "Gender Equity, Social Institutions and the Future of Fertility", *Journal of Population Research*, Vol. 17(1), pp. 1-16.

McDONALD, P. (1996), "Demographic Life Transitions: an alternative theoretical paradigm", *Health Transition Review*, Supplement 6, pp. 385-392.

MHLW (2001), *Basic Survey on Wage Structure*, Ministry of Health, Labor and Welfare, Tokyo.

MHLW (2001a), *Basic Survey on the Employment of Women*, Ministry of Health, Labor and Welfare, Tokyo.

MHLW (2001b), *National Survey of Lone Parent Households*, Ministry of Health, Labor and Welfare, Tokyo.

MHLW (2001c various), *Monthly Labour Survey*, Ministry of Health, Labor and Welfare, Tokyo.

MHLW (2001d), *Survey on Wage Increase*, Ministry of Health, Labor and Welfare, Tokyo.

MHLW (2001e), *Report on Correction of So-called "Service Over-time Work" by Supervised Inspection*, Labour Standards Inspection Office, Ministry of Health, Labor and Welfare, Tokyo.

MHLW (2001f), *Survey on Employment Trends*, Ministry of Health, Labor and Welfare, Tokyo.

MHLW (2001g), *Vital Statistics*, Ministry of Health, Labor and Welfare, Tokyo.

MHLW (2001h), *Survey on Social Welfare Institutions*, Ministry of Health, Labor and Welfare, Tokyo.

MHLW (2001i), *General Survey on Wages and Working Hours*, Ministry of Health, Labor and Welfare, Tokyo.

MHLW (2002), *Basic Survey on the Employment of Women*, Ministry of Health, Labor and Welfare, Tokyo.

MHLW (2002a), *General Survey on Working Conditions 2002*, Ministry of Health, Labor and Welfare, Tokyo.

MHLW (2002b), *General Survey on Part-time Workers 2001*, Ministry of Health, Labor and Welfare, Tokyo.

MHLW (2002c), *Vision and Viewpoint on the Framework of Pension Reform*, Ministry of Health, Labor and Welfare, Tokyo.

MHLW (2002d), *General Survey on Working Conditions*, Ministry of Health, Labor and Welfare, Tokyo.

MHLW (2002e), *Present Situation of Working Women and Equal Employment Opportunity Policies in Japan*, Ministry of Health, Labor and Welfare, Tokyo.

MHLW (2003), Report by "Expert committee on society where people can work regardless of age", Ministry of Health, Labor and Welfare, Tokyo.

MHW (1998), *White Paper on Health and Welfare for 1998: Reflecting a society with fewer children to build a society where people can have dreams to bear and rear children*, Ministry of Health and Welfare, Tokyo.

MHW (1998a), *A Society with a Decreasing Population: Responsibilities and Choices for the Future*, Policy Planning and Evaluation Division of Minister's Secretariat, Ministry of Health and Welfare, Tokyo, Gyosei.

MOL (1991), *Survey on Employment Trends*, Ministry of Labor, Tokyo.

MOL (1997), *General Survey on Part-time Workers 1995*, Ministry of Labor, Tokyo.

MOL (1997a), *General Survey on Working Hours and Salaries*, Ministry of Labor, Tokyo.

MOL (1997b), *Report on the Results of the 1996 Survey on Women Workers' Employment Management*. Women's Bureau Investigation Paper No. 28, Ministry of Labour, Tokyo.

MOL (1999), *Basic Survey on the Employment of Women 1999*, Ministry of Labor, Tokyo.

MOL (1999a), *General Survey on Working Hours and Salaries*, Ministry of Labor, Tokyo.

MOL (2000), *Basic Policy on Measures for Gender Equality in Employment Opportunities*, Ministry of Labor, Tokyo.

MOL Study Group on Human Resource Management (1999), "Interim Report of the Working Group on Corporate Management and Employment Practice", Ministry of Labor, Tokyo.

MOL and JIWE (2000), *Employment Management Study Group on Part-time Work Report*, Ministry of Labor (Women's Bureau), Tokyo and Japan Institute of Workers' Evolution.

MORISHIMA, M. (2002): "Pay Practices in Japanese Organizations: Changes and Non-changes", *Japan Labor Bulletin*, Vol. 41, No. 4, Japan Institute of Labour, Tokyo, pp. 8-13.

MCA (1990), *Labour Force Survey*, Management and Coordination Agency, Tokyo.

MCA (1996), *Survey on Time Use and Leisure Activities*, Management and Coordination Agency, Tokyo.

MPMHAPT (2001), *Special Survey of the Labour Force Survey*, Ministry of Public Management, Home Affairs, Posts and Telecommunications, Tokyo.

MPMHAPT (2001a), *Survey on Time Use and Leisure Activities*, Ministry of Public Management, Home Affairs, Posts and Telecommunications, Tokyo.

MPMHAPT (2002), *Labour Force Survey*, Statistics Bureau, Ministry of Public Management, Home Affairs, Post and Telecommunications, Tokyo.

MPMHAPT (2002a), *Family Income and Expenditure Survey*, Ministry of Public Management, Home Affairs Post, and Telecommunications, Tokyo.

NAGASE, N. (2002), "Wife Allowance and Tax Exemption behind Low Wages for Part-time Workers", *Japan Labor Bulletin*, Vol. 41, No. 9, Japan Institute of Labour, Tokyo.

NATIONAL FORUM SECRETARIAT (1998), *Report on the National Forum for Early Childhood Education*, The Stationery Office, Dublin.

NESF (1997), *A Framework for Partnership- Enriching Strategic Consensus through Participation*, Forum Report No. 16, December, The National Economic and Social Forum, Dublin.

NESF (2001), *Lone Parents*, Forum Report No. 20, July, The National Economic and Social Forum, Dublin.

NIKKEIREN (2001), *The Current Labor Economy in Japan*, Japan Federation of Employers' Associations, Tokyo.

NIPSSR (1997), *Basic Survey on Fertility 1997*, National Institute of Population and Social Security Research, Tokyo.

NIPSSR (2000), *The Second National Family Survey 1998*, National Institute of Population and Social Security Research, Tokyo.

NIPSSR (2002), Population Projection for Japan 2001-2050. With long-range population projection 2051-2100, January, National Institute of Population and Social Security Research Tokyo.

NIPSSR (2002a), *Social Security in Japan 2002-3*, National Institute of Population and Social Security Research, Tokyo.

NOACK, T. and ØSTBY, L. (2002), "Free to Choose – But Unable to Stick With It?, Norwegian fertility expectations and subsequent behaviour for the following 20 years", in E. Klijzing. and M. Corijn (eds.), *Fertility and Partnership in Europe: findings and lessons from comparative research*, Vol. II, United Nations, Geneva/New York.

O'CONNELL, P.J. (2002), "Adaptability – Flexible Working Arrangements", *Impact Evaluation of the European Employment Strategy in Ireland*, Department of Enterprise, Trade and Employment, Dublin.

O'CONNELL, P.J., McGINNITY, F. and RUSSELL, H. (2003), "Working Time Flexibility in Ireland", in J. O'Reilly (ed.), *Regulating Working-time Transitions in Europe*, Edward Elgar, Cheltenham, UK, forthcoming.

O'DONNELL, R. and O'REARDON, C. (1997), "Ireland's Experiment in Social Partnership 1987-96", *Social Pacts in Europe*, European Trade Union Institute, Brussels, pp. 79-95.

O'DONNELL, R. and O'REARDON, C. (2000), "Social Partnership in Ireland's Economic Transformation", *Social Pacts in Europe – New Dynamics*, European Trade Union Institute, Brussels, pp. 237-256.

O'DONNELL, R. and THOMAS, D. (2002), "Ireland in the 1990s: Policy Concertation Triumphant", in S. Berger and H. Compton (eds.), *Policy Concertation and Social Partnership in Western Europe*, Berghan Books, New York/Oxford, pp. 167-190.

OECD (2000), *Employment Outlook*, Paris.

OECD (2001), *Economic Surveys – Ireland*, Paris.

OECD (2001a), *OECD Social Expenditure Database*, CD-ROM, Paris.

OECD (2001b), *Starting Strong: Early Childhood Education and Care*, Paris.

OECD (2001c), *Economic Surveys – Austria*, Paris.

OECD (2002), *Economic Outlook*, No. 72, Paris.

OECD (2002a), *National Accounts of OECD Countries, Main Aggregates – Vol. 1, 1989-2000*, Paris.

OECD (2002b), *Economic Surveys – Japan*, Paris.

OECD (2002c), *OECD Employment Outlook*, Paris.

OECD (2002d), *Labour Force Statistics*, Paris.

OECD (2002e), *Education at a Glance*, Paris.

OECD (2002f), *Babies and Bosses – Vol. 1, Australia, Denmark and the Netherlands*, Paris.

OECD (2002g), *Revenue Statistics 1965-2001*, Paris.

OECD (2002h), *Society at a Glance: OECD Social Indicators*, Paris.

OECD (2003), *Economic Outlook*, No. 73, Paris.

OECD (2003a), *Main Economic Indicators*, Paris.

OECD (2003b), *OECD Database on Population and Labour Force Projections*, Paris, forthcoming.

OECD (2003c), *Ageing and Employment Policies: Japan*, Paris.

OECD (2003d), *Trends in International Migration*, Paris.

OECD (2003e), *Benefits and Wages: OECD Indicators – 2003 Edition*, Paris.

OECD (2003f), *Taxing Wages – 2003 Edition*, Paris.

OGAWA, N. and RETHERFORD, R. (1993), "The Resumption of Fertility Decline in Japan; 1973-92", *Population and Development Review*, Vol. 19(4), pp. 703-741.

OISHI, A.S. (2002), "The Effect of Childcare Costs on Mothers'Labor Force Participation", *Journal of Population and Social Security*, pp. 50-65.

ONO, H. and REBICK, M.E. (2002), "Impediments to the Productive Employment of Labor in Japan", SSE/EFI Working paper Series in Economics and Finance, No. 500.

OPPENHEIM MASON, K., TSUYA, N. and CHOE, M.K. (eds.) (1998), The Changing Family in Comparative Perspective: Asia and the US, East-West Center, Honolulu.

ORTEGA, J.A. and KOHLER, H.P. (2002), "Measuring Low Fertility: Rethinking demographic methods", Working Paper 2002-001, Max Planck Institute for Demographic Research, Rostock.

OSAWA, M. (2001), "People in Irregular Modes of Employment: Are they really not subject to discrimination" Social Science Japan Journal, Vol. 4, No. 2, pp. 183-199.

ÖSTAT (1992), "Berufsunterbrechungen. Ergebnisse des Mikrozensus 1990" (Career Interruptions. Results of the 1990 microcensus), Beiträge zur österreichischen Statistik, Heft 1044, Vienna.

Österreichische Bundesregierung (2003), "Regierungsprogramm für die XXII. Gesetzgebungsperiode" (Government Programme for the XXII Session), Vienna.

OUCHI, S. (2000), "Telework in Japan", Japan Labor Bulletin, Vol. 39, No. 8, Japan Institute of Labour, Tokyo.

PEARSON, M. and SCARPETTA, S. (2000), "An Overview: What do we know about policies to make work pay?", OECD Economic Studies, No. 31, OECD, Paris.

PRINZ, C. (1995), Cohabiting, Married, or Single, Avebury, Aldershot.

POOCOCK, B. (2001) "The Effect of Long Hours on Family and Community Life: A Survey of Existing Literature", August, Center for Labour Research, Adelaide University, Adelaide, Australia.

RETHERFORD, R., OGAWA, N. and MATSUKURA, R. (2001), "Late Marriage and Less Marriage in Japan", Population and Development Review, Vol. 27(1), pp. 65-102.

RETHERFORD, R., OGAWA, N. and SAKAMOTO, S. (1999), "Values and Fertility Change in Japan", in R. Leete (ed.), Dynamics of Values in Fertility Change, Oxford University Press, Oxford, pp. 121-147.

RØNSEN, M. (1999), "Impacts on Fertility and Female Employment of Parental Leave Programs. Evidence from Three Nordic Countries", paper presented at the European Population Conference, 30 August–3 September, The Hague.

ROWLAND, D. (1998), "Cross-National Trends in Childlessness", Working Papers in Demography No. 73, Australian National University, Canberra.

RUHM, C. (2000), "Parental Employment, and Child's Cognitive Development", NBER Working Paper 6554, National Bureau of Economic Research, Cambridge, MA.

RUSSELL, H., SMYTH, E., LYONS, M. and O'CONNELL, P.J. (2002), Getting out of the House: women returning to employment, education and training, Liffey Press in association with the Economic and Social Research Institute, Dublin.

SATO, H. (2001), "Is Atypical Employment a flexible form of Working Life", Japan Labor Bulletin, Vol. 40, No. 4, Japan Institute of Labour, Tokyo.

SCHATTOVITS, H. (2000), Kinderbetreuungsscheck: Modellentwicklung und Analysen, Austrian Institute of Economic Research (WIFO), Vienna.

SHIRAHASE, S. (2002), "Women's Working Pattern and the Support to Working Mothers in Contemporary Japan", Working Paper Series No. 14, National Institute of Population and Social Security Research, Tokyo.

SOCIAL POLICY BUREAU (1999), *National Survey on Lifestyle Preferences F.Y. 1997, People's Life Indicators F.Y. 1998*, Social Policy Bureau, Economic Planning Agency, Government of Japan.

STEWART, W. and BARLING, J. (1996), "Fathers' Work Experiences Effect Children's Behaviours via Job-related and Parenting Behaviours", *Journal of Organisational Behaviour*, Vol. 17, pp. 221-232.

SUZUKI, T. (2001), "Leaving the Parental Household in Contemporary Japan", *Review of Population and Social Policy*, No. 10, pp. 23-35.

TAKAYAMA, N. *et al.* (2000), "Economic Costs of Marriage, Child Rearing and Fertility (Syussan Ikuji no Keizai Kosto to Syusseiryoku)", *Population Study*, Vol. 56(4), National Institute of Population and Social Security Research, Tokyo.

TAX BUREAU, MINISTRY OF FINANCE (2002), *An Outline of Japanese Taxes 2001–2002*, Japanese Ministry of Finance, Tokyo.

TAX COMMISSION (2002), *Policy Guidance on the Establishment of a Desirable Tax System*, June, The Tax Commission, Tokyo.

TCD (2002), *Off the Treadmill: Achieving Work/Life Balance*, October, Report for the Family Friendly Framework Committee, Trinity College Dublin.

TSUYA, N., BUMPASS, L. and CHOE, M.K. (2000), "Gender, Employment and Housework in Japan, South Korea, and the United States", *Review of Population and Social Policy*, No. 9, pp. 195-220.

UENO, C. (1998), "The Declining Birthrate: Whose Problem?", *Review of Population and Social Policy*, No. 6, pp. 103-128.

VAN IMHOFF, E. (2001), "On the Impossibility of Inferring Cohort Fertility Measures from Period Fertility Measures", *Demographic Research*, Vol. 5, Article 2.

WAKISAKA, A. (2002), "Work-sharing in Japan", *Japan Labor Bulletin*, Vol. 41, No. 6, Japan Institute of Labour, Tokyo, pp. 7-13.

WALDFOGEL, J., HIGUCHI, Y. and ABE, M. (1998), "Maternity Leave Policies and Women's Employment after Childbirth: Evidence from the United States, Britain and Japan", Centre for Analysis of Social Exclusion, London.

WALDFOGEL, J., HAN, W.J. and BROOKS-GUNN, J. (2002), "The Effects of Early Maternal Employment on Child Cognitive Development", *Demography*, Vol. 39, No. 2.

WALKER, J.R. (1995), "The Effect of Public Policies on Recent Swedish Fertility Behaviour", *Journal of Population Economics*, Vol. 8(3), pp. 223-251.

WEATHERS, C. (2001), "Changing White-collar Workplaces and Female temporary workers in Japan", *Social Science Japan Journal*, Vol. 4, pp. 201-218.

ZA (1990), *International Social Survey Programme 1998: Family and Sex Roles*, Zentralarchiv für Empirische Sozialforschung, Universität zu Köln.

ZA (1997), *International Social Survey Programme 1994: Family and Gender Changing Roles II*, March, Zentralarchiv für Empirische Sozialforschung, Universität zu Köln.

ZHOU, Y. and OISHI, A.S. (2002), "Latent Demand for Licensed Childcare Service in Japan", paper presented at the 2002 Japanese Economic Conference, Hiroshima University, Japan.

ZHOU, Y., OISHI, A.S. and UEDA, A. (2002), "Childcare System in Japan", paper for International Workshop on Low Fertility and Social Policies, 19-22 November at the National Institute for Population and Social Security Research, Tokyo.

Background Annex to the Review

This annex gives a more detailed description of public family spending (Section A1), child-related leave schemes (Section A2), and the main family benefit programmes (Section A3).

Average earnings and exchange rates

Throughout, "average earnings" refer to the annual earnings of an Average Production Employee (APE). This concept refers to the average gross wage earnings of adult, full-time workers in the manufacturing sector in each country. In 2002, these were EUR 23 963 (USD 22 543) in Austria, EUR 25 330 (USD 23 829) in Ireland and JPY 4 254 270 (USD 33 926) in Japan (OECD, 2003e *forthcoming*).

The exchange rate used is the average of the daily rates in 2002, with USD 1 equivalent to EUR 1.063 and JPY 125.4 (OECD, 2002).

Purchasing power parities (PPP) eliminate the difference in price levels between countries. This report uses OECD estimates, with PPP per USD equal to EUR 0.910 in Austria, EUR 0.989 in Ireland and JPY 150 (OECD, 2003).

A1. Public Family Spending

In 2001, public family spending as a proportion of GDP was highest in Austria at 3.27%, around OECD average at 2.1% in Ireland and lowest in Japan at 0.88% (Table A1). The majority of family spending in Austria and Ireland is in the form of cash benefits with 31% and 23% respectively spent on family services. The reverse is true in Japan, where cash benefits are a smaller proportion of overall public family spending, and 70% of spending is on family services.

A2. Leave programmes

All three countries have some form of maternity and parental leave while none of them have compulsory paternity leave regulations. Table A2 describes the main characteristics of existing child-related leave schemes. Maternity leave provisions are similar across the three countries: there is a cash benefit for those on maternity leave, and the maximum length of paid leave is

Table A1. **Variation in public family spending**

Percentage of GDP, 2001

	Austria	Ireland	Japan
Cash benefits[a]			
Maternity benefit	0.15	0.07	0.10
Childcare (leave) benefit	0.22	–	0.01
Lone parent benefit	–	0.60	0.06
Family allowance and other cash benefits	1.89	0.97	0.09
Total	2.26	1.64	0.26
Services			
Childcare services	0.43	0.07	0.22
Pre-school services	–	0.25	0.10
Other services	0.58	0.16	0.30
Total	1.01	0.48	0.62
Total public family spending	3.27	2.12	0.88
Share of services in % of total	31	23	70

– No Lone parent benefit in Austria and no childcare leave benefit in Ireland. In Austria, there are no pre-school services. Children are in childcare.
a) The value of family tax allowances and tax credits (with the exception of the Austrian Child Tax Credit) are not included in these calculations.
Source: OECD Secretariat calculations from information supplied by national authorities and OECD (2001a).

16 weeks in Austria, 18 weeks in Ireland and 14 weeks in Japan. In Ireland, a further eight weeks of unpaid maternity leave is available.

There is far more variation in parental leave provisions. The Austrian system was reformed in 2002, separating leave entitlement from income support (Chapter 5). The former is within the jurisdiction of Labour law and provides for employment-protected leave until the child's second birthday. Meanwhile, the Childcare Benefit is no longer related to the leave period and generally lasts for 30 months and is an income-tested benefit paid to parents of young children irrespective of their previous employment status (Section A3). In Ireland, each parent is entitled to 14 weeks employment-protected parental leave, with no public income support. In Japan, employment-protected parental leave lasts until the child's first birthday. Japanese parents taking leave receive 30% of their previous wage during leave (paid through Employment Insurance), and an additional payment worth further 10% which is paid as a lump sum if they return to work for at least six months.

In Austria and Ireland, all workers are eligible for some leave to care for sick children, lasting a maximum 2 weeks in Austria per annum (where children are under 12), whilst Irish force majeure leave is a maximum 5 days in three consecutive years. In Japan, employers are obliged to endeavour to provide such leave for pre-school children.

Table A2. **Major characteristics of child-related leave schemes, 2002**

	Austria	Ireland	Japan
	Maternity leave		
Eligibility	Currently in covered employment.	In covered employment for at least 10 weeks (employees and self-employed) and 39 weeks of paid contributions.	Currently in covered employment (employees and self-employed).
Duration	8 weeks before and 8 weeks after confinement; work during this period is prohibited.	18 weeks of paid leave in total; work is prohibited four weeks before and four weeks after confinement; an additional 8 weeks of unpaid maternity leave is available.	6 weeks before and 8 weeks after confinement; work prohibited until six weeks after confinement.
Cash benefit	100% of average earnings of the last 3 months paid through Health Insurance (average benefit of EUR 1 050 per month).	70% of gross earnings subject to a minimum net payment of EUR 135.60 and a maximum net payment of EUR 232.40 paid through health insurance (just under half of APE).	60% of average standard earnings paid through health insurance.
	Parental leave		
Eligibility	Currently in covered employment.	One year of continuous service with the current employer (individual entitlement for either parent).	One year continuous service with the current employer; several groups of workers are excluded (*e.g.* working less than three days per week or having a fixed-term contract or having a spouse that can take care of the child).
Duration	Up to the second birthday (three months can be deferred until school age), or, with employers consent, part-time work for up to 48 months.	14 working weeks for each parent (for twins, 14 weeks for each parent for each child), to be taken as a block or, with employers consent, in a broken format until child reaches age 5.	Until one day before child's first birth day, *i.e.* 44 weeks, to be taken by one of the two parents (no possibility to split the entitlement).
Cash benefit	No payment under parental leave legislation, but leave-taker may receive the income-tested Childcare Benefit of EUR 436 for 30-36 months.	Unpaid leave.	30% of the employee's wage plus another 10% (of their annual wage) after returning to work.
	Nursery leave (*force majeure* leave in Ireland)		
Eligibility	Currently employed; care for a sick child or close relative, or in cases where the normal carer is ill.	Currently employed; urgent family reasons owing to the injury or illness of a child or a close relative.	Employers are obliged to endeavour to introduce nursery leave for children under the school age (in 1999, 11% of all companies had such a system).
Duration	One week per year, or two weeks per year if child is under age 12.	Three days per year up to a limit of five days in three consecutive years.	Not legally determined, in practice a few days per year.
Cash benefit	Full wage payment.	Full wage payment.	Full wage payment.

Source: National authorities.

A3. Family benefits

Family benefits subsidise some of the costs associated with child-rearing, and are particularly important for low-income families. Table A3 describes the main family benefit programmes, and Table A4 gives the rates of payment. Maximum family payments are most generous in Austria and lowest in Japan.

The similarity across the three countries is that they all recognize the extra costs faced by large families – with higher benefit rates for third and subsequent children. Otherwise the main differences between countries in the nature of public income support for families are:

● The main Japanese benefit (child allowance) is only payable to those with children aged under 6, whilst most Austrian (with the notable exception of the Childcare Benefit) and all Irish family benefits are payable to those with older children. Austria is the only country to have benefit rates that vary with the age of children.

● In both Austria and Ireland there is a mixture of universal and income-tested family benefits, whilst in Japan most financial support for families is income-tested. The main Austrian income-tested benefit is the Childcare Benefit for those with very young children, which is only paid if the annual earnings of one parent are below EUR 14 600. In Ireland, the Family Income Supplement is an income-tested in-work benefit, but it is relevant to relatively few families – with only 11 570 recipients in 2001 (DSCFA, 2002).

● The treatment of lone parent varies: in Austria there are no specific lone parent benefits provided by central government, in Ireland there is a benefit for lone parents, and in Japan there is a benefit for lone mothers.

In Japan, financing of the child allowance is split between national and local authorities, and employers. The relative contributions vary according to whether the child is older or younger than three years old and differ for non-employees, employees and public servants. As well as paying a portion of child allowances, some employers pay benefits for those with dependents – as detailed in Table A5. Just over three-quarters of companies provide family benefits, and half provide benefits for spouses – the latter are mostly only provided if the spouse has limited earnings. These are generally only paid to the head of household or main earner (MHLW, 2002).

Table A3. **Main family benefit programmes, 2002**

	Recipient group	Features
Austria		
Childcare Benefit	Families with children aged up to 30/36 months if individual income of parent receiving the benefit does not exceed EUR 14 600 per year.	Per family, individual income includes earnings and other income of the receiving parent. Payable for 30 months if one parent receives the benefit, or 36 months if parents alternate. Low-income and single parent families may be eligible for a (loan) supplement, which has to be re-paid once earnings increase. Non-taxable.
Child Tax Credit	All families with dependent children. Paid for all children up to the age of 18, and for those aged 19-26 and in full-time education.	Per child, paid with family allowance. Not income-tested, non-taxable.
Family Allowance	All families with dependent children. Paid for all children up to the age of 18, and for those aged 19-26 and in full-time education.	Per child, age-related payment. Not income-tested, non-taxable.
Sole Earner's and Sole Parent's tax credits	Single- or no-earner, families with dependent children, and those with low second incomes.	Per family, income test on second earner, non-taxable. Can be paid as a negative income tax.
Ireland		
Child Benefit	All families with dependent children. Paid for all children under the age of 16, and for those aged 16-18 and in full-time education.	Per child, higher rate for third and subsequent children. Not income-tested, non-taxable.
Family Income Supplement	Low-income working families with dependent children.	Income-tested, paid to families with earnings around 80% of APE. Exact threshold and amount depends on family size. The individual or couple must be employed for at least 19 hours per week between them. Non-taxable.
Home Carer's Tax Credit	One-earner married couple families with dependent children, and those with low second incomes.	Per family, income test applies to second income only. Paid only to couples filing for joint tax assessment (except those claiming the increased standard rate tax band), where one parent works at home to care for children (or other relatives). Non-taxable.
One Parent Family Payment	Low-income single parents with dependent children. Payable to lone parents with children under the age of 18, or aged 18-22 and in full-time education.	A personal rate with increases for each dependent child. Income-tested, non-taxable. Earnings up to one-third of APE completely disregarded.
Japan		
Childbirth Allowance	Paid at the birth of a child to all families.	Lump sum payment, twice the usual amount is paid for twins. Not income-tested, non-taxable.
Child Allowance	All families with children aged under 6, except high-income families.	Income-tested, paid to 85% of families with children aged under 6. Non-taxable. Per child, higher rate for third and subsequent children.
Child Rearing Allowance	Low-income lone mothers with dependent children up to the age of 18.	Income tested, paid in full to those with income around one-third of APE. Exact threshold and amount depends on family size. Non-taxable.

Source: National authorities.

Table A4. **Comparison of family benefit rates, 2002**

Details		Annual rates			Income tests (annual income levels)
		National currency	US dollars	As a percentage of APE[a]	
Austria					
Childcare Benefit	Children aged 0-30/36 months per family	€ 5 303	4 989	21.8	Only payable where the earnings of one parent is less than EUR 14 600, no payment for those on higher earnings.
	Loan supplement to low-income families	€ 2 212	2 081	9.1	Supplement payable where individual income is below EUR 3 997, and for couples, if partner's income is below EUR 7 200 plus EUR 3 600 per child. Has to be paid back once earnings exceed EUR 10 175 (single parents) or EUR 25 440 (couples).
Child Tax Credit	Per child	€ 611	575	2.5	Not income-tested.
Family Allowance	Per child, aged:				Not income-tested.
	0-9	€ 1 265	1 190	5.3	
	10-18	€ 1 483	1 395	6.2	
	19-26	€ 1 745	1 641	7.3	
	Supplements (per child):				
	2nd child	€ 154	144	0.6	
	3rd and further children	€ 306	288	1.3	
	Severely disabled	€ 1 572	1 479	6.6	
Sole Earner's and Sole Parent's Tax Credits	Per family	€ 364	342	1.5	In a couple family, second earner taxable earnings must be below EUR 4 400.

Table A4. **Comparison of family benefit rates, 2002** *(cont.)*

Details		Annual rates			Income tests (annual income levels)
		National currency	US dollars	As a percentage of APE[a]	
Ireland					
Child Benefit	Per child aged under 16, or aged 16-18 and in full-time education				Not income-tested.
	1st and 2nd child	€ 1 411	1 328	5.6	
	3rd and subsequent children	€ 1 770	1 665	7.0	
Family Income Supplement	One per family	60% of difference between net family income and income limit			Income tested. Income limit depends on family size, EUR 18 824 for one child, EUR 20 176 for two children, EUR 21 476 for three children.
Home Carer's Tax Credit	One per family	€ 770	724	3.0	Payable in full where home carer's taxable income is below EUR 5 080. A partial amount payable for those with income between EUR 5 080 and EUR 6 620.
One Parent Family Payment	Personal rate (under age 66)	€ 6 178	5 811	24.4	Income-tested.
	Per dependent (aged under 18, or 18-22 and in full-time education)	€ 1 004	944	4.0	Earnings below EUR 7 618 completely disregarded, thereafter withdrawn at 50%, and a reduced amount payable up to earnings of EUR 15 236.
Japan					
Childbirth Allowance	Per birth	¥ 300 000	2 392	7.1	Not income-tested.
Child Allowance	Per child aged 0-6:				Income-tested. Thresholds vary depending on family size, whether or not the family is employed and the earnings level.
	1st and 2nd child	¥ 60 000	478	1.4	
	3rd and subsequent children	¥ 120 000	957	2.8	
Child Rearing Allowance	Children aged 0-18:				Income-tested. Full amount payable where income is below JPY 1.3 million, a tapered amount payable for incomes between JPY 1.3 million and JPY 3.65 millions.
	One child	¥ 508 440	4 055	12.0	
	Two children	¥ 568 440	4 533	13.4	
	Addition for third and subsequent children	¥ 36 000	287	0.8	

a) Individual benefits or elements of them, are expressed as a proportion of gross APE.

Source: Austria (national authorities), Ireland (DSCFA, 2001), NIPSSR (2002) and OECD Secretariat calculations.

Table A5. **Employer-provided family benefits in Japan**

	Family benefits (1999)	Spousal benefits (1997)
Percentage of companies paying	77.3%	49.9%
Average annual amount (as a proportion of APE)	¥ 225 000 (5%)	¥ 126 000 (3%)
Features	This amount includes benefit for both dependent children and spouses. In 1997, 76.6% of companies paying family benefits included an element for spouses.	Spousal benefits are mostly only paid to families with low spousal earnings. Of those companies paying benefits for spouses, 76.4% only pay the benefit if spousal earnings are below JPY 1 030 000, and 15.4% if they are below JPY 1 300 000.

Source: MOL (1997a, 1999).

Unemployment and social assistance benefits

Table A6 describes the main income support systems for non-working families in each country. In all three countries unemployment insurance (UI) is paid to those covered by contributory-based schemes. In Austria and Japan, the payment rates are related to previous earnings (subject to a ceiling), whereas Ireland has a flat rate payment. Increases for dependent children are paid in Austria and Ireland, but not Japan. The duration of UI benefits is shortest in Japan, and the longer payment durations in Austria and Ireland are followed by income-tested unemployment assistance payments which are payable for indefinite periods. In Japan a lump-sum re-employment benefit is paid to those who return to work earlier than one-third of the way through the UI payment period (Table A6) and, in Ireland, benefit recipients moving into work may be eligible for Back to Work benefits for the first 3 or 4 years of employment (Box 6.3).

Means-tested social assistance is available in all three countries for those not eligible for other benefits. In both Austria and Japan, other relatives have a legal obligation to support those in need before social assistance payments will be considered. Assistance with housing costs is provided as part of social assistance in Ireland and Japan, whereas in Austria, such assistance is the responsibility of the provinces, and treatment varies – they may be part of social assistance or a separate Housing Benefit for those on low income.

Net replacement rates (net income out of work expressed as a proportion of net income in work) vary across the three countries, between lone parents and couples, and depending on whether they are in receipt of UI or social assistance. The NRRs for UI recipients are most relevant, especially in Austria and Japan, because only a limited number of families receive social assistance (and social assistance recipients are not often considered ready for work). With NRRs for couples on UI of around 71% in Austria, 54% in Ireland and 57%

Table A6. **Unemployment and social assistance benefits for those of working age with children**

Type of system	Account taken of children in rates of payment	Net replacement rates[a] (%)	
		Couple	Lone parent
Austria			
UI benefits are related to previous earnings (subject to a maximum) and are payable for 20-52 weeks depending on employment record and age. Duration can be increased for those taking part in specific labour market programmes.	Increases paid for dependent children.	71	70
Indefinite income-tested unemployment assistance is payable after exhaustion of UI benefits. It amounts to 92% of previous UI benefits, or 95% for low-income groups.	Increases paid for dependent children.	67	66
Means-tested social assistance is a provincial benefit, and eligibility and rates vary between provinces. Under family law, other relatives have a duty to provide financial support.	Increases paid for dependent children. Some provinces pay other supplements – for example for children going to school for the first time.	72	63
Ireland			
Flat-rate UI benefits are payable for 15 months to those covered by UI. Reduced payments are made where weekly earnings whilst in employment were below certain levels. Lone parents receive half the personal rate (they will be in receipt of One Parent Family Payment).	Increases paid for dependent children (not paid to lone parents).	54	54
Indefinite means-tested unemployment assistance is payable to unemployed people who are not entitled to, or have exhausted their entitlement to, UI benefits and are genuinely looking for work. The rates are the same as for UI payments.	Increases paid for dependent children.		
Means-tested Supplementary Welfare Allowance is payable to those not entitled to other benefits. Supplementary support for rent and mortgage interest payments exists. It is seldom paid to the unemployed.	Increases paid for dependent children. An annual Back to School Clothing and Footwear allowance is available for children aged 2-17 and those aged 18-22 and in full-time education.	72	59

Table A6. **Unemployment and social assistance benefits for those of working age with children** (cont.)

Type of system	Account taken of children in rates of payment	Net replacement rates[a] (%)	
		Couple	Lone parent
Japan			
UI is payable for between 90 and 300 days, the exact duration depending on the period of employment insured, the age of the recipient and whether the termination of previous employment was voluntary or involuntary. The amount is related to daily wages in the previous 6 months (subject to a ceiling). A unique feature is the lump-sum re-employment benefit that is paid if steady employment is found earlier than one-third of the way through the payment period.	No increases for dependent children.	57	59
Means-tested Public Assistance is payable to those considered below minimum living standards. The rates are calculated according to monthly income and minimum living expenses (depending on the region). Under civil law, relatives and family members are required to help those in need. Entitlement is subject to strict assets tests.	Takes account of family size.	67	54

a) NRRs express the net income out of work as a proportion of the net income in work (accounting for tax payments and benefits). These calculations are for families with children aged 4 and 6, assuming they earn the APE when in work.

Source: OECD (2003e), NIPSSR (2002) and national authorities.

in Japan, immediate financial returns to work appear to be weaker in Austria than the other two countries.

Social assistance support ensures that family resources do not fall below a certain minimum standard. For couple families with children the level of social assistance (including family benefits), as a share of APE, is very similar across the three countries, though the structure of assistance varies between them, with Austria giving the highest weight to the costs of children (Table A7). Equivalence elasticities give some idea of the extent to which these benefits take account of the costs of children by showing the relative value of extra income that an additional person brings to the household for those on social assistance.

Table A7. **Benefit income as a share of average wages and equivalence elasticities for additional children**

Family type[a]	Austria[b]		Ireland		Japan[c]	
	% APE	Elasticities	% APE	Elasticities	% APE	Elasticities
Single person	19	–	24	–	24	–
Lone parent, 1 child	34	0.79	62	1.55	46	0.94
Lone parent, 2 children	48	0.75	75	0.55	60	0.57
Lone parent, 3 children	63	0.78	90	0.60	74	0.59
Couple	28	0.48	41	0.66	38	0.60
Couple, 1 child	43	0.79	50	0.38	47	0.38
Couple, 2 children	57	0.75	59	0.38	59	0.50
Couple, 3 children	72	0.78	70	0.44	71	0.50

Note: Base rate for elasticity equivalence calculations is the single person rate for social assistance. The social assistance rates are those payable where there is no other income, and do not include housing benefit. The calculations include other family assistance benefits.

a) The benefit rates for children are for those aged 4 (families with one child), aged 4 and 6 (families with two children), aged 4, 6 and 8 (families with three children).

b) Refers to SA rates in Vienna.

c) Refers to SA rates Grade 1-1, as paid in Osaka and Tokyo and assume the adults are aged 20-40. Assumes the lone parent is female, and therefore entitled to the Child Rearing Allowance (see Tables A2 and A3).

Source: OECD Secretariat calculations.

OECD PUBLICATIONS, 2, rue André-Pascal, 75775 PARIS CEDEX 16
PRINTED IN FRANCE
(81 2003 14 1 P) ISBN 92-64-10418-6 – No. 53167 2003